HERALD

MBER 16, 1940

ONE PENNY

This is the Gin

on's

Stands Supreme

IES DOWN

Triumphs In st Air s Of War

ORCE HAD LOST 175 MACHINES UP OCK LAST NIGHT FOLLOWING A UGHT THE FIERCEST AIR BATTLES HTERS BROUGHT DOWN 171 AND

were brought down, but ten of the pilots are

day the total of enemy aircraft destroyed was passed the two thousand mark to 2,158.

STOP PRESS

BOMB SCARE IN NEW YORK

NEW YORK, Sunday.

Traffic between Brooklyn and Manhattan, over the Williamsburg Bridge, was suspended for 40 minutes this afternoon while the police examined a package, which it was feared might contain a bomb.

Experts plunged the package in oil and carried it to the river bank.—British United Press.

NAZIS HOLD UP FRENCH TRAIN

The German authorities have tightened restrictions on the border of occupied and unoccupied France, turning back three carriage loads of passengers on the night train to Paris.

RAF PUTS GOERING IN SHADE

GERMAN air raids on this country appear small compared with the fierce offensive the RAF is carrying out against Germany's invasion bases.

Foreign reports state that the Navy is taking part in the attacks.

Wave after wave of RAF bomber formations are, hour after hour, day after day, keeping up a continuous bombardment of shipping and troop concentrations at Channel and North Sea ports.

On the other hand, German mass raids on London rarely last more than an hour, and seldom are there more than two in a day.

Single planes or small formations do the rest of the Nazi raiding.

Bigger Formations

The R.A.F., it became apparent last night, has during the past 24 hours dealt Germany one of the heaviest blows since the war started.

Its bombers, in bigger formation than ever before, has smashed away with tremendous fury at the enemy.

The Air Ministry told how large forces of British bombers ranged on Saturday night and early yesterday over Germany, France, Belgium and Holland, systematically seeking out and breaking up the German High Command's invasion machine.

Flying through appalling weather—aircraft were struck by lightning, radio aerials were burned off in violent electric storms, and many machines were "iced up"—the raiders struck heavily at the German "front line" in the ports.

(Continued on Back Page, Col. 5.)

RAIDERS CHASED BACK TO THE CHANNEL

TWO ITALIAN PLANES RAID LONDON

By a "Daily Herald" Reporter

TWO Italian planes took part in the midday raid on London yesterday.

"I am not suggesting

THE two main bodies of raiders over the London area yesterday received such a gruelling as never before.

Spitfire and Hurricane squadrons, many of them veterans in London defence, fought them over the Kent coast as they came in, fought them over Maidstone and Canterbury, fought them above the Medway and Thames Estuary.

Many they turned away. The survivors they fought again over London itself, squadron after squadron of fighters flying fresh into action.

Finally they chased them back

WE REMEMBER THE BATTLE OF BRITAIN

Frank and Joan Shaw

HINCKLEY · LEICESTERSHIRE · ENGLAND · 1990

Typeset and Printed by Echo Press (1983) Ltd., Loughborough, Leicestershire

FOREWORD

As those who have vivid and mature recollections of the Battle of Britain grow fewer with the passing years, it becomes ever more important to record their memories and recollections of those momentous events of the summer of 1940 as they saw them.

Then Britain stood alone. The Royal Navy was fully stretched in getting convoys through to feed the nation. The Army was still being re-organised and re-equipped for the day it would return to continental soil. But for three months in that long, hot summer of 1940, the fate of our country hung in the balance and in the hands of the Royal Air Force. In particular, in the hands of a few hundred young men of Fighter Command.

There is no glory in war. I have personal experience of that. But there are times in one's life when one has a great pride that enables one to face tremendous danger, enormous stress and deadening fatigue. Hugely out-numbered, the young men of the Royal Air Force faced all of these problems and saw them through to enable this country of ours to survive.

But for the dark and seemingly all powerful evil forces at that time to conquer Great Britain the Royal Air Force had first to be defeated. It was not. The young pilots and all the ground staff saw this country through. In the words of Sir Winston Churchill, which have now become immortalised into the English language: "Never in the field of human conflict was so much owed by so many to so few".

The Army eventually returned to Europe to liberate the nations of that continent and so lead to the peace and harmony in which we have now lived for so many years. The Royal Navy played its full part in taking the Army back to Europe, and in the long years of war before the Liberation kept the trade routes open so that we could all be fed and clothed.

But that particular summer of 1940 belongs to the Royal Air Force and to the young men, whether pilots or ground staff, who gained that vital period of time necessary for the nation to recover its strength and so lead to the eventual freeing of all Europe.

Many of those young men died fighting for our freedoms that perhaps today we take too much for granted. Many more are, of course, no longer with us as a result of the passing years. But there are still those living quiet, unassuming lives amongst us as friends, workmates and neighbours. To them all we owe an incalculable debt.

INTRODUCTION

The first book in the series "We Remember …" told the story of Dunkirk and the miraculous escape of the British Expeditionary Force. The second book told the story of the Home Guard and the measures that were taken to resist an invasion that seemed a certainty.

But before an invasion could be mounted, the Luftwaffe had to have command of the air, and to achieve that it had effectively to destroy the Royal Air Force, or at least its capacity to resist.

The Battle of Britain really began on 8th August 1940. General "Hap" Arnold of the American Air Force described it in one neat sentence. "On 8th August the Royal Air Force Fighter Command took off to save everything, and between then and the end of September they saved it".

When the battle began, Air Chief Marshall Hugh "Stuffy" Dowding could find about 550 fighter planes to defend Great Britain. In contrast the Luftwaffe had some 2,500 aircraft, a ratio of over 4 to 1 against.

August 8th, Adlertag, "Eagle Day", was the first day of the fortnight in which Goering promised to destroy the Royal Air Force. Already attacks had been mounted against convoys in the Straits of Dover and along the English Channel, but had been discontinued. With "Eagle Day" the tactics switched to raids on airfields in the South East and to attacks on the radar masts. Throughout this period Fighter Command was at full stretch. When we mentioned earlier "about 550" fighter planes to defend Great Britain, that was the number available at any one time. But planes have to be serviced, and repaired, not to say armed. The figures for the total number of fighters available, after allowing for repairs etc., show how stretched the Royal Air Force was, and how its resources were dwindling in the face of remorseless attacks.

	Hurricanes	Spitfires	Total
21st August	615	326	941
30th August	580	287	867
8th September	530	275	805
15th September	472	256	728
2nd October	482	281	763
18th October	512	285	797

By 15th September the Royal Air Force had 213 fewer planes than four weeks' earlier – almost a quarter of its strength. But the period had also "bought time" and, as it proved, victory. Suddenly and inexplicably, Goering switched his Luftwaffe attacks to terror bombing, just as they were causing deadly harm to both the fighter stations and the radar installations. It was the respite the R.A.F. needed desperately. The figures above show how recovery started after 1st September. In the words of the Duke of Wellington at Waterloo, "It was a close run thing"!

The switch to terror bombing gave the Fighter Command the chance to recover not only in terms of actual planes available but, of even greater importance, in terms of pilots available.

Lord Beaverbrook rapidly organised and accelerated production so that in a comparatively short period of time the number of aircraft available was back to pre-August levels and higher.

But 50 fighter planes can be built whilst one pilot is being trained. The failure of Goering to persevere with any one of his three varying tactics and to discontinue them at decisive moments, not only gave Fighter Command the opportunity to train new pilots. It allowed the experienced pilots a respite from the strains of those weeks and pilots who had their nerves destroyed by weariness or had suffered injury an opportunity to recover.

Air Chief Marshall Dowding has been almost universally described as a kind, caring, sensitive man. As a pilot of the First World War he knew personally the almost unbearable strains and tensions that he was placing on his young pilots. He constantly referred to them as his "chicks" and to ease the strains he rotated postings as much as his resources permitted to allow for short, quiet periods away from the centre of battle. But even so, some Squadrons were suffering 50% pilot losses, not through combat, but through stress and weariness.

Ultimately the indecision of Goering, and the advantages of radar, led to the failure of the Luftwaffe to destroy the Royal Air Force. But the decisive factor was the courage and tenacity of the young pilots of Fighter Command who faced death daily and overcame fear and weariness so that others could, at a later date, free Europe and indeed the world.

Churchill's speeches on the Battle of Britain are well known and documented. But there is perhaps one comment he made which is shorter and more profound in its simplicity, and which is not known.

September 15th, 1940, was the culmination date for Goering. After then he could no longer claim any real hope of mastering Fighter Command. On that date every plane had been engaged and every pilot strained to exhaustion and there were no reserves left. But somehow Fighter Command had survived.

Churchill's first words that evening were: "Don't speak to me; I have never been so moved".

Five minutes later he was still emotionally affected, and then said, as if to himself, "Never in the field of human conflict has so much been owed by so many to so few". Of course he went on to write down these words and they became a part of the English language. But his first reaction, "Don't speak to me; I have never been so moved", perhaps really says it all.

And on 19th September 1940, four day's later, Operation Sealion for the invasion of Britain was "postponed indefinitely".

Frank and Joan Shaw

THE BATTLE OF BRITAIN

"One left in the morning to go out and die. If death was not at the rendezvous one went back for a drink with the boys.

Between leaving in the morning and returning, or not returning, when the day's work was done there might have been two, three, four sorties. This was a rare strain on the women …

Back in the Mess at Digby the party had already begun as the last few Pilots were coming in to land. They entered by ones and twos until there were two 19 year old wives without husbands.

These girls knew they need not wait any longer … They just slid out of the room.

There was no fuss, no tears. They just left. They could have wrecked the morale of the Squadron; but they never did."

GROUP CAPTAIN PETER TOWNSEND

*Battle of Britain Pilot and later Equerry to
His Majesty King George VI*

THE LAND THAT WE LOVE

The Heinkels are over, the sirens wail loud
Take heed of the warning, don't stand in a crowd
Be calm in your shelter and quieten your fear
The ground barrage lightens – the fighters are here!

For Britain and Freedom, straight into the fray
The Knights of King Arthur in modern array
Eight guns sing a rhythm, three short bursts – one long
How mournful the music – A Nazi's death song.

The battle is over, turn your thoughts from above
And look to the future, of the land that we love
When our sons have conquered, then what's the reward?
The same "Special Areas" and the old "Yellow Card"?

Make a land "fit for heroes" for those we love dear
And then in our conscience we can sound the "all clear".

This poem was written by my father, also called Frank Shaw, in 1940, when he was aged 31. He is still alive now, aged 81 and living in the same house at 27 Northwall Road, Deal.

The poem was written one afternoon when he had returned from working at Betteshanger Colliery in Deal, Kent, where he worked as a Coalminer. He recalls how he had seen an air battle right overhead involving German bombers and fighters and British Hurricanes and Spitfires. He then went straight indoors and sat down at the table on which was still all the cutlery and crockery from his dinner of the early afternoon following his morning shift at the colliery. The poem expresses not only his feelings about the battle he had just witnessed, but also his feelings of the wider "battle" that would follow the end of the war and the need to ensure that all the miseries of social deprivation of the 1930's did not return. The "Special Areas" were areas of high unemployment and social misery, and "the old Yellow Card" refers to "Unemployment Cards".

But the poem is especially interesting for another reason. It was written in September, 1940, and at a time when Britain stood absolutely alone. Everyone was awaiting invasion and the world saw nothing for Great Britain but total defeat. But the poem shows that even then ordinary men and women all had a total confidence of victory and never once doubted it would come. The words "the battle is over turn your thoughts from above, and look to the future, of the land that we love" and "make a land fit for heroes" can have no other meaning.

I find it amazing that at that time these otherwise "ordinary" men and women of this country had that total confidence. The "experts" throughout the world gave us no hope. The "ordinary" men and women had no reason to feel that way. But they were right!

ACKNOWLEDGEMENTS

This is the third book in our series of "We Remember". But this book is different in that what had started as a "leisurely" process of publication in September became a "mad rush" when we realised that the Battle of Britain commemorations were starting in July.

To get this book out, effectively two months early, has required enormous help and co-operation.

The book itself, however, could of course only have been produced in the first place with the assistance of all those who wrote of their experiences. They have proved a most valuable insight into conditions and attitudes in Britain at a time of National Crisis. What they revealed is most peculiar – an almost universal recognition of that crisis but a stubborn refusal to be humbled or hustled by it. Those who have written their stories have given us a privileged view of "Britain Alone", almost a "time warp", so that we are taken back as it were to 1940.

So our thanks must go to:

All those who took the time and trouble to tell their stories and record those many incidents in 1940 which "fill in" the historical information we already have of the Battle of Britain.

Stephen Gamble for yet another brilliant painting for the jacket. He produced the Home Guard cover and the only puzzle is why he remains in Local Government with that level of talent!

The Imperial War Museum for almost all the full page photographs. However an extra "thank you also" for a service that might otherwise go unrecorded. When we pulled the publication date forward, the Museum staff were already fully committed on other projects and it appeared impossible to get the photographs within the period required. Our special thanks must therefore go to Jane Carmichael of the Museum who pulled out all the stops and got them for us. Without her we would have been lost!

"The Daily Express" for allowing the reprint of their issue of 12 September 1940. Also "The Daily Herald" of 16 September 1940.

The Printers, Echo Press Limited, who like the Imperial War Museum were asked to produce everything two months ahead of the planned date – and did it. Many thanks.

And for the third time, special thanks to Jane Stew, Shirley Cartwright, Judy Crawshaw and Margaret Young for converting handwritten personal stories into a format that could be used by the Printers. Our thanks may seem repetitive – but they are real because without you the whole project would be, to use an understatement, "difficult"! Many, many thanks.

The Battle of Britain was a unique event and experience. For the first time in history the outcome of a War was decided in the skies, whilst the population watched and wondered. These stories and recollections make sure that the feelings and views of the "ordinary" man and woman will not be forgotten. Enjoy the stories – but never forget the debt we owe.

Frank and Joan Shaw

R.A.F. FIGHTER COMMAND ORDER OF BATTLE

09.00 hrs., 1st July 1940

Sector	Sqdn.	Aircraft	Combat Ready (Unserviceable)	Base Airfield	Pilots on State	Commanding Officer
No. 11 Group, H.Q. Uxbridge, Middlesex						
Biggin Hill	32 Sqdn.	Hurricanes	12 (4)	Biggin Hill	16	Squadron Leader J. Worrall
	79 Sqdn. (1)	Hurricanes	12 (5)	Biggin Hill	14	Squadron Leader J. D. C. Joslin
	245 Sqdn. (2)	Hurricanes	15 (1)	Hawkinge	16	Squadron Leader E. W. Whitley
	600 Sqdn.	Blenheims	8 (6)	Manston	22	Squadron Leader D de B. Clarke
	610 Sqdn.	Spitfires	14 (3)	Gravesend	20	Squadron Leader A. T. Smith
North Weald	25 Sqdn.	Blenheims	6 (10)	Martlesham	22	Squadron Leader K. A. K. McEwan
	56 Sqdn.	Hurricanes	16 (2)	North Weald	20	Squadron Leader G. A. L. Manton
	85 Sqdn.	Hurricanes	15 (3)	Martlesham	21	Squadron Leader P. W. Townsend
	151 Sqdn.	Hurricanes	14 (4)	North Weald	20	Squadron Leader E. M. Donaldson
Kenley	64 Sqdn.	Spitfires	10 (4)	Kenley	19	Squadron Leader N. C. Odbert
	111 Sqdn.	Hurricanes	12 (4)	Croydon	17	Squadron Leader J. M. Thompson
	501 Sqdn.	Hurricanes	10 (5)	Croydon	18	Squadron Leader H. A. V. Hogan
	615 Sqdn.	Hurricanes	12 (6)	Kenley	21	Squadron Leader J. R. Kayll
Northolt	1 Sqdn.	Hurricanes	10 (6)	Northolt	18	Squadron Leader D. A. Pemberton
	257 Sqdn.	Hurricanes	13 (5)	Hendon	17	Squadron Leader D. W. Bayne
	604 Sqdn.	Blenheims	10 (6)	Northolt	21	Squadron Leader M. F. Anderson
	609 Sqdn.	Spitfires	15 (2)	Northolt	18	Squadron Leader H. S. Darley
Hornchurch	54 Sqdn.	Spitfires	12 (3)	Rochford	18	Squadron Leader J. L. Leathart
	65 Sqdn.	Spitfires	11 (5)	Hornchurch	16	Squadron Leader D. Cooke
	74 Sqdn.	Spitfires	10 (7)	Hornchurch	20	Squadron Leader F. L. White
Tangmere	43 Sqdn.	Hurricanes	13 (4)	Tangmere	18	Squadron Leader C. G. Lott
	145 Sqdn.	Hurricanes	11 (7)	Tangmere	17	Squadron Leader J. R. A. Peel
	601 Sqdn.	Hurricanes	15 (2)	Tangmere	19	Squadron Leader the Hon. M. Aitken
	F.I.U	Blenheims	4 (4)	Tangmere	10	Wing Commander G. P. Chamberlain
Filton	92 Sqdn.	Spitfires	11 (6)	Pembrey	19	Squadron Leader F. J. Sanders
	213 Sqdn.	Hurricanes	14 (4)	Exeter	20	Squadron Leader H. D. McGregor
	234 Sqdn.	Spitfires	9 (6)	St. Eval	21	Squadron Leader R. E. Barnett
Middle Wallop	236 Sqdn.	Blenheims	11 (4)	Middle Wallop	19	Squadron Leader P. E. Drew
	238 Sqdn. (3)	Hurricanes	10 (2)	Middle Wallop	17	Squadron Leader H. A. Fenton
Debden	17 Sqdn.	Hurricanes	14 (4)	Debden	19	Squadron Leader R. I. G. MacDougall
No. 12 Group, H.Q. Watnall, Nottingham						
Duxford	19 Sqdn.	Spitfires	8 (5)	Fowlmere	24	Squadron Leader P. C. Pinkham
	264 Sqdn.	Defiants	11 (7)	Duxford	23	Squadron Leader P. A. Hunter
Coltishall	66 Sqdn.	Spitfires	12 (4)	Coltishall	25	Squadron Leader R. H. A. Leigh
	242 Sqdn.	Hurricanes	10 (4)	Coltishall	21	Squadron Leader D. R. S. Bader
Kirton-in-Lindsey	222 Sqdn.	Spitfires	12 (4)	Kirton-in-Lindsey	21	Squadron Leader H. W. Mermagen
Digby	29 Sqdn.	Blenheims	10 (5)	Digby	15	Flight Lieutenant J. S. Adams
	46 Sqdn.	Hurricanes	15 (3)	Digby	17	Flight Lieutenant A. D. Murray
	611 Sqdn.	Spitfires	3 (11)	Digby	21	Squadron Leader J. E. McComb
Wittering	23 Sqdn.	Blenheims	10 (6)	Colly Weston	20	Squadron Leader L. C. Bicknell
	229 Sqdn.	Hurricanes	14 (2)	Wittering	20	Squadron Leader H. J. Maguire
	266 Sqdn.	Spitfires	8 (5)	Wittering	21	Squadron Leader J. W. A. Hunnard
No. 13 Group, H.Q. Newcastle, Northumberland						
Church Fenton	73 Sqdn.	Hurricanes	8 (5)	Church Fenton	22	Squadron Leader J. W. C. More
	87 Sqdn.	Hurricanes	14 (4)	Church Fenton	23	Squadron Leader J. S. Dewar
	249 Sqdn.	Hurricanes	10 (4)	Leconfield	23	Squadron Leader J. Grandy
	616 Sqdn.	Spitfires	11 (4)	Church Fenton	19	Squadron Leader M. Robinson
Catterick	41 Sqdn.	Spitfires	11 (6)	Catterick	21	Squadron Leader H. West
	219 Sqdn.	Blenheims	10 (4)	Catterick	19	Squadron Leader J. H. Little
Usworth	72 Sqdn.	Spitfires	12 (4)	Acklington	19	Squadron Leader R. B. Lees
	152 Sqdn.	Spitfires	8 (4)	Acklington	25	Squadron Leader P. K. Devitt
	607 Sqdn.	Hurricanes	10 (6)	Usworth	17	Squadron Leader J. A. Vick
Turnhouse	141 Sqdn.	Defiants	14 (5)	Turnhouse	20	Squadron Leader W. A. Richardson
	253 Sqdn.	Hurricanes	13 (5)	Turnhouse	19	Squadron Leader H. Starr
	602 Sqdn.	Spitfires	12 (4)	Drem	19	Squadron Leader G. C. Pinkerton
	603 Sqdn. (4)	Spitfires	10 (6)	Turnhouse	19	Squadron Leader E. H. Stevens
	605 Sqdn. (5)	Hurricanes	8 (6)	Drem	17	Squadron Leader W. M. Churchill
Dyce	262 Sqdn. (6)	Hurricanes	3 (2)	Grangemouth	7	Squadron Leader H. Eeles
Wick	3 Sqdn.	Hurricanes	12 (2)	Wick	18	Squadron Leader S. F. Godden
	504 Sqdn.	Hurricanes	12 (4)	Castletown	15	Squadron Leader J. Sample

ix

End of a Messerschmitt.

THE BATTLE OF BRITAIN

by

AIR VICE MARSHALL JOHNNIE JOHNSON
C.B., C.B.E., D.S.O., D.F.C.

'When all the world is young, lad,
And all the trees are green;
And every goose a swan, lad,
And every lass a queen.'

When you flew high over Dover during that fine early summer of 1940 you saw the French coast and the *Pas de Calais* until it was lost in the blue haze, and here lay the crack fighter squadrons of the Luftwaffe ably led by young and experienced leaders, including Adolf Galland, Werner Mölders and Helmut Wieck.

You could not see the scores of airfields which dotted the land between Hamburg and Bordeaux and which housed two air fleets, *Luftflotte 2* and *Luftflotte 3*, while *Luftflotte 5* rested on Danish and Norwegian bases. This powerful air armada, with some 2,800 combat aeroplanes was thus dispersed along a wide front so that air attacks against Britain could be mounted from different directions. The airfields were well stocked for the coming assault, and the aircrews, flushed with victory after their successful *Blitzkrieg* campaign in the Low Countries and France waited for *Reichsmarschall* Göring to give the signal.

Operation *Sealion,* the strategic plan for the invasion of Britain followed the usual pattern of *Blitzkrieg,* except that the air fighting over Dunkirk had made Göring realise that the R.A.F. would prove a harder nut to crack than some air forces, who, without radar had been surprised and largely written-off on the ground because they had little or no warning of the approach of enemy fighters. Once again the Luftwaffe would be used as a big stick to bludgeon all opposition, and the panzers would cross the Channel, as they had crossed the Meuse, with strong packs of dive-bombers taking the place of the artillery, and gain foot-holds on suitable beaches between the Isle of Wight and Dover.

The Luftwaffe would destroy the fighter defences in the south and then extend their offensive further inland, so that the bomber fleets could roam unopposed over England, taking out the old cities, reducing civilian morale, and paving the way for invasion against a British Army short of the weapons lost at Dunkirk. The enemy planners estimated that four days of intensive operations would subdue our southern air defences, and a further four weeks would be required to write-off the remainder of the R.A.F. Adler Tag (Eagle Day), scheduled for early August, would mark the beginning of the attack against 11 Group and, if all went well, the panzers would cross the Channel four or five weeks later.

The Luftwaffe possessed some excellent aeroplanes, and the Messerschmitt 109E had a higher ceiling and better guns than either the Spitfire or the Hurricane. The enemy fighter carried either four machine guns or two machine guns and two cannon; the latter compared very favourably with our eight Browning machine guns. The 109F, which was soon to make its appearance over England, had one cannon which was centrally mounted and fired through the hub of the airscrew, and later versions of this splendid fighter had three cannon.

During the fighting over Dunkirk our pilots found that their Spitfires had slight margins of speed and climb over the 109E. But most of these fights took place below

20,000 feet, and later, when we had to fight well above this height, it was soon discovered that the enemy fighter was decidedly superior because its super-charger was designed to operate more efficiently at the higher altitudes. When the Messerschmitt took evasive action by half-rolling and diving vertically for the deck, we found that we couldn't stay with it in this manoeuvre. Certainly the Spitfire was more manoeuvrable, but manoeuvring does not win air battles, and tight turns are more of a defensive than an offensive tactic. The Spitfire's rate of turn would get you out of trouble if you saw your attacker in time, but only superior height would save you from the 'bounce'.

In his subsequent Despatch, the Commander-in-Chief said that the Battle divided itself broadly into four phases. First, the attack on shipping convoys, ports, coastal airfields and radar stations; second, the onslaught against inland fighter airfields; third, the bombing of London; and, fourth, the fighter bomber stage.

The bombing of our sector airfields, with their operations rooms and essential communications, was the most critical phase of the battle. Between 24th August and 7th September there were thirty-three major bombing attacks, and twenty-three were concentrated against our vital nerve centres – the fighter airfields and sector stations of 11 Group whose job was to defend London and the South East. By 5th September Park was reporting to Dowding that the damage by bombing was having a serious effect on the fighting efficiency of his group.

Thanks to their large fighter escorts the enemy bombers were getting through to our airfields and their casualties were reduced. During a four day period of fighting we shot down 106 enemy aeroplanes, including a small proportion of bombers, and lost 101 fighter pilots.

It was at this critical time that I was posted to the South Yorkshire Squadron at Kenley, which together with Biggin Hill guarded the eastern flank of London. Ideally, a fighter squadron would be in the front line for about six weeks before moving to a quiet sector to rest the veterans and train replacement pilots. 616 (South Yorkshire) Squadron had within the past two weeks suffered four pilots killed, another five wounded, and one a prisoner of war. Dowding wisely pulled them out of the line, and we were sent to Coltishall where J. Johnson, with a total of 195 flying hours (twelve on Spitfires) was barely able to fly a Spitfire let alone fight it.* We newcomers lacked experience and were mere passengers on our first few operations.

During the first three days of September the bombing attacks, with packs of escorting fighters, continued and we shot down 90 enemy aeroplanes and lost 85 pilots. The total wastage in our fighter pilots was about 120 pilots each week. Our operational training units produced 65 inexperienced pilots each week and it was quite apparent to Dowding and Park that they were fighting a battle of diminishing returns. They realised that if the Luftwaffe kept up the pressure the control and reporting system would gradually disintegrate, and it would only be a question of time before the Germans dominated the air over Southern England.

Fortunately at this time the conduct of the battle changed. On the night of 24th/25th August the first bombs fell on central London. Winston Churchill ordered a retaliation raid against Berlin, and during the next week there were four more. Hitler demanded immediate reprisals and shouted in an hysterical broadcast: "If they attack our cities, we will rub out their cities from the map. The hour will come when one of us two will break, and it will not be Nazi Germany."

Göring eagerly responded, and late in the afternoon of Saturday, 7th September, sent over 372 bombers and 642 fighters to make two concentrated attacks against London in rapid succession. Dowding, however, anticipating daylight attacks against our capital, made more use of the big wings from 10 and 12 Groups, and Park intstructed that whenever time permitted his squadrons were to be used in pairs.

The attacks on London and its suburbs continued with little respite from 7th September until 5th October. It was the crux of the Battle and its turning point, for it gave Park the opportunity to repair his battered airfields and restore his communications. On Sunday, 15th September, Göring provided the strongest escort so far, five fighters for every bomber, to try and saturate our defences. These big enemy formations took a long time to assemble; our radar gave ample warning, and Park had the precious time to form his squadrons into wings and to ask for reinforcements from the flanking groups.

The fighting on this day cost the Luftwaffe fifty-six aeroplanes against our twenty-six pilots. More bombers struggled back to France, on one engine, badly shot-up, and with many crew members dead or injured. At the debriefings the bomber captains complained bitterly of incessant Hurricane and Spitfire attacks from squadrons that had long ceased to exist – if they could believe their own Intelligence and the Berlin radio.

The fighting on this day clinched the victory, for two days later, on Hitler's instructions, the German invasion fleet left the Channel ports for safer places, and Operation Sealion was called off, never to be repeated.

The daylight offensive against London continued for another six weeks (phase four), but from the beginning of October enemy bombers only operated at night and the Blitz, in all its fury, was upon us. The daylight offensive passed to enemy fighters and fighter bombers. These raids, flown at great heights and taking every advantage of cloud cover,

*Later, pilots flew at least fifty hours on Spitfires before joining their squadrons.

set Dowding new problems about high altitude interception, but they achieved little else, and Fighter Command continued along the path of recovery which had begun on 7th September.

Morale and leadership are closely interwoven, and there can be no doubt about the tremendous influence of Air Chief Marshal Sir Hugh Dowding on his subordinate commanders, and on our young fighter leaders like Douglas Bader, Bob Tuck, Mike Crossley, Don Kingaby, Victor Beamish, Archie McKellar, Jim Hallowes, H. M. Stephen, Finlay Boyd, 'Sailor' Malan and 'Dutch' Hugo from South Africa, 'Jamie' Jameson, 'Hawk Eye' Wells, Colin Gray and Alan Deere all from New Zealand, Frank Carey from Australia, Gordie McGregor and Willie McNight from Canada, and Witold Urbanowicz from Poland, to mention but a few ... *We few, we happy few, we band of brothers'.*

And so the great battle was fought and won over the Channel, over the fields of Kent and Sussex, over the wolds of Hampshire and Dorset, over the flat marshes of Essex and the sprawling mass of London. Unlike the previous battle of destiny – Waterloo, Trafalgar, the terrible roar and devastation of the Somme bombardments – there was little sound or fury. People on the ground went about their business with little idea of what was taking place high in the sky. They saw a pattern of white vapour trails, slowly changing form and shape. Sometimes they saw the contestants as a number of tiny specks scintillating like diamonds in the splendid sunlight of those cloudless days. The skilful parries of the defence continued throughout those long days of the late summer – had they not done so London would have suffered the fate of Warsaw and Rotterdam.

The Battle of Britain was one by the gayest company who ever fired their guns in anger. Thanks to their Commander, morale was very high throughout Fighter Command, and this combination of stout hearts, good aeroplanes, radar, excellent leadership in all levels and devoted service on the ground, proved too much for the Luftwaffe.

The prestige of the fighter pilots stood high. They were the defenders of the people and sometimes they, and they alone, stood between victory and defeat. They led a strange life, which alternated beween short periods of intense excitement and danger, in the air when they did not have enough time, and long spells on the ground when they had too much. Once in the air they had the gift of becoming part of their fighters. Their devotion was well hidden beneath their casual demeanour. Of those 449 fighter pilots and other aircrew who lost their lives in the Battle of Britain let it be said:

'All the soul
Of man is resolution which expires
Never from valiant men till their last breath.'

These then are my recollections of the Battle of Britain as an operation that saved this country. As for my own personal emotions, I can distinctly remember that they were as follows. Despite what I regarded as my inexperience, I had a strong natural instinct to survive and so far as I was concerned that took the form of using every opportunity possible to fly a Spitfire in whatever capacity! If a Spitfire was needed for ferrying or, in fact, for whatever task, I can tell you that I was there!

I can also tell you that my other particular emotion I remember is that I was especially conscious at the time that I was a member of a very select body of men. Of all the millions of people who were intimately involved in our war effort, we were just a few hundred up there in the blue sky on whom, at that particular time, everything depended. Many of that select body of men were from the old "Empire" and we must never forget the debt we owe to them also. We were here to do a job for our country. Those men from the old "Empire" volunteered to come and face the most formidable of foes, and the most fearsome odds.

Finally, I have to say that we were inspired by Churchill and Dowding, and it was their qualities of leadership that produced that priceless pearl called high morale. We were fighting for our lives, and we were fighting for our country. We had many disadvantages but we also had other advantages like radar. But taking all those factors into account I still believe without any doubt at all that the greatest single factor in the winning of the Battle of Britain was that high morale amongst all of the R.A.F. but especially the Pilots who had to go into battle, that was produced by the leadership of Winston Churchill and Air Chief Marshall Dowding. It is something that we shall never forget because if it hadn't been there, however much courage and tenacity and skill was shown by the Pilots, without that high morale that was produced by the quality of leadership, things might have turned out differently.

Note: A young pilot officer in the Battle of Britain in 1940, Johnnie Johnson quickly displayed exceptional talent as a fighter pilot. He went on to command his own Wing by 1943 and flew and fought throughout the war. By the end of the war he was the Allied airforce's top scoring fighter pilot. His decorations included the D.S.O. and D.F.C.

My Army experiences started in June 1940 when I had to report at Dover Castle. This was just after Dunkirk. In fact we received some kit which had been salvaged from those who had lost their lives. We were supposed to be trained in our Unit in Signalling for the Royal Artillery. Because of numerous air raids and shelling this training virtually went by the board. After spending some damp nights in the old Castle dungeons, a small group of us were put on coastal defence.

We were sent to man a pill box on the cliff tops at Swingate between Dover and St. Margaret's Bay. I remember a young sub-altern officer visiting us and saying in a grand tone of voice "You are in the front line now you know!" Some "front line troops" to be sure! We didn't even have experience in using a rifle!

We lived well, sleeping and eating in a Nissen Hut when not on duty. One of our party was an excellent cook, and we just couldn't believe it was the same food we had found so difficult to eat when in Dover Castle. We were all told the code word "B" would mean the German invasion had started. It was glorious weather even as September came along. We often looked at the German guns firing from the French coast and counted to see how many seconds passed before the shell landed somewhere near us.

When on duty in the pill box once or twice the code word was given. But it was only as a warning just to be ready! Then one Saturday night three of us were doing our shift in the pill box with a Lance Bombardier of the Regular Army as our "Commander". He was quite unnerved when the Army field telephone rang and he heard loud and clear "CODE WORD B".

This was the real thing! His first reaction was to order us to take all the rifles and ammunition as well as the Bren gun and ammunition outside of the pillbox.

"I am not staying in this so and so place" were his reassuring words!

For the rest of that night we all stood and shivered on that cliff top until daylight came and still nothing had happened! We were "off duty" at 6.00 a.m. and were very relieved to get back into our Nissen Hut home.

After washing and having breakfast I set out for Dover. I always went to the Baptist Church when "off duty". I soon discovered a road block had been set up, but I talked my way through it and arrived at the Church a little late. The Minister was praying when I entered, but before he had finished his prayer the air raid siren went.

All the congregation trooped outside and went down the nearest shelter which was underneath Woolworths. After a little while a lady approached me and said if I wished, I could go home with her and could have an informal service with a few other friends. I accepted her invitation and a service was duly started in her home.

It hadn't lasted long before a bomb dropped very close to her house, shattering windows and causing her 12 year

Air Chief Marshal Sir Hugh C. T. Dowding, GCVO, KCB, CMG

old daughter to panic. I had lunch in that house, and my host put on the radio and I heard then the report "all troops must report to barracks". I knew I must go. I thanked my kind friends and walked back to Swingate.

My mates seemed very restless when I met them and all thought the German troops would soon appear. I was eventually left alone in the hut whilst they went to a pub to build up their courage with a drink!

I retired to my bed but not to sleep. I remember the others returning some time later quite the worse for wear. I must admit my faith was not as strong as it should have been! I remember somewhere about midnight pulling the Army blanket over my head and my last thoughts before going to sleep were "I will be taken prisoner by the Germans before waking up".

Of course life was just the same as usual on that Monday morning with no Germans in sight anywhere! We did hear, however, that more enemy planes had been shot down by the Royal Air Force that Sunday than on any day since the war had commenced. Of course that Sunday was "Battle of Britain Sunday" and it is one that I will always particularly remember.

Ben Angell, 14 Queens Drive, Halesworth, Suffolk

My father, mother, brothers and myself lived on the farm called 'Wills Farm', Newchurch on Romney Marsh in Kent. Father and brothers, with the help from men employed, worked on a farm of 100 acres which we owned. All the land we owned was immediately around the farm.

After Dunkirk things began to happen. Plans were made to flood the Romney Marsh, by breaching the sea wall at Dymchurch. We were told that it would take two tides to flood the Marsh. All persons living on the Marsh were told to go to the hills, about 2 miles away, and await orders from the military.

The sheep had to be shorn early to get the wool stored away. Then orders came that the War Office at Maidstone wanted to collect the young sheep, and take them to Wales which they thought was a safer place. The reason being the Kent or Romney Marsh sheep are a hardy breed and good for lamb and mutton to eat. We had quite a few sheep taken. The farmers were paid market price for animals taken. Reports came through later, however, that most of the sheep had died as the weather was too wet and cold in Wales for them during the winter.

No persons could enter the Marsh across the Royal Military Canal which runs from Hythe to Rye. Every other bridge was blown up, soldiers were posted at all bridges, and all persons had to have a pass to show they lived on the Marsh.

A few enemy planes came over and dropped bombs, but never doing any damage. Several persons who had no business or work left the Marsh. We had plenty of soldiers in the village. All the empty houses and farm buildings were taken as billets for them. The following is my own report of the Battle of Britain and of the planes and bombs around us.

May 21st 1940 bombs dropped at Burmarsh.

July 3rd saw first German plane. A Dornier 215 in the afternoon. Ack Ack fire bursting around. Bombs dropped at Lympne.

July 10th over 100 enemy planes attacked a convoy in the Channel. 14 fetched down in early afternoon. Planes looked like specks in the sky.

July 17th bombs dropped at Ashford and Brookland.

July 26th an enemy plane came right over the farm in the afternoon.

July 27th delivered petrol to tractors working away from the farm, and saw the bomb crater at Brookland.

August 11th enemy lost 66 planes.

August 12th enemy lost 62 planes.

August 13th enemy lost 78 planes.

August 14th enemy lost 31 planes.

August 15th had air battles all day. Bombs dropped at Lympne, Dymchurch, Brenzett, New Romney. Croydon had very heavy raids. Enemy lost 169 planes. Bombs dropped at New Romney while men were working on engines. Told to stop work.

August 17th no air raid in England. Enemy lost 467 planes in one week. We lost 110 planes. 42 pilots safe.

August 18th planes coming in dropped bombs at Newchurch at midday. Tried to reach London, turned back. Enemy planes came down in flames at Snargate and Bilsington. ME110 landed safely at Newchurch. One of our Spitfires crashed at Ruckinge in the evening. Pilot safe. First time used dyke as an air raid shelter. Spent large part of afternoon there. Called out to see two enemy planes on fire trying to get home. Never made it. Came down in the Channel.

August 24th planes coming in the evening met our fighters and turned and dropped bombs at Ruckinge, Newchurch and Dymchurch. The bomb at Newchurch was in our field. Walked and saw crater in the evening. No other damage done.

August 31st Dornier made a crash landing at Newchurch in the evening across the Bilsington

Generalfeldmarschall Hermann Goering.

Road. Laid in dyke. Plane came right over us very low. Saw R.A.M.C. from Newchurch go out to the plane with ambulance. Walked and saw the plane in the evening.

September 1st ME110 came down at Bilsington intact in afternoon. Laid in dyke. Plane came right over us. Plane was later sold to America intact.

September 2nd ME109 came down in flames at Bilsington in afternoon.

September 7th heavy raid on London in evening. Wave after wave of bombers came over us. Hurricane came down at Newchurch. Pilot safe.

September 11th Heinkle III made a crash landing at Burmarsh. Crew set fire to plane. Spitfire crashed in Newchurch burying itself deep in the ground.
(*Note* In 1976 this plane was found a memorial to the pilot was placed along the road where the plane came down).

September 15th ME109 came down at Ruckinge at lunchtime killing a mother and her baby daughter. The plane was a yellow nosed fighter. Went and saw the plane in the evening. Saw 4 parachutes in the sky in the morning.

September 22nd air raid in afternoon. Hurricane came down in flames in Newchurch. Pilot baled out. Shute never opened. Landed close to our farm.

September 26th bombs dropped at St. Marys bay blocking the road.

October 1st bombs dropped at New Romney in same field as engines cutting the steel rope. Told to stop working.

October 11th while driving to Ashford market in the morning bombs were dropped in Ashford. Stopped by police and told to get out of car and go to the shelter in a church.

October 12th planes came in and were turned back, dropping bombs at Ivychurch close to my brother threshing corn.

October 20th ME109 crashed at St. Mary in the Marsh. Plane burned out.

October 24th bombs dropped beside canal at Bilsington.

October 26th bombs dropped at St. Marys in the Marsh blocking the road.

November 5th bombs dropped while we were in Ashford market. Had to go to shelter.

November 7th ME109 crashed to the ground at Newchurch. Bomb exploded as it hit the ground. Buried itself deep in the ground.

November 23rd ME109 crashed at Ivychurch in the early morning.

November 25th found glass from enemy bomber in our field at Newchurch.

During the Battle of Britain my brothers found packets of leaflets from the enemy, printed in English, telling us the state of the war. We also had several packets of English leaflets printed in German and French giving our version of the war! Glass from the enemy bombers was found in the fields after a heavy raid from London. They made the glass into rings and bangles for us local girls! I still have some left to this day.

The next was when my father received a letter from the Air Ministry stating they would be taking 100 acres of our farm to help make a runway as a landing ground for fighters. There were several such landing grounds on the Marsh. They could only be used in the summer as the Marsh is too wet in the winter. All the dykes were piped and filled with beach. Spitfires were used on the runway which was close to our house. Sad to say some planes never returned. We used to count them out and on return.

However, after the Battle of Britain it became much quieter with only a few raids doing no damage.

After the war was ended we had our land returned to us, but I have to say that it took several years to get it back into a decent state of cultivation!

Mrs. Ivy Homewood, Invicta, The Street, Newchurch, Romney Marsh, Kent

(*Sadly we record that Mrs. Homewood died at the end of May 1990.*)

A formation of Hurricanes setting off to intercept enemy bombers.

I suppose my story should be entitled "The day I nearly lost my head"! To appreciate this story it is necessary to understand the geography of our area. I lived in an estate consisting of wooden bungalows, commonly called "the huts". These estates with up to 350 dwellings were built during and after World War 1 to house workers drawn from all over the country to work in the Woolwich Arsenal situated about 4 miles to the north west.

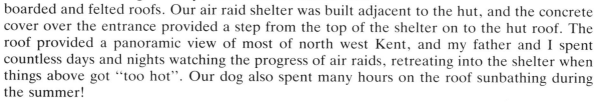

Our "hut" was on the Bostall Heath estate which was one of the highest areas in the district. Approximately 300 yards to the north is Bostall Heath proper, being a large open space surrounded by woodland. During the war it was an anti aircraft gun site boasting 4 4½″ naval guns manned by Royal Marines.

The huts were single storey, timber construction with boarded and felted roofs. Our air raid shelter was built adjacent to the hut, and the concrete cover over the entrance provided a step from the top of the shelter on to the hut roof. The roof provided a panoramic view of most of north west Kent, and my father and I spent countless days and nights watching the progress of air raids, retreating into the shelter when things above got "too hot". Our dog also spent many hours on the roof sunbathing during the summer!

This story concerns a day raid. Without warning a group of German aircraft flew at low level along the valley formed by the North Downs where we were, and the hills of north Kent. There had been no warning so we were all unprepared. The aircraft headed for London, and after they had gone the air raid warning then sounded! So we were well prepared for their return. That came about 20 minutes later. In the meantime (as we heard later) they had bombed a school in Brownhill Road, Catford and caused many casualties.

My father and I were in our usual position on the roof awaiting the return of the aircraft. So were the Royal Marines with their 4½″ guns.

The aircraft duly arrived, retracing their inward journey. From our high position we were almost looking down on the aircraft, about 5 miles away, because they were flying at low level.

Suddenly there was an almighty crash. There was a rush of hot air, and a cloud of smoke which seemed to envelope us. The guns were firing at zero elevation! The shells must have passed over our heads almost within touching distance. Needless to say we retreated to a lower and safer position.

The excitement ended as quickly as it had begun. Within a few minutes the all clear had sounded. However, about 10 minutes later a Royal Marines Officer appeared in the vicinity asking the whereabouts of the "two idiots who nearly had their heads shot off".

After a cup of tea and a conducted tour of our spotting post he admitted that the guns should not really have been fired at such a low elevation because of the stress of the mountings caused by the horizontal thrust. My view was that the guns shouldn't have been

fired at such a low elevation because they were firing at us!

Needless to say this experience did not interrupt our spotting, and in fact there was to be a time when I can modestly say that I was responsible for saving serious injury and possible death to many of our neighbours because of our early warning system. But that of course is quite different from the day we were nearly shot to pieces by the Royal Marines!

Frank Kirby, 45 Mount Road, Bexley Heath, Kent

Heinkel 111.

7

I was one of the first Militia, a group of 20 year olds who were called up six months before the war started. My AB64 – the soldiers record book – shows my age at the time as 20 years 364 days. If I had been one day older I wouldn't have had to go! It was the day that changed my life and I have never regretted it.

I was a junior engineering and ship building draughtsman, which was then a reserved occupation, and my future career was designed to be in engineering. Instead I am now a retired schoolmaster, having seen the world and followed a respected profession. But in those pre-war months I was sent to Harrogate and was trained as a Special Wireless Operator for interception work.

When war broke out I was in 110 Special Wireless Section stationed in a large country house at Frant near Tunbridge Wells. Our wireless sets were accommodated in what we called "gin palaces" in the grounds of the house. Our job was the interception of German Air Force communications during what came to be called the Battle of Britain in July 1940, right through the Summer to the Blitz and night bombing of November 1940.

The Luftwaffe used a three letter wireless code and each plane in each flight remained in communication with its base until it was either shot down or reached its target. Then the one word message was sent back – ABU. That meant "I have dropped my bombs".

I shall never forget that summer of 1940. When we were off duty we would lie on our backs on the village green at Frant and watch the dog fights going on high above us. In the balmy air the faint chatter of machine guns would filter through to us as two or three lonely Spitfires would dart like sparrows in and out of the massed bombers that droned seemingly unconcerned on their way to London.

In August 1940 I and Frances – my childhood sweetheart – decided to get married in order to qualify for a marriage allowance! On the 24th we were duly married at Becket Street Methodist Church in Derby, where we first met at Sunday school.

I had 48 hours leave and we arranged to stay at Frances home with her mother and grandmother for the wedding night. After a crowded day we prepared for bed, tired and happy, but then, as if on cue, the sirens went!

I paid little attention to them, but Grandma, a gentle lady who I remember could blush like a schoolgirl with embarrassment, announced that we must all go to the Nissen shelter in the back garden. Furthermore she was adamant!

I who had never been in a shelter before and who was stationed on the flight path of every

raid on the south of England in those hectic days, who had survived the numerous coastal raids carried out by the Luftwaffe, and even travelled on a Green Line bus through a daylight bombing raid on London only the day before, was thus forced to spend my wedding night on a bunk a yard away from my bride, with her mother and grandmother to keep us company. So much for war time romances!

Arthur W. Dalby-Phillips, Grasmere,
155 Bagnall Road, Nottingham

Plotting the movement of enemy aircraft.

When the Battle of Britain started I was working in a shop in Grays, Essex. I remember that the siren sounded for an air raid in the late afternoon one day, and we in the shop, that is 6 of us, went down to the shelter in the back gardens. Although there was shrapnel from the guns still falling about we couldn't resist eventually coming out to see what was going on!

Our first thought was that the invasion had started, even though the church bells weren't ringing. The sky was full of aeroplanes almost like swarms of bees. They were flying in tight formation. I can still see in my mind our fighter planes weaving in and out of them trying to break up the formations and separate them, making it easier for them to be shot at.

There were a number of parachutes coming down. Of course as the planes were shot down the pilots were baling out, but at the time we girls thought they were paratroopers and part of the invasion force!

The planes I remember scored a direct hit on the oil works at Purfleet, which was near to us at Grays, and it meant that trains to Barking station where I had to get to were unable to get through. Fortunately we had a van, and we managed to get home by road.

We often had aerial "dog fights" going on in Grays and would see our fighters go back to base at the nearby aerodrome very often doing a victory roll, although I am told that that was not allowed.

When they got the trains running again we saw at the side of the line numerous damaged aeroplanes, some of which had been forced to do a "belly" landing.

Being only 23 years old it was all a very frightening but exciting time. I was once walking on my rounds when I was nearly hit by shrapnel from our guns, and sheltering in a doorway I could clearly see the bombs leaving the German bombers. I ran very very quickly into the nearest shelter in someone's garden!

We soon lost our excitement over falling bombs and air battles going on above us, because we were more concerned with staying alive, and we just wanted to get home from work before the sirens went. After a while it started to get raids in the evenings and the siren seemed to go almost regularly between 6 and 7 p.m. So if we were lucky we just had time to have dinner and then it was straight down to the shelter until the all clear went usually at 7 a.m. next morning.

When the winter came it was cold and wet and we would shelter under the stairs or under a table instead of in the shelter in the garden.

People were being killed and houses being demolished all around us, and I can still remember the feeling each day when we went to work but despite all our troubles you still considered yourself lucky to be alive!

Mrs. Dorothy Southgate,
4 Warwick Road,
Broughton Astley, Leicestershire

11

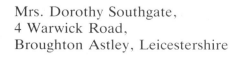

Pilot Officer W. D. McKnight, awarded the Distinguished Flying Cross for destroying 3 enemy aircraft in one day and then attacking an artillery train on the French Coast with his remaining ammunition.

In the early stages of the Battle of Britain many south coast towns were the targets of the German "hit and run" aircraft. At this time I was a Corporal Physical Training and Drill Instructor in the Royal Air Force, attached to one of the Air Navigation Schools centred in Eastbourne.

The cadets were billeted in hotels in the town, some of them on the seafront. As a matter of policy it was decided that the R.A.F. would supplement the Army defences by setting up machine gun posts on the flat roofs of some of the hotels and these would be manned by the cadets.

I was up on the roof one day when a new crew was being briefed by an Officer about what to expect.

After he had finished I remember him saying "Now lads, you don't have to worry about those Germans. They're rotten shots. Only yesterday they opened fire on us, and they missed us by a good yard!"

I remember that a few very white faces appeared amongst the young lads!

Edward Fensome, 3 Birchfields, Camberley, Surrey

My memories start in June 1940 when as a Royal Artillery man, aged 18, I was stationed at Portland in Dorset. I was manning, with about 60 other gunners, a Heavy Coastal Defence Battery, situated on the west side of the Island. There were steep cliffs about 300 feet high.

As you can appreciate the view from our Battery position gave us a fantastic panoramic view over the surrounding coast area, including Chesil Beach and more important over a naval base at Portland Harbour which a fortnight earlier had witnessed some troops of the B.E.F. and French forces being evacuated from France.

During the month of July I remember German air activity increased considerably, with daylight attacks by small numbers of enemy aircraft resulting in bombs being dropped in and around the Naval Dockyard installations, doing some damage and causing casualties to naval ships and personnel.

However, what these raids did achieve for our defences and civil defence units was to prepare them for what was to follow during the next 2 months.

I remember the following events clearly. One fine day during that fateful summer we heard the sound of aircraft engines, and we were suddenly alerted to a large mass of enemy planes headed for the Harbour about 8,000 feet high. Seconds later about 50 aircraft became visible a few miles away. The air raid sirens immediately gave warning, although belated for some, for as the sirens were still sounding all hell was let loose!

About 20 Junkers 87 dive bombers broke formation and started diving on the Dockyard area, and in particular the Anti Aircraft Defence Ship H.M.S. Foylebank. At this time all the Ack-Ack defences opened up on the raiders. The noise was deafening and frightening. There were our own guns firing and enemy bombs bursting. Several planes had already been hit by the terrific barrage being put up against them, and parachutes were coming down over the Harbour from crews who managed to use them, and jump from their stricken planes.

The Foylebank itself was now a sorry sight, and had obviously been hit very badly. She was now enveloped in dense smoke and flame. However, some guns were still firing and we were to learn afterwards that one of the gunners, a seaman named Jack Mantle, had continued firing his gun until he was killed although severely wounded. His effort was probably seen by many in our Battery. It came as no surprise to us when he was posthumously awarded the Victoria Cross. It was the first I believe awarded to the Royal Navy in British Home Waters in World War 2. He was buried in the Royal Naval Cemetery at Portland. Regretfully H.M.S. Foylebank sank shortly after this action, and the casualties were very heavy.

Towards the end of this raid enemy aircraft were still flying low over the Island, trying to get out of the intense fire still being directed against them. I, and a mate of mine, were manning the machine gun near our Observation and Fire Control Post, when we saw an enemy fighter, an ME109, heading straight for our Battery! We started firing at several hundred yards range, and observed tracer very close to the plane, but although some hits may have been scored, the plane carried on without any apparent damage!

After the raid it was announced that many enemy aircraft had been destroyed, some being caught out over the Channel by our fighters. JU 87 bombers were in fact gradually phased out of service towards the end of the Battle of Britain owing to the heavy losses inflicted on them!

An Observer Post attached to a Coastal Defence Battery.

13

By late evening that day large clouds of smoke were still coming from the dockyard area, and some oil tanks, which had been hit, added to the general dismal scene. For many of us, servicemen and civilians, this raid had certainly been our baptism of war and will always be remembered by all who witnessed this raid at Portland. That night I remember turning in with quite a headache after a day of high excitement, drama and tension, and very thankful to be fit in mind and body!

During August I was to witness many more such raids and it was common to see large numbers of enemy aircraft passing high overhead en route to bomb inland targets. Very frequently we witnessed air battles between Hurricanes and Spitfires against enemy fighters, usually ME 109E's and 110's, and also bombers such as HE 111's, Dornier 17's and 117's and JU 88's. I personally saw about 12 enemy planes brought down within about 5 miles radius of Portland and relate the following incident which occurred on 11th August, 1940. It was a lovely morning, and as I was on guard duty that suited me fine! I had visions of doing a bit of sun bathing in the fields behind our Battery. How wrong I was to become!

About mid morning we could hear the now familiar drone of heavy bombers approaching. The sirens started their wailing warning and I thought ruefully, here it comes again! Within seconds large stacks of enemy planes could be clearly seen in the clear skies to the south east, and machine gun fire could be heard in the distance. Our fighters were already in action!

Some of the enemy formations were breaking up and within seconds bombs were bursting in the dockyard area and the long Chesil Beach, where the oil tanks were and also regretfully on civilian homes situated near this area. At this stage I took cover in a sandbag emplacement in the Battery where I also got a better view! By now the scene below was looking like Dante's Inferno, and "dog fights" were going on all over the sky. Several planes had already been shot down, and one I saw crashed near Weymouth harbour.

At about this time one of our chaps yelled out "one of the buggers is coming down". I looked quickly in the direction he pointed, and sure enough a JU 88 was about to crash land in a field about 250 yards away. A Spitfire fighter was about 100 yards behind pumping fire into it with long bursts of his machine guns. The pilot must have been OK because he pancaked down roughly, knocking telephone wires down in the process, and skidding to a halt in a turn facing our Battery! Without any further thought I grabbed my rifle and started running towards the plane. I was soon joined by a friend of mine, and another guard and the three of us arrived at the plane together. By this time the fighter was zooming over the scene, doing the Victory Roll before leaving the area.

Three of the bomber crew were helping a fourth chap out of the cockpit canopy, and laid him down on the grass a few yards from the plane. At this time we took the 3 prisoners without any trouble! A civilian Defence Ambulance chap appeared on the scene and he immediately put a tourniquet on the injured airman's leg, or what was left of it. By this time a stretcher had arrived from our Battery, and two of our chaps carried the injured navigator back to the Battery where he was made as comfortable as possible. I couldn't help noticing the plane had been peppered with bullet holes. How the crew had got out alive I will never know. They were certainly very lucky chaps!

When we got back to the Guard Room with our prisoners we carried out a proper examination on them, and apart from a few cuts and bruising they were OK. We gave them some food and drink before they were taken away by a guard and medical team in an ambulance. We heard the next day that the navigator had had his leg amputated, which didn't surprise me at all!

I remember another incident during a raid at this time but with perhaps a more humourous outcome. A lone enemy plane, probably a HE111, flying at about 20,000 feet, after being attacked by Ack-Ack fire and pounced on by a fighter, had released his bomb load so that he would increase his speed to get away! At this time I was working on fatigues doing repairs to our perimeter barbed wire fencing, which surrounded our Battery.

I saw the plane zig-zagging and was suddenly aware, by the shrill whine, that bombs were on the way! The first bomb exploded in a church yard about 400 yards away. I dived for cover, which turned out to be a covered dug out used by the guard. As I took off the rest

15

German Reconnaissance photographs of burning oil storage tanks at Newhaven, 7th August 1940.

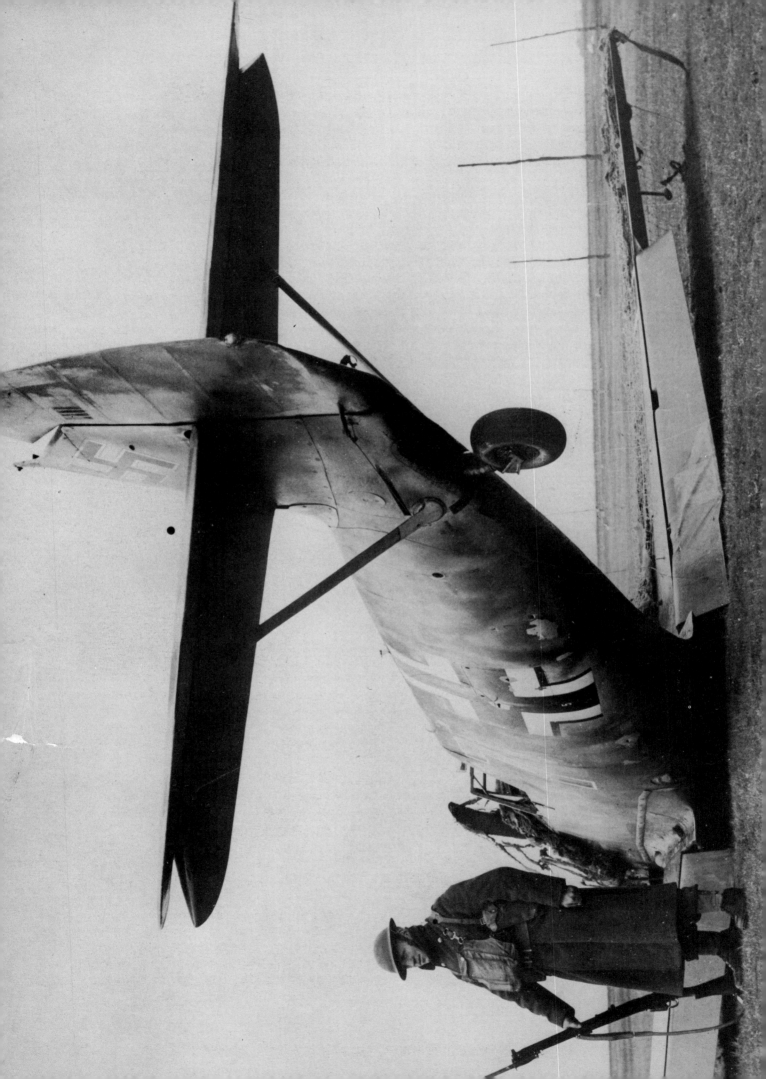

of the stick of bombs started exploding at about 60 yard intervals in a more or less straight line towards the Battery! I was surprised at the softness of my landing and then more so as I hard an angry growl of protest. I had landed on no such other person as our Guard Commander, who no doubt had taken refuge before I did!

The last bomb of a stick of five landed about 50 yards away from us. We were showered with debris from the crater, but as I had taken most of the muck and shielded the Guard Commander, no charge was forthcoming! On reflection, I am sure my journey through the air was assisted by the last bomb blast, but thankfully it was the last bomb in the stick. Or else...!

Later I had to walk to a cemetery and inspected the results of the first bomb. Not a pretty sight! Bones and coffins everywhere. The other bombs had exploded harmlessly thank God!

The reason I was only 18 in 1940 was that I had joined the Territorial Army at the age of 17. I had been trained as an Infantryman in the 1/5th and 2nd/5th Leicesters, but because I was under 19 I was too young to be sent abroad with the above Battalions. So I had been sent and transferred to the Royal Artillery and Weymouth and Portland in May 1940. Apart from home leave, we had one day off every seven days. I was stationed in and around Portland until 1943, when I was transferred to a Mobile Unit for the invasion of France. But that of course is another story!...

Gordon W. Kennely, 52 Balmoral Road, Mountsorrel, Nr. Loughborough, Leicestershire

---

In 1940 I was a paperboy earning 30 shillings (£1.50) a week from a Mr. Len Wiltshire of South Willesborough, delivering in the Romney Marsh area as it is known. It was a very long round, especially on a bike! This is why I got all that extra money!

I was very small and thin. We used to start at 6 o'clock in the morning and my round was Sevington, Mersham, Bilington, Bonnington, Newchurch, Ivychurch, Ruckinge and Home! Anyone would be able to trace this route on a map of Romney Marsh. I can recall many things. The rat-a-tat of machine gun fire of battles overhead, with the Hurricanes and Spitfires getting in amongst the hordes of German bombers and fighters.

One incident I remember particularly. A Dornier bomber crash landed across the road between Bonnington and Newchurch, near to a farm cottage, after being shot down. I remember that the farmer's wife held the crew up with what transpired to be a toy pistol!

I remember next day the reporters came down from London to get her story and I met them all as they borrowed the papers I was delivering to read their reports of the previous day!

On many occasions I used to sit in the crashed planes although they were guarded by soldiers and police. I also remember the local policeman we had who captured a German pilot! The pilot's plane had crashed on a farmhouse, killing the farmer's wife and a child. The pilot was found in a field wandering around. He was over 40 years old and belonged to the Yellow Nosed Crack Squadron. I remember a few of these planes were shot down.

Another incident involved myself. I used to deliver on to several Army searchlight camps that were dotted about Romney Marsh. I used to bring them cigs, sweets etc. This day in question a Dornier bomber came down on fire. It was very low and you could see the markings and the men inside.

17

Messerschmitt 109 shot down so quickly on 25th October 1940 over Romney Marsh that its guns had not been fired.

What happened next I will remember all my days.

All the soldiers got their rifles and were firing at it. It continued down in flames until it hit the ground and exploded on impact.

Next morning when I arrived, they told me that I had a lucky escape. Where I had been standing was a bullet implanted in the side of the hut. In fact they thought that it had been fired from the plane!

The worst incident was when a German fighter was shot down. The pilot jumped out but his parachute did not open. He landed in a field by the camp, but they would not let me see him. When they showed me the spot the next day, the ground was badly marked and it is something I will never forget.

On several occasions I would have to jump off my bike whilst delivering papers, as "dogfights" took place overhead. I got to know the soldiers at the camps quite well, and even one day invited two of them home to my mum and dad's house, which they accepted, and came to tea. They were from the Royal Ulster Rifles.

Funnily enough, another thing I remember from this time was the local baker who baked his own bread! I used to help him and he used to help deliver some of my papers! His bread rolls were very good. The Battle of Britain only lasted a few months but I can remember all these things and more as if it was only yesterday.

Fred Smith, 41 Herbert Road, South Willesborough, Ashford, Kent

I particularly remember the Battle of Britain because I served in the W.A.A.F. on a Fighter Station at Hornchurch in Essex as a plotter in the Operations Room. We had Spitfires stationed at the Station rather than Hurricanes. Our work was of the utmost secrecy. We were on both day and night shifts.

One day we had a daylight raid of low flying German planes. They bombed the airfield and because of the lack of warning they caught the Spitfires as they were taking off. We were not on duty. We were down in the shelters. But when it was over and we came up we saw a terrible sight. There were huge craters and bits of Spitfire planes spread around. We were all given shovels and we filled in the craters to get the airfield operational again.

After that our Operations Room was moved to a grocer's shop near the river. We were in Grays in Essex. It was rather a make-do place, cramped and with little space to move around, and here one day whilst I was on duty the Battle of Britain really got underway.

We had information of the movement of aircraft from the Observer Corps in Kent and Essex who were watching from the coastline. We plotted on the table with little arrows the route, height and number of the planes, and the numbers seemed to grow and grow. Then we heard the actual sound of the Battle itself. Guns, bombs, planes coming down, it was deafening. Then the bombs fell on the oil refinery on the Thames opposite us. There were huge black clouds floating over. It became quite dark except for the flames, and it was as if all hell had been let loose.

Then all our lines went dead and we had no means of communication until they were hurriedly repaired.

Because our work was very very concentrated we could not afford to make a mistake with our plotting. Pilots' lives were in our hands. We returned to camp in a lorry, all very tense and wondering how many unexploded bombs we were driving over. After that we were moved to the Masonic Hall in Romford. After the little shop it seemed a palace! But many a time we had to throw ourselves flat on our face on the way to our bus that took us to our Operations Room in Romford. Very often there was a stick of 5 or 6 bombs coming down and as we lay flat on our way to night duty in the dark we could almost count them from the different explosions. If 2 or 3 landed to our right and then the fourth landed to our left we would get up and run to the bus!

In the beginning we did 3 shifts. A 12 hour night duty and then 2 day duties. Later on we did a 6 hour night duty, because we had more people. Most of our rest time on the camp we spent in the shelters!

We lived in married quarters on the camp. Two girls to a room. The houses had little gardens of which we were very proud. When we had any spare time we grew tomatoes, but we had no idea how to do it! Not knowing that one had to pinch out the green shoots, we had tomato trees! Nevertheless they were full of tomatoes!

I can remember that we used to shake our fists at the German planes in frustration and after we got our tomatoes well underway it was often said that if Hitler dropped a bomb on our tomatoes we were going to be very annoyed! Luckily they never did or otherwise it's likely I would not be here to tell this tale.

We stayed in the Operations room in Romford all through that time, but the only result of that when the Battle of Britain came to an end was that we then had to stay through the Blitz. But that is another story.

Mrs. Muriel E. Vlaanderen, 19 Alledge Drive, Woodford, Kettering, Northants

The Operations Room of an RAF Station, Fighter Command, in 1940.

When the Battle of Britain was on we played out in the street a lot, and I remember one day the air raid siren had gone off. The barrage balloons were up, and an aeroplane got caught in the balloon's wires and it crash landed in the grounds of Dagenham & County High School.

My friends, girls and boyfriends, ran to see if it was a German plane, and we were all very excited. Then when we reached the plane it was a Spitfire that had crashed and out stepped the pilot with a white silk scarf round his neck. All of a sudden all the school children gave him a cheer for landing safe even though we were disappointed he wasn't a German!

I was never evacuated as my mother wouldn't let me go. She said if we were to be killed we would all be killed together! My father worked in London in a tobacco factory called Lambert & Butlers, and he was on fire watch duty. I remember one morning he should have come home and he didn't arrive. We were all getting quite worried as that was the night of the first blitz on London, and then we got a phone call from our local sweet shop saying he was alright but a bit shaken. He would be home shortly.

When he arrived we kissed and hugged him and Mum made him a nice cup of tea. Then he told us that he had had a narrow escape as he had got blown down a staircase. But two men were killed. He also said that the canteen had got bombed and he brought some tea home as we were always short of tea!

I think we grew up very quickly in the war time. When the air raid siren went we would grab our homework and Mother's insurance books, birth certificates, identity cards and any other papers and run to the shelter. One day I was seeing to my Mum's chickens and the siren went and I went to go to the shelter that was in our back garden. Funnily enough I remember that sitting there on the shelter was the largest toad you have ever seen! I could not move as I was frightened, but my father picked it up by the leg and threw it over someone else's garden! Then we all got into the shelter.

It was a tragic time but at the same time we had some fun in the dark old days 1939/1945. I can remember when the war was over in 1945 we went round to all the different streets in Dagenham to see if we could get in on any of the street parties that they were having. But sad to say no luck! Still never mind!

Mrs. J. Dalton, 2 Weyland Road, Dagenham, Essex

One of my recollections during the Battle of Britain was when I was with a Searchlight Detachment in Headcorn, Kent, when one particular alarm was sounded for us to take up battle stations. I was in P.T. shorts, with no shirt, because I was sunbathing about 200 yards away from the site. I was running up the road when a German fighter started to machine gun the

area. Bullets started to hit the road behind me and so I took avoiding action by diving into the hedge. Unfortunately I did not realise that it was a bed of stinging

nettles! Afterwards my mates had to give my body a good scrub with vinegar taken from a pickled onion jar, and the results were that I was called "Stinker" for a week afterwards!

Ossie Lloyd, 2 Bishopstone Drive, Beltinge, Herne Bay, Kent

21

Spitfire pilots coming in from combat.

I was 12 when war was declared and I had been warned not to stray from home as there would be some important news on the wireless. I was talking and laughing with a school friend in the street when suddenly there was the eerie wailing notes of the air raid siren filling the air. I can remember that our laughter stopped straight away, and I recall feeling chilled and scared. Doors were opened and people came out of their houses looking up to the sky. My mother ran down the street to push a gas mask (which was still in its cardboard box) into my arms, and told me to follow her to the shelter at once. Doors were quickly closed and our neighbours also sought their air raid shelters. It was a Sunday morning, just after 11.00 a.m. on a beautiful summer's day with blue skies and really warm sunshine. But within minutes our lives had changed, and the child in me had gone never to return. From then on it seemed that we were constantly facing a time of responsibility and danger.

We sat on the wooden bunks in the shelter for a while and then the all clear sounded. Apparently it had all been a false alarm, and we then had quite a few months of the "phoney war" as we called it. Then the raids started on the coastal towns and into Kent and then to London.

The Anderson shelters were a construction of steel sheets bolted together in a curved shape. This was then sunk deep into the earth of the garden with sand bags filled and the rest of the earth piled on top. Later on we grew a patch of flowers on ours as camouflage!

We tried to make them as comfortable as possible with cushions and small blankets etc., but our only means of lighting was a hand torch or candles.

The days were hot and sunny, but we had to spend long hours in the shelters, coming up between in a quiet lull if possible to make a cup of tea or a sandwich. Quite often, however, this would be impossible either because the gas was just a glimmer, or it was too dangerous.

We lived only a matter of yards away from the Barracks, and had factories by the riverside. Also we were near an aerodrome, and Tilbury Docks was on the opposite side of the river, so there was plenty of gunfire at times. When the Heavy Ack Ack guns boomed out the ground seemed to shake, and the Bofor guns on the lorries and trailers would tour the streets, firing with a "pom pom" sound. The tracer bullets were often called "flaming onions". After the raids we would sweep up pieces of shrapnel or broken glass from the street, but some brown sticky paper in cross strips often helped to prevent glass breaking.

In between raids we tried to carry on as normal. My Mother was working so I was often in the company of an aunt. Her twin sons had been captured in France, and I recall when we were shopping one day I told her that I could hear a German plane. She thought this was nonsense as the siren had not given its usual warning. But then suddenly from behind a cloud and quite low the huge grey shape of a German bomber appeared. I can clearly remember it had black swastikas on the side.

This was followed by others, moving quite slowly, and then the air raid siren sounded and the guns started firing. But instead of going to the shelter I remember my aunt dancing with rage on the pavement, shaking her fists in defiance of the bombers! I looked on quite amazed at this display and then an Air Raid Warden ran up and shouted, telling us to take cover in a nearby shelter for the public.

The blackout was a problem. I could recall in the past I had

J.U. 88 Bomber.

run home from school. It was turning dark, and I loved to see the lamp lighter. He rode his bicycle with a long pole balanced over his shoulder, and one touch of the pole to the tall lamp post and the street was lit with a comforting glow. But now with the war it was all pitch dark. We walked with the aid of dim torches, and a few cars moved slowly with headlights dimmed, and not a glimmer of light showed from the houses. When we had a full moon everywhere was lit up with a silver light. Then we could see. But so could the planes and we came to dread "the bombers moon" as it was called. Sometimes on a dark night I had seen the search lights sweep the skies, and then a plane was caught in the crossed beams, and the guns would crash out their fire and the enemy plane would spin towards earth in flames.

One night I can remember seeing white parachutes floating down, and my first thought was of an invasion. But the planes were dropping flares to light up their targets. You just lived each hour as it came, but there was a wonderful spirit everywhere and it was a time I can never forget.

Mrs. Mary Earle, 1 St. Albans Close, Valley Drive, Gravesend, Kent

---

I was an Apprentice Carpenter with 9 months still to finish my time when I was called up to report to Dover on 16th September, 1940. That is the day after that which is celebrated as Battle of Britain Day because of the number of planes reputedly shot down.

A man who worked with my father was going to the same place so we travelled together, catching a train from Aylesbury about 7.45 a.m., which should have got us to Baker Street by 9.15, finishing the journey from Rickmansworth, behind an electric engine. However, we stopped at one of the stations beyond Harrow. "Everybody off. Buses in the forecourt." They delivered us to another station with an underground service, and eventually we arrived outside Charing Cross where we were confronted with a line of Redcaps turning everyone away. There seemed to be hundreds like ourselves with little suitcases!

"Try Blackfriars". "How do you get there?" "Use the Underground if you don't know the way." We knew the trains were not moving because there was a raid on, and the flood gates were shut because we had been held up on the Bakerloo on account of it. It was midday by now and as we had had enough gumption to pack some sandwiches we went into a pub and waited for the "all clear". Having got to Blackfriars and on to the platform, we were then instructed to catch an Orpington loop-line train, but before one arrived there was another warning and we had to go down to ground level and only go up when the train came in.

We got within one or two stations of Orpington and once again it was "everybody off, buses outside". Having regained the train at Orpington we went on to change during that afternoon and evening at Tonbridge Wells and Ashford, to arrive at Dover about 7 o'clock. We had been travelling for nearly 12 hours on a journey of less than 150 miles.

During the next four weeks whilst doing initial training the air activity was confined to high flying fighters and fighter bombers carefully keeping just out of range of the guns around Dover. There were, however, raids on the barrage balloons, and convoys going through the Dover Straits. Having joined one of the gun sites in the area in the middle of October, by the end of the month we were treated to a most amazing sight. A large formation of heavy bombers, of unusual design, some even bi-planes, fairly slow and at only 10,000 feet as against the normal 30,000 feet. They were heading straight over us!

It was the Duce's Italian effort! It was a gunner's paradise and they had a rough ride especially when the fighters got at them over Kent!

Soon after that, following some attempts to bomb the gun sites, though without doing much damage, we were pulled out and the fighters took over the defence of the area. As regards Dover itself, during this period, the long range shelling from across the Channel was much more unhealthy than that of the bombers, although neither could be recommended!

Philip Roche, 1 St. Mary's Row, Aylesbury, Buckinghamshire

A barrage balloon at the docks.

I first joined the Army in 1938 and by the time the war started I was in the 452 Company of the 67th Searchlight Regiment. The result was that in those regiments instead of being called a "Private" I was called a "Gunner". This caused a lot of amusement at home where my brothers and sister and my step brothers and sisters found it all highly amusing because they said I couldn't fire a pop gun!

Our Searchlight Regiment had a number of jobs. Apart from the obvious one of trying to pick out enemy planes so that the gunners could fire at them the other was to if needs be dip our searchlights in the direction of the nearest airfield for any of our planes that were returning home having lost their bearings or at dusk. By lighting up enemy aircraft we could have also given the general direction to where they were so that our fighters could engage them.

We moved around the country a great deal, and very often we were left in remote places for months at a time. We had a ration lorry that used to come every other day which also used to bring us our mail. A lot of us used to have a parcel now and then mostly from churches and charities of different kinds. The sad thing was that people were rationed so tightly that all the poor dears of the country seemed to do was knit mittens and scarves and woollen helmets. Every parcel seemed to contain a set of mittens, a scarf and a woollen helmet! Our kit bags were full of them!

So we started to change them with the local farmers for eggs and rabbits, and sometimes a chicken. The problem was that eventually every farmer or labourer and even the farmer's wife seemed to have woollen mittens, scarves and woollen helmets. I remember one day even seeing a clergyman on a bike wearing one near a village in Devon!

The farmers eventually had so many mittens and scarves and woollen helmets that we lost all our bargaining power with them. However, suddenly they started to ask for them again, and we couldn't understand this till one of our chaps found out that they were undoing them and reknitting them into jerseys and pullovers! So then we saw all the farmers in the vicinity wearing them, all in khaki of course.

Talking of bargaining power I must mention one item that I always remember had no bargaining power at all. This was food sent over by the Americans! They were dreaded tins of soya sausages. I never found one person in the whole of the British Army who liked them, and I cooked for some different chaps I can tell you. I used to try disguising them with onions, or even mixing small quantities in with cottage pie, but always the taste came through and nobody would eat any of it once they tasted it.

The farmers tried them but after the first lot weren't interested in them anymore! We then suggested that they use them in the pig swill. One farmer came back and said he'd tried it, but all it had done had brought his pigs out in a rash! We rather doubted that tale! But it gives you some idea of the aittitude that we had to American food. I never heard of the civilians having any of our soya sausages but I always remember our Sergeant saying that if they had Britain would have surrendered straight away! My mind boggles to this day at the thought of those soya sausages.

Anyhow back to the Battle of Britain and the involvement of my Searchlight Regiment in all that happened. We were at a little village called Huntley just outside Gloucester. It was a Search-light Camp of 40 men and our supply of water came from a family who had a little lorry hire business next door to the camp. They had a very deep well and the water was quite delicious. You could imagine that the well was soon in constant use with 40 men at the camp. I think the family's name was Blanford or something like that, and I still have a photograph that was taken with the lady at the house. However, to get back to my story.

Re-arming a Hurricane for action.

We were allowed 7 days privilege leave, to be taken 2 men at a time. Came my time and I set off for home in Clydach. It wasn't a very happy home. My dad had remarried after the death of my mother in 1930, and my step mother had children and so I had brothers and sisters and step brothers and sisters and we didn't all get on very well at all.

But I loved my Dad very dearly, because he had been both a mother and father to me since 1930, and I always said that if I could grow up to be half the man he was I'd have been alright. When I arrived I was generally greeted by my step mother saying "Your father is over the allotments". What a greeting! He spent most of his time off work there.

But on this particular occasion after spending my leave with Dad on the allotments, and when he was at work roaming the hills and mountains around the town, I returned to the Army camp site at Huntley to resume my duties as the camp cook. After a few days I received a very disturbing letter from my Dad. I relate roughly now what he wrote.

"Whatever have you brought home with you son? Your brother has got them, so has your sister, step sister, step brothers, step mother (that made me laugh!), myself and now my workmates at work are walking about scratching like monkeys. I find they are what are commonly known as "crabs" and if you are in any way embarrassed by this and don't want anyone to know about it, I will tell you how to get rid of these tormenting parasites. But you will have to be very careful. If you can get hold of a little petrol, put some on a rag and rub it on your pubic hairs and under your armpits, but whatever you do, do keep away from the fire!" Well I had noticed these little insects on me, and I must admit that I was constantly scratching! I had tried picking them off, but they seemed to bore into my skin, especially around my private parts, and I was concerned that they seemed to be multiplying at an alarming rate as well! So I decided to take Dad's advice and try his remedy.

Now we had a very large Thorneycroft lorry on the site which was used to generate the searchlight so with that in mind I decided on my course of action. I waited till night and everyone was asleep. I then got a long stick and tied a piece of cloth on the end, and crept quietly to the lorry and dipped it into the petrol tank. It came out dripping wet with petrol.

That task completed without incident, I crept behind the huts and proceeded to rub this cloth over all the relevant parts! After having completed what I had set out to do I returned to my sleeping hut and quietly got into bed to await the results of my secret operation!

It wasn't long before I had to abandon any thoughts I might have had of having a peaceful night's sleep. Slowly at first, then rapidly I started to burn all over, especially my private parts and rear! It reached such alarming discomfort that I had to leave my bed. Firstly I ran around the field in my underpants. The night was quite cool but it did not cure my terrific burning sensation! Not feeling much relief from that I then got a bowl of ice cold water and a cloth, and kept dabbing myself all over. Remember this was in the middle of a field at 1 o'clock in the morning and I can tell you that my teeth were soon chattering. After some time I decided to give bed another try. I eventually did manage to drop off to sleep.

The next morning my first thought on awakening was to investigate the results of my night's work. The crabs had gone alright, and I haven't seen a sight of a crab from that day to this but I couldn't get the smell of petrol to disappear from my blankets and clothes for a very long time. Funnily enough the following day I observed a large Army lorry entering our site gates, and then half a dozen or so of the men proceeded to unload two large boilers and four galvanised baths. There was also all sorts of soaps and boxes of ointment, also flannels and brushes. Accompanying all this equipment was our Medical Officer, giving out instructions. Soon they had the boilers alight and full of boiling water, and for days there was quite a lot of scrubbing and bathing and shaving going on till finally the Medical Officer gave the "all clear". It had been an operation to get rid of "crabs" in the camp and if I had just hung on a few days I could have done it the easy way. The funny part was that he remained puzzled by the fact that there were 40 men in the camp, 39 of whom had crabs all over them, and one didn't! I always remember him saying that he had never heard of anyone being immune to crabs! I never said anything, so I remained a mystery to him. The final irony of it all is that I think my current girlfriend at that time must also have caught crabs, because after one particular night with her I never saw her again!

Kenneth "Rosie" Barfoot, 76 Bournes Hill, Halesowen, West Midlands

Flt. Lt. Ball DFC; Sqd. Ldr. D. Bader, DSO and Pilot Officer W. D. McKnight, DFC, at Duxford, September 1940.

I joined the R.A.F. in 1938, and after training as an Air Craft Rigger I was posted to a Squadron working on Wellington bombers. It was those Wellington bombers that carried out the first raid of the war on Germany. There were 6 involved and on the first raid 2 of them did not return. I knew the crews personally.

After the first few weeks of the war when we had finished servicing aircraft and they had to go on a raid, we then had to go to the middle of the airfield and to the side of the Flare Path and wait for our planes to return. As soon as we heard engines we had to light the paraffin flare with matches and then run out of the way! As soon as the planes had landed we then had to dash like hell to put the flares out so that there could not be any possibility of any guiding light for German planes to bomb the air strip.

One thing that I shall never forget was one afternoon. I was taking a load of bombs by tractor with about 8 trailers full of bombs. I had to go past the hangars to get to the dispersal points across the other side of the airfield.

As I got to the hangars the air raid warning went, and I parked my tractor and bombs outside the administrative building and went to dash into a shelter. It wasn't a very bright thing to do.

However, before I could get into the shelter the Duty Officer stopped me and asked me what I was doing! I told him! He turned round to me then and said "Get those bloody bombs to the dispersal point. You'll have us all blown up"!

He was right of course. But I had to take the bombs straight across the open air field in the midst of an air raid, and I can tell you I wasn't decidedly happy about that arrangement! However, I came out unharmed. But it is my one major recollection of the events of the Battle of Britain and even though the Duty Officer was right, it wasn't him who had to drive the tractor with 8 trailer loads of bombs behind it while bombs were dropping all round!

I was based at R.A.F. Honnington near Bury St. Edmunds and I knew most of the air crews. There was James Smalley, big and untidy, who regularly brought show girls down from London to the parties, and then would sit other evenings when he had nothing to do sitting quietly on a sofa knitting! There was Bill Macrae who was a Canadian who was almost passionately alcoholic, and who delighted in carrying out stunts with his Wellington bomber over the churches of Norfolk lifting his wing tips at the last second almost before crashing into the spires. There was Peter Grant who was a fair haired lad and almost a Hollywood caricature of the sporting youth English public schoolboy. He was a General's son who had joined the R.A.F. after failing to get into Cambridge and he had a stylish approach to life both on the ground and in the air.

One major incident everyone remembered was when he brought his Wellington in at almost zero level over the rugger pitch, scattering players to all points of the compass. However, there was no trouble from the Commanding Officer because he believed that spirited flying bred spirited fighters. Perhaps he was right!

I can remember the time when the first contingent of the Women's Auxiliary Airforce girls, called the W.A.A.F. arrived at the airfield. It created unprecedented excitement, and caused the Station Commander to make one of his rare public appearances to supervise the rigging up of a barbed wire entanglement around their quarters!

The only discordant note that was struck was when it was found that the most glamorous and sought after of the girls had ended up in the arms of a non commissioned SERGEANT PILOT!

Sam Jones, 21 Manor Road, Tipton, West Midlands

Pilots resting prior to take off.

As soon as we heard the news that war had broken out I went with my mother, brother and sister to find my father who was working out on the farm. As we walked through the orchard, we three children were plying mum with all sorts of questions.

"Why do the Germans want to fight us? Will we be bombed out? When will the sirens go off? Will the bombers come over and drop bombs on us? Will dad have to leave us here to help fight the Germans? Do we still have to go to school?

All these thoughts were going through our young, innocent but confused minds. We were living in the Weald of Kent, not far from the coast, and our peaceful, idyllic lives

Mrs. Rowland, front right.

were suddenly thrown into turmoil with activity everywhere. All signposts were taken away, as were all iron gates and railings, which were melted down to make guns.

Army troops moved into surrounding orchards and fields with anti-aircraft guns, all heavily camouflaged. Only a mile away from us was a Searchlight Battery which scanned the skies for enemy aircraft as soon as a siren sounded.

During an air raid we had to stay indoors because of the flying shrapnel caused by the Ack-Ack guns nearby. Many a time we had to delay leaving home for school because of an air raid and as the school was over two miles away, we quite often had to jump into a ditch, this being the only shelter available. As soon as the sirens sounded, our own fighters would take off and were soon engaged in "dogfights" with the enemy planes. It was a familiar sight to see planes shot down and pilots baling out. If a plane came down close by we would chase off to the crash scene. If an enemy was shot down we would watch until the British pilot did a victory roll, at which we would all cheer and jump up and down with excitement.

One day some War Office officials came to our farm with an Ordnance Survey map and requested to see a certain field which was flanked on either side by a large wood. As this field was pasture land, they told my father that he must dig a wide ditch in the shape of an "L" through the centre of the field to prevent enemy aircraft from landing after darkness and depositing troops who would then hide in the woods. After this we children were kept well away from the woods in case a German pilot was hiding there!

During the Battle of Britain we had to endure air raids day and night. No sooner had the "all clear" sounded than it seemed the siren went again!

During the early hours of one morning we were surrounded by bombs. It seemed that a bomber was being attacked and the pilot decided to drop his bomb load and make a run for it! What we thought was the plane coming down in flames turned out to be a basketful of incendiary bombs on fire. At the same time there were terrible explosions everywhere; windows shattered, the back door was blown off its hinges, our beds shook and moved across the floor. Then the dog howled and the cats were charging everywhere! My father and brother immediately rushed across the fields to put out the incendiary devices which had

fortunately landed conveniently near our pond! When it was daylight my father discovered three unexploded bombs in the field about 150 yards from our house. These were dealt with by the Bomb Disposal Squad. Another larger bomb had fallen some 400 yards away. This one had buried itself into the earth so far that it took almost a week to dig out! Two other large craters were found close by and it appeared we were very lucky not to have received a direct hit that night. I am sure that my parents offered many prayers of thanks to the Lord. Incidentally, after the war the farmers were paid to fill in their own bomb craters.

33

A German pilot shot down, 29th October 1940.

I can remember picking up propaganda leaflets that had been dropped by enemy aircraft overnight as well as handfuls of silver, metallic strips which had been dropped to try and confuse the radar. Many different posters were displayed in school – "Dig for Victory", "Save All Waste Paper", "Careless Talk Costs Lives", "Don't Answer Questions should a Stranger approach you, even if he is in uniform, he may be a Spy". Many posters carried pictures of bombs telling us not to pick up any but to notify our parents or teacher.

Looking back over the war years there were many amusing and many sad incidents but I think we were so young that we didn't really appreciate the true significance of it all.

Mrs. Doreen Rowland, 22 Greystoke Road, Caversham, Reading, Berks

One glorious late June morning, when all should have been right with the world, the air raid siren went. The last wail died away with its lingering low pitched moan, and within minutes, seconds even, aircraft were directly overhead with engines screaming and machine guns blazing into the clear blue sky. It was not to be the last time in 1940 that the Battle of Britain would rage over Dorset's gentle countryside.

I was an Apprentice Printer on the local newspaper in Dorchester. I had just turned 18 and had a year's deferment from military service, much to my disgust! I wanted to be a Fighter Pilot, but my boss convinced the powers that be that I could serve the war effort much more effectively by tapping the keys of a Linotype machine! When the sirens went, the paper's staff were under instruction to down tools and take cover but the Chronicle staff didn't take cover, for this was all history in the making, and we wanted to be part of it, even if only in our memories. So we all made for the flat rooftop of the paper's front office in Trinity Street everytime the siren sounded!

On one particular day, I remember the fighter planes from Warmwell, a wartime airfield just a few miles away, were more vicious than usual. Their gunfire was more persistent. The enemy aircraft from across the Channel seemed more determined than ever to break through the force that was slowly destroying their arrogance.

We watched enthralled. We wanted to cheer when aircraft, belching smoke and wobbling crazily screamed towards the ground beyond the rooftops and we pointed at parachutes which mushroomed starkly white against the sky. The planes that were destroyed were Nazi war machines. The bodies beneath the parachutes were usually German aircrew – but we didn't really know, not for certain.

I was looking upwards, towards the south, almost overhead, when suddenly a huge orange flash dimmed the brilliant sunshine. It was followed by a pall of dense black smoke, out of which spewed a mass of debris. Parts of aeroplane started to flutter gently to the ground, leisurely twisting and turning whilst large black objects sped swiftly past them.

From amongst the debris a parachute appeared but the familiar reassuring white mushroom was missing. In its place was a useless fluttering thing, little thicker than a line, to which was attached a sandbag like object beneath it. I followed it down and within seconds it disappeared behind the rooftops.

It was after the war that I read an account of a Polish pilot who had emptied his guns and then in desperation, rammed a Nazi bomber and both aircraft exploded. It may not have been him I saw that day but I have often wondered.

Later on I remember German bombers came over Dorchester again. The siren wailed and a couple of us went on to the flat roof. The Battle of Britain had been virtually won by now, and interest in the war was becoming academic!

We waited for five minutes or so, and then we heard the drone of aircraft. A squadron of twenty or so German bombers finally came into sight. Dorchester was its quiet, rural self. People gazed curiously upwards as the Nazis passed serenely overhead at no more than 1500 feet. Almost every mark on every plane was visible. The Swastika on the tail, the Iron Crosses on the fuselage and wings. They were heading inland. They had no interest in Dorchester. Rumour had it that they were after the Westland Aircraft factory at Yeovil, which at that time was manufacturing the Westland Lysander, a single engine reconnaisance plane.

The German bombers approached their supposed target. On a single command, it seemed, something like the Nazi equivalent of "bombs away – Now!" or "Bloody hell, a Spitfire!" and the squadron released their deadly cargo in one simultaneous action.

The bombs whistled down on to the ancient and lovely old abbey town of Sherborne, which was completely innocent of any serious war effort but is only about four miles from Yeovil.

Was it a Spitfire which caused such panic action? This is what the wartime bush telegraph

35

Fighter pilots of a Polish Squadron.

told us – that a single Spitfire had dived on the Germans from out of the clouds. The pilot supposedly committed suicide in an act of remorse. But was it just another rumour? We will never know.

The damage to Sherbourne was not as bad as might be supposed, although it was bad enough. It was confined mainly to roads, gas mains and water mains. Surrounding fields had large holes in them, the odd cow was knocked out, and an unlucky house or two or three. We never got to hear the extent of any casualties.

I never did become a Fighter Pilot! When I finally joined the R.A.F., they packed me off to India, where I served most of my time in Signals H.Q. in New Delhi as a Wireless Operator – again much to my disgust!

Finally, there was one one extra thing I remember. The Dorset County Chronicle, in common with many other organisations of all sorts and types, ran a Spitfire Fund. The idea was to collect sufficient money in private donations to "buy" a Spitfire, the price of which was generally reckoned to be £5,000. I remember typesetting never ending lists of donations for publication week by week when the Fund was first opened.

As the weeks went by, however, enthusiasm died and the Fund was eventually closed at about £3,500. We never did get a plane with "The Dorchester Chronicle" painted on the fuselage. The money disappeared anonymously into Air Ministry coffers! Times don't change!

Dudley (Doug) E. Gardiner, 65 Broadmeadow Road, Wyke Regis, Weymouth, Dorset

---

It was August 1940. During the afternoon my friend and I had cycled into the countryside as the weather was fine and warm. At about 4 p.m. we were sitting at Portsdown Hill, looking over the land and sea to the Isle of Wight when suddenly we saw and heard a large formation of aircraft coming from that direction.

We had not heard any air raid sirens and moments later to our surprise explosions erupted all over Portsmouth which was soon covered in smoke. By this time some Ack Ack guns were firing and the aircraft were overhead. We felt very exposed, but there was no cover, and when the shock had passed we cycled like mad homewards!

As I rode through areas of devastation my fears grew. At the end of my road a policeman stopped me. I could see chaos everywhere. Smoking piles of bricks where houses had been. The road was strewn with rubble and water seemed to be gushing everywhere.

The Officer let me pass when I explained that my home was at the other end of the road, but he warned me that there were unexploded bombs close by. I made my way down the road, carrying my bicycle over the debris.

Then I realised that there was a huge crater on the corner where the grocer's shop had been. My home was on the opposite side, with the roof damaged, windows gaping, and I will always remember the awful feeling inside me as I got through the front door to look for my family. To my relief they were alright, but dazed with shock. The next day I was helping to clear up the road. My thoughts were still of the neat grocer's shop with the fl'†dbFgerald.....0000 21297 's of shining tins of biscuits. The owner and his wife had been so proud of their business and employed a young girl. They would have all been working that afternoon as usual. As I worked my way along the road I saw the shop on the other corner of the road. The front had been blown in and inside I saw a sad looking upright piano.

The front of the piano was missing and the strings were all exposed. Later I met the owner of the shop and I remarked to him that it was a shame about his piano being wrecked.

"A piano?" he exclaimed. "That shop has been empty for months!" That piano has remained a mystery to this day. Nobody ever did find out where it came from!

Eric Adams, 66 Testlands Avenue, Nursling, Southampton, Hampshire

Heinkels on a bombing raid.

My first encounter with the actual "combat" side of the 1939-45 war was when I was posted from Hereford Barracks. All our military knowledge had been instilled there and we were trained as Anti-Aircraft Searchlight Operators. We were landed around the Thames Estuary as reinforcements for the Coast Batteries there.

I arrived in Sheerness in June and the Battle of Britain developed from small "hit and run" raids in late July and all through August with raids on selected targets around the coast. The local Dockyard and Garrison and then the nearby Fighter Station at Eastchurch was blitzed by JU 87's Stukas and also Heavy Bombers (JU 88's) and Fighter Bombers, and knocked out with heavy casualties and loss of material. The sky began to fill with vapour trails as the fighters of both sides clashed and fought for mastery of the skies over Southern England and especially Kent. On one occasion the sky over Sittingbourne looked like a mass of tangled knitting wool as the fight went on. Occasionally parachutists would be seen coming down, followed and shot at to prevent a return to battle. Despite claims that are made, that was done by both sides. Planes could be replaced. Trained pilots not so easily.

By then we had started to receive shot down German airmen, mostly from the Air-Sea Rescue Launches that constantly went out from Sheerness to pick up any pilots who had been shot down. These German airmen were lodged in our Guardroom Cells until interrogation and then shipped up to Hyde Park Concentration Area, and ultimately off to Canada!

Some of them spoke fluent English, and fully expected that Hitler would be in Buckingham Palace by Christmas and the war would be over! I remember one in particular. He clasped in his hand his "Iron Cross" and, in fact, he offered it to me, telling me to give it back to him after the war when I went to visit his family in Munich! Apparently it was all he had left. Souvenir hunters had taken everything else of any value from him. He wanted to make sure that his "Iron Cross" was looked after. His name was Toni Meier, and apparently his father was the then Head Postmaster of Munich. He made his offer to me because I had lent him some toiletries and a cigarette or two. He vowed to grow a beard in Canada and shave it off when he went home again! Of course I never saw him again, and I have often wondered since at the turn of his fortune after he left us.

The issue of guarding the German Airmen shot down in our vicinity of Kent did give rise to some unusual situations, at times friendly and other times resentful and antaganistic. As mentioned earlier, different personalities emerged amongst them as we kept them in separate cells, only singly bringing them out for meals, exercise and ablutions, etc. One particular Kapitan surprised us one morning as he shaved by bursting into song, "I lift up my finger and say tweet, tweet, shush, shush, now, now, come come" and laughing at our expressions. He'd learnt it from English students before the War. He hit the ceiling on finding that some of his insignia had been removed from his tunic whilst it was drying and the red faced Orderly Sergeant was ordered to return them by the Orderly Officer!

Some prisoners virtually advised us to look after them and they'd see us right when we were conquered! One assured us that Hitler would be in Buckingham Palace by Christmas 1940. We laughed at them and assured them that we didn't think so.

Exercises and interrogation were always observed by hostile and naturally angry dockyard civilian workers, and when we were escorting prisoners at those times, we marched with loaded rifles and fixed bayonets. I often wondered who we were supposed to use them on when

39

Fighter trails in the sky over Kent.

these people pressed too near at times! The Guard Commander gave the order to "load" on one occasion, and frightened us all to death! But we got through and never risked it again.

Sheerness was then a large, Naval Dockyard and Shore Station. H.M.S. Wildfire and a Garrison also had severe bombing, the cookhouse being demolished and the Dining Room, with loss of life including many A.T.S. personnel. The head cook, a married man from Gravesend, lost his home, his wife and children in a raid on the riverside town.

The first mass formation raids saw hundreds of bombers flying in formation towards us. It seemed they reached the full width of the Estuary as they flew unhindered on and on towards waiting London, some sixty miles away to the west. Above the bombers, twinkling in the sunlight, flew swarms of fighter planes and only occasionally did a puff of smoke appear in the sky from some of our then few Ack-Ack guns.

But they didn't fly back in formation! Their fighters had to get back to base or ditch when out of juice. Then the Royal Air Force pounced! Helter-skelter back over the way they came with "Spits" and "Hurris" in hot pursuit and down they went all over the Thames and Medway area. I remember that night that the Thames glowed red from the fires burning all the way up to London.

The Coast Battery stationed at Sheerness was a locally raised T.A. Unit and, of course, their homes and families suffered grieviously. They regarded me as some sort of "foreigner" but couldn't have been kinder in every way. I was married then and my wife was invited down to stay the following Summer and was made very welcome.

A particular act of kindness I will always remember from those dark days was when we had to mount a Guard on the Garrison and Dockyard. Every Friday evening about 7 p.m., a girl in her teens, probably 18 or 19 years old, came through the barrier and left a brown paper carrier bag of fruit for those of us on duty! Never could we get to know her name or ever thank her properly, but I will always remember that kindness and thoughtfulness and may God bless her wherever she is today.

Jack Lattimer, 27 Slant Lane, Mansfield Woodhouse, Nottinghamshire

The Sheerness Unit at The Garrison. Jack Lattimer, 4th row from front, far right.

German fighter pilot with Iron Cross, shot down 30th August 1940.

I have some very funny memories of the Battle of Britain. Just behind our house was Ilford football ground, and there was a barrage balloon which was called "Sally" by the locals, and also two Ack-Ack guns. To me Sally looked like a fat elephant as she swayed in the wind at the end of her cable, and one day I remember the cable broke and she floated away, dragging the cable with her. The best part was that it took the top off Garwood's fish shop sheds where they smoked the haddocks. The shed was never rebuilt.

During the day the two Ack Ack guns were usually on standby with just a couple of soldiers on them, and if the gates of the football ground were left open for a time it wasn't long before us local lads were inside getting near the guns and talking to the soldiers.

I remember clearly that amongst the questions always asked by them was "Have you got an older sister?" "No" was my innocent reply. "But my Aunt Vie who lives with us is only 18"! I remember this caused a great deal of interest! I was told instantly by one of them to tell her to meet him outside by the main gate at 8 o'clock that evening and the reward for doing all this was a few bars of chocolate and sweets. I managed to maintain that for a couple of weeks, but as she already had a steady boyfriend and didn't turn up at the main gate obviously it didn't last!

My other memory at this time of the Battle of Britain was that near us was a sandpit and after one particular raid the rubble from one of the bombed buildings was brought and dumped at the sandpit. We boys used to go regularly to sort through it and see what we could find. On one particular day the lorries dumped rubble from the sweet shop and so we loaded our pockets and jumpers full of sweets and chocolate and returned later with a barrow! God knows what condition the sweets were in, but by the end of the week we were sick of sweets anyway! That tip is now under a housing estate.

Looking back I don't know why, but one of the most important things we did at this time was to collect shrapnel. We had tins and tins of splintered metal from shells and bombs everywhere, and I was constantly being nagged by my mother to get the bloody tins out of the house, and then nagged for tearing the pockets of my new trousers that mum had made for me out of a new blanket. It itched all the time because we didn't have underpants in those days!

I remember a German bomber crashing on a house near to us, and as my dad was on the rescue team I remember him bringing home a German Pass which belonged to one of the airmen. He gave it to me and I was the local celebrity for weeks showing it to all the boys. A Pass with a real Swastika on it!

But that story has a nice ending. I kept that Pass until after the war and in about 1975 my brother traced the grave of the airman to Crannock in England, and then traced the airman's

family and visited them in Germany. It was a nice personal touch to end what was a dreadful time for everybody.

The awful thing is that even as a child I can remember the sense of relief when the "all clear" went, and it meant there would be no more bombs for a while, and you were thankful that any bombs that had come down had missed you. But at the same time thinking that some other poor sod would not be seeing the end of the war. A terrible thing for children to have to be thinking at that time.

Peter F. Mann, 18 Lake Walk, Clacton, Essex

43

Flight of Spitfires on patrol.

The windows of the house, showing the criss-cross tape to stop glass shattering from blast.

I suppose there are many things I remember, but the Battle of Britain took place right above us, and all around me, and so it has left many memories. I lived with my parents on a small holding. It was a market garden and poultry farm about 1½ miles from Hawkinge aerodrome, and we worked at home. That particular corner of Kent was well fortified with guns and troops as well as planes.

As I am sure you know everyone was issued with identity cards, but we had to take them everywhere. The road we lived in was Coach Road, and if I went on my bicycle to the local shop I had to show the card to a soldier posted where Coach Road joined the main Folkestone to Canterbury Road! It was really like living in a military camp!

The pilots of the fighter planes lived away from the aerodrome, either in large houses, or if they had their wives with them they stayed in private houses. I got to know one couple who stayed with friends. He flew a Spitfire. I have the cuttings from the Folkestone paper about his exploits. He was only 23.

Once in half a minute its recorded that he shot down 2 planes, and he received the Distinguished Flying Cross and Bar. He autographed a photo for me which I still have. Unfortunately the terrible part was that he didn't survive the war.

The weather was wonderful in that September of 1940. There were clear blue skies every day so that one could see way up high. Sometimes the sirens sounded before the planes arrived, but quite often they were over before the sirens were sounded at all. It was difficult at the height the planes flew to tell them apart. All we could see were small silver machines weaving and diving and looking like small silver moths against a clear blue sky. Then there would be a rattle of machine gun fire and sometimes a whirring scream when a plane was hit and came crashing down. Then one looked for the parachute in the hope that the pilot had got out in time. In the field next to us there was an Anti Aircraft Battery, placed there to guard the aerodrome. At first I think they were Territorials, but certainly later they were replaced by a Royal Marine Battery.

We used to sell some fruit and vegetables locally, more like the farm shops of today, and I suppose news got around and we used to have service men buy fruit or veg when they were going on leave etc. The Sergeants in the Royal Marine Battery also used to buy as well I suppose to supplement their ration. The Royal Marine Battery consisted of 2 companies one from the north of England and one from the west. I can't remember the exact date, but for some time after they arrived one heard the orders for the gun crew to raise the guns to fire, then false alarm, and after a while they lowered them. Then one day it was for real. They fired! They couldn't fire when our planes and the enemy were mixed in with each other, but this particular day there were enemy formations alone and without any British planes in sight.

That same evening the Sergeant of the Northern Detachment came for some vegetables. He said when he gave the order to raise the guns and centre on the given target one of the gun crew said (and this Sergeant came from Cumberland and had a real accent), "Ist real?" Then he replied "Ay lad, ram thome" and the "it home" spoken as one word! I have never forgotten that sentence.

Of course there was also the shelling from the German guns in France. Dover and Folkestone both used to get shell warnings – after the first shells had landed! I also remember looking towards Dover many times and seeing the barrage balloons being shot down.

The enemy planes were often overhead before the sirens sounded and so otherwise of course we had no warning. When the aerodrome was bombed we had no warning, so we hadn't time to get into the dug out. I remember we had clothes brushes on a wooden mount hanging in the hall of our house, and I remember watching those swing to and fro as the ground shook.

45

Flying Officer Haines who shot down 7 enemy aircraft, 2 after pursuit across the Channel to France.

Later on I remember seeing the bombers go over towards London. They were flying very high and had a different drone of engine to our planes. When the enemy planes came over and the Ack Ack guns fired we used to watch the puffs of white smoke in the clear blue sky. I still have some pieces of shrapnel I picked up. I also have a copy of a four page leaflet in French, dropped in France in 1942 for the French patriots. I suppose it must have got caught up somewhere on the plane distributing it in France, because it came down over this side in our garden!

Although at one time we were told what to do if the enemy came I don't think we really thought it would happen. I have been more concerned on what I have read since the war on our real position with regard to weapons etc.!

As a matter of personal interest after Hawkinge aerodrome was bombed that same Royal Marine Ack Ack Battery was moved to Dover. Then after a while there it moved again and eventually finished up in Crete. They formed part of the rear guard in 1941, and were left on the island at the evacuation. They were captured and made prisoners of war and were four years in prison camps.

I know that somebody is going to say "Well how do you know all that?" The answer is simple. In August 1946 I married one of the men who had been in the West Country Detachment and so life came its full circle!

Mrs. Joan Webb, 3 Ringwood Close, Canterbury, Kent

During the fine August of 1940, I was living as a young "teenager" on the Isle of Wight. This story is of one day from the Battle of Britain.

The Isle of Wight formed a triangle with Southampton and Portsmouth, with the Solent in between and was heavily attacked and defended during this period. The day started as many others during that short intense period. It was a clear blue sky, warm and sunny. My usual anticipation of the day's action to come was heightened when about mid morning the air raid siren sounded. We soon spotted the raiders approaching over the Channel. This day was to be one of dive bombing by Stukas. The target being shipping in the Solent and the dock installations at Cowes. The Stukas having unloaded their bombs then turned their attention to the local area for a spot of low level machine gunning.

I was watching with my mother from the back of the house as seven Stukas flew in line up the River Medina. They then disappeared behind a Cement Works and as we counted them coming into view again only three appeared. We stood outside in our back lane, which backed on to fields leading to the river. Our house was No. 9, one of a crescent, so our view to the left was blocked by Nos. 1 and 2. Suddenly over the roof of No. 1 appeared a Stuka, just missing the house. The pilot opened fire and as the plane passed by the rear gunner opened fire. My mother and I dived over a two foot wall and into a sandbagged dugout! Besides the Stukas fire power, the general noise was added to by a Bren Gunner from the nearby Barracks opening fire!

Suddenly all went quiet, so after a few minutes we ventured from our dugout, only to be met by another aircraft coming from the opposite direction at low level and firing his machine

guns! We immediately dived for the dugout again, and the Bren Gunner once more joined in the melee!

A few seconds later an aircraft was heard to crash in the next field. Feeling safe we regained our feet and went to see what had happened. To our amazement the crashed aircraft was a Hurricane of Fighter Command. It turned out he had been shot down and was getting rid of his ammunition before crashing. By this time the Stukas had gone home, and so we went in for tea.

Tom Burt, 12 Jesty's Avenue, Broadwey, Weymouth

Junkers 87 Stuka dive bomber releasing its bombs.

It was the Summer of 1940. The skies over London were a glorious blue. I was 10 years old at the time and living with my parents and sister at 37 Skeena Hill, Southfields, S.W.19, near Wimbledon. Though slightly apprehensive that we were at war, life was a great adventure for a 10 year old then, watching the vapour trails of fighter aircraft involved in "dogfights" miles above our heads. One day I counted the formation of twenty-five German bombers cruising towards London, completely unmolested by anti-aircraft guns or fighters, at least not over our district on that particular day!

The house next door to ours had been empty for a time and was requisitioned by the Army to use as a billet for soldiers. I and my sister, Yvonne, who was three years younger, were on holiday from school but as we couldn't go away for our holidays that year we spent a lot of time chatting with our military neighbours. They let us put on their helmets and helped us into their Army trucks parked outside in the street. After a few months of air raid warnings we became more accustomed to the fact that not a great deal occurred in the way of danger to ourselves during the raids, and we had long given up the practice of taking cover, although we did remain close to home watching the aircraft twisting and weaving amongst themselves. Some occasionally spiralling to earth, leaving a corkscrew of dense black smoke behind them.

One day during an air raid my sister and I were outside the soldiers' billet, watching some of them board a truck, when all hell broke loose. Out of the corner of my eye I noticed the dark, ominous shape of an enemy plane approaching, very fast, at low level, the sound of its motors having been drowned by the trucks revving up.

No sooner had we spotted the plane, and we were standing almost transfixed with terror, staring at it closing in on us, than we were whisked off our feet by a couple of soldiers who grabbed us and dashed with us in their arms into the open garage. As the plane passed overhead, the roar of its twin engines shaking the building, we heard the stutter of machine gun fire. From the doorway of the garage we saw a Heinkel 111 banking to the left as it regained height. The twin plexiglass machine gun pods slung under the fusalage and the swastika on the tail clearly visible.

Quite a few soldiers were picking themselves up off the pavement where they had taken cover. Others were peering our of the trucks and swearing at the departing bomber. By some miracle there wasn't one injury! Many people came out to see what had happened, all chattering excitedly to one another. But the only apparent damage was some bullet holes in the tarpaulin covers of some of the lorries! Our mum, who had been indoors at the time, came looking for us, as white as a sheet and fearing the worst. But she was overcome with emotion when she saw us running towards her, trying to describe simultaneously and excitedly our experience of having been straffed by the Luftwaffe!

Thank goodness no bombs were released on that low level attack, as the outcome would have been vastly different. Fortunately the Heinkel never returned for a second go. That was the day I suddenly became aware that war was a reality and not a game, and it was all getting a bit too close for comfort!

At the Lycee Français in Kensington 1939. Andre Fontaine third row from front, extreme right.

Formation of 5 Heinkels on a raid.

During one daylight raid I remember we were sitting in our communal shelter when a Warden rushed in slamming the metal door behind him. It was rarely shut so that people could dive in if danger was imminent. The Warden said "brace yourselves, I think this is going to be a close one." Then we heard the unmistakable scream of a bomb hurtling to earth followed by an almighty bang. The Warden ventured out and came back in almost immediately to tell us that the house opposite had been hit by an oil bomb. A lady sitting further down the shelter exclaimed in horror "I hope it's not my house".

But it was her house as we discovered when we all left the shelter to inspect the damage. An oil bomb was designed to spread oil everywhere as it exploded with the intention that it would ignite and cause widespread fire damage. Luckily this one didn't. It hit the corner of the house where the roof met the two adjacent walls, making a big hole and exposing a small bedroom to the world! My first impression was of the brownish dust and masonry and plaster drifting in the air, and the incredible mess of oil stain scattered over the area, as if someone had exploded a huge can of creosote in the front garden. Fortunately the damage to the house was none too serious but as a child at the time I remember the shock I felt that someone's home could be smashed up so quickly. I also remember hoping fervently that ours would not suffer the same fate one day!

Andre Fontaine, 33 Druce Way, Thatcham, Newbury, Berkshire

My memory of the Battle of Britain is when I was in the bomb disposal squad before I was sent to Burma, and there were a number of humorous incidents quite apart from the tragic ones, and I think the one that might interest you is when I met my wife. I had recovered an unexploded time bomb, and after making the bomb safe by removing the fuses I made the fuses comparatively safe and destroyed the bomb casing and any explosive. I took the two fuses back to our terraced house where we were billeted, and placed them on the mantlepiece as a souvenir.

The following morning without any warning at all and for some reason I have never been able to explain, one of them blew up blowing all the doors in the billet open, and when I went to investigate an Officer, a Lieutenant Else, was standing there with all his top clothing burnt off and the upper part of his body burned. Of course I rushed him straight off to hospital for attention. The next day when I visited him all of his upper part had been painted with a violet colour material, and I am afraid that in my ignorance I laughed. The result was that I was severely reprimanded by a lovely young nurse whom I eventually married! How fate affects one's life. Fortunately I survived many incidents, often dangerous, involving bomb disposal, but recently I was involved in a car accident which has made me a virtual cripple. However, life goes on and I remain cheerful. Incidentally on bomb disposal we removed bombs in their order of priorities,

and we were surprised one day when we were told to remove one from the middle of a huge field because in relation to other bombs that we knew of it was of a low priority. Then we found out that it was close to the residence of the Queen Mary. When we had defused it she came and shook us by the hand and asked all about the work that we did and she was a lovely lady. It was one of those wonderful memories of my life.

W. F. Moore, 4 Cleveland View, Marske by Sea, Cleveland, Yorkshire

Hurricane of No. 85 Squadron on patrol, October 1940.

In September 1940 a friend of mine, a Mrs. Mac who with her husband had an antique shop, asked me if I would join her in taking a hop basket at a local farm. I hadn't enlisted as I'd had my appendix out, and the idea was to make a bit of money, and so I agreed. The farm did not have hopper huts so the pickers were all locals, mostly mothers and children.

There were of course others who were "old hands". But we were terribly slow and always got left behind in our row. It was lovely weather and most mornings we could hear the German aircraft starting their trip across the Channel, and then the sirens went. The mothers gathered their children together and the mother next to me was always shouting "Doreen, the SI-REEN". When actual dog fights were overhead we got in a ditch by a hedge, and some of us who had baskets put them on their heads! I could never understand why they did it but they did. After the raids the sky was always full of vapour trails.

One morning I saw Aunt Kathleen who lived nearby, running over a field. She was over 60! It was to tell me that a stray bomb had fallen on our house. This was the other side of town which took me about half an hour by bike, and when I got there my mother had been taken to hospital but was not badly injured. She was saved by a door falling on her in the centre of the house. I burst into tears and was consoled by an old friend, a Colonel Cussans who with British sang-froid said "Have a pear!" As a matter of interest he'd been in the Rhodesian Cavalry and was in charge of raising the local "Home Guard". He was elderly and had a bad chest and when some VIP's came to see him at his office he was wrapped in a shawl. So they got someone else in better health!

Anyway, my mother went to Aunt Kathleens from the hospital, but missing was my little dog John who had been sitting in front of the house when the bomb fell. I looked far and wide near the house but no luck. He was eventually found at the house we had recently moved from, sitting on the lawn! To get there he must have gone all through the town where he had never been before. John had to go to kennels and then my mother and I went to a small hotel near Aunt Kathleen. The proprietor kindly gave me an early breakfast each day so that I could get to the hop garden at 7 o'clock in the morning! Thank you very much! But he was very kind and gave me sandwiches but they were always "sandwich spread"!

Meantime as the air action increased it was decided that mothers with young children should be evacuated. A lot of our hopper friends asked our advice, and we said we thought they should go. So eventually very few baskets were left.

The farmer eventually had to get help and parties of troops and miners came at different times. The picking which usually lasted three weeks now lasted for six weeks and the cry never seemed to go up that the oast was full and now we could stop work! The farms with hopper huts had no trouble, as if any of the locals did leave, there were plenty of Londoners to take their place who were only too pleased to get out of London!

Mrs. Mac and I learned we had earned about £5 a week each, so we hadn't made our fortunes, although that wasn't bad money in those days. We missed all the jolly locals. I'd led a very sheltered life and I was amazed at all the b'...ing and f'...ing in casual conversation. We found it very tiring sitting all day and any clothes you wore were stained brown, but I have to say the hops had a lovely smell.

Of course we didn't realise we were seeing history in the making. I'm afraid that when any aircraft came down we fiercely hoped it was "ONE of THEIRS"! Funnily enough I can remember that the farm was at Nackington, owned by Finn & Sons just outside of Canterbury.

Betty Green, Bob-Lo, 172 Old Dover Road,
Canterbury, Kent

53

A fighter pilot "scrambles" and is airborne in 15 seconds.

I remember the War alright, I was almost 8 when it broke out and I can recall very clearly my feelings on September 4th. A dark foreboding filled us as we pictured the battle to come. At school anti-blast strips of paper were gummed across the windows. Our air raid shelter was a shallow dry ditch under a hedge, some distance from the playground.

My home was in the country, some 5 miles out of Ludlow in Shropshire. The Clee Hills formed a barrier to the east of the village, yet when Coventry got it, the shivering of the ground and sky lit like the dawn told us of the damage, as did the muttering explosions and the searchlight fingers querulously probing the darkness. Mostly the War was a distant thing for me, yet I was to become inadvertently involved in it.

Briefly, my great-aunt and uncle had a shop in Glossop in Lancashire. On my uncle's death my aunt sold the business and went into a large terraced house near Glossop Station. When she was near to death from cancer, my mother had a telegram. Apparently, the nurse who looked after aunty had been sent away. There was a three week gap between her leaving and getting a new one. Was my mother able to fill the gap and stay with her? Mother had my sister and me to look after, but father was down south at work in Christchurch, Hampshire. He came home every eight weeks or so. Naturally my mother sent off a reply in the affirmative and so we set off by train for Glossop.

When everything settled down I went down to the shop and saw Joe, my uncle's erstwhile chauffeur, whom I knew very well. He seemed pleased to see me. "Are you coming with me to Manchester on Wednesday, Michael?" he asked. This was a weekly journey for supplies, and was carried out in his lorry. Of course, I said I would be happy to go with him! So on Wednesday morning off we went.

Just as we went over the swingbridge over the Manchester Ship Canal, the sirens went. They let us drive into the Docks where a Warden met us. "Drive that wagon up the side of that warehouse" he said to Joe "and then go and find the shelter! It's just round the corner." Even as he spoke I could hear the thrum of planes overhead. Joe drove the lorry alongside the warehouse as instructed. "Get under the wagon, Mike" he urged me, "I'll come back as soon as I've found the shelter".

I did as I was told. Lying on my stomach I peered out from under the tailboard, looking towards the canal. At the canal side was a big concrete apron, sloping down all along its length towards the water, and no more than 20 yards from where I lay. I later discovered that the apron was used to launch barges sideways into the water, after being taken out for overhaul. To my left was an open space and then the wall of another warehouse.

I lay quite still, waiting for Joe to come back. The sounds of the raiders grew louder. Still Joe remained absent. Later I discovered that once he found the air raid shelter they refused to let him come out to get me! I understand that he was forcibly restrained. Soon the anti-aircraft guns began to thunder some distance away. Their fire ceased, however, almost as suddenly as it had begun. Then I began to hear the very clear thrum of the raiders overhead, overlaid by another kind of engine. An engine I knew. Spitfires!

I eased myself out slightly and stared up. A regular "dogfight" was in progress. The raiders were trying to keep a straight line and one by one they were being shot up. The fighters slid over and under them, guns spitting venom.

But soon I sank back under the lorry as I heard the frightening, fearful scream of a tortured aircraft coming down, ever down. Then I saw the machine curve down, coming straight at me, fire pluming from its belly. The noise of it grew to a bellowing scream and the aircraft, its pilot with hands outstretched against the perspex of the cockpit, and his mouth wide open in terror, smashed with a tremendous force into the concrete apron in front of me.

Instantly the ground heaved under me but the blast from what must have been a full bomb load went up and away from me. My ears went deaf and the lorry I was under lurched off

55

the ground but I could still see that pilot a split second from hell as the dust and smoke began to clear. Very little was left of the apron. A Spitfire followed him down, but when its pilot saw the enemy blow up, he pulled back and roared off into the blue sky again.

Still numbed from the crashing bomber, I kept to my place under the lorry. God alone knew what was likely to happen next. I hadn't long to wait. All around me came the sound of sudden explosions. The devils were dropping their bomb loads.

A stick of bombs is one of the most terrifying experiences in creation. It's like dangling over a pit and knowing the exact moment the rope will snap. I heard a stick of bombs coming down like a mechanical banging upon a drum. The first one whistled down some distance away, and "BLAM!". Its explosion didn't hide the whistle of the next. "Whe-e-e-e-w-w-Blam! That was closer.

"Whe-e-e-w-w-BLAM!" Closer still.

"BLAMM! BLAMMM!! BLAMMM!!!" and the world exploded!

A huge grain silo near to me took off and went up about 200 feet and disintegrated, whilst the adjoining warehouse caved in with an ear battering roar. The ground heaved under me as the lorry literally left the ground and crashed down again. My head hit something underneath it and ached for days afterwards. Bombs were still exploding somewhere but everything seemed quiet after that stick of bombs. I could hear myself breathing and discovered that I and everything else in the area was covered with a layer of pulverised grain. I was white from head to foot! Presently I heard voices and the tramp of feet.

"He's dead, the poor little devil", I heard Joe telling someone.

"The poor little bugger's dead, thanks to you lot! God knows what I'll tell his mum...".

That was when I clambered out from under the lorry and a couple of minutes later came the sound of the "all clear".

The warehouse, or what was left of it, was burning furiously. The canopy extending from the warehouse over the lorry had gone. The ground was a mess. Rubble lay everywhere, even in the bed of the lorry. I could not understand why Joe was crying. I was alright! The bomb didn't get me! "What about the supplies Joe?" I enquired.

He bit his lip and looked at me. "You're right lad. We've got away with it!" he declared. "By gum, we have that. An' we'll have them supplies as well, and sod Jerry!" He grinned at me. "Into the wagon with you, and let's see if she'll start up!"

We clambered back into the cab. When Joe cleaned off the instruments we found that every bit of glass in the cab was smashed. The windscreen, mirrors, even the side windows (which Joe had earlier wound down just in case) were in smithereens. But the engine started at the second burst on the starter, and after a bunch of about 20 men had cleared the rubble from the immediate area, we drove away to a cheer from our willing helpers.

An hour later we were on our way back to Glossop in the draughty lorry. The roads out of the City were cluttered with cables which had been overhead for the trolley buses. Here and there had been a bomb burst, but there was surprisingly little damage to be seen along the main road. People gave us a wave as we went past them. What we must have looked like I can't imagine. Back in Glossop I told my mother about the bombing.

"Fancy" she said slowly "lucky you got back in time for tea aren't you? But you'll change out of those horrible clothes first my boy. What the blazes have you been doing?"

Three weeks after the new nurse arrived to look after my great-aunt, and my mother and I went home, my great-aunt died.

One odd thing I remember about that raid. We were never allowed to go anywhere without our gas masks. Mine was in a battered old cardboard case, and I took it with me that morning. But after that raid in the Docks I never saw it again. It was on my seat in the cab. Where it went to I'll never know! It's haunted me ever since, partly perhaps because I never did get another one to replace it! You know, I missed my gas mask. Despite the fact that the tape cut into my shoulder when carrying the thing, if you put the mask on loosely and blew, you got a noise like a horse breaking wind!

Michael A. A. Lloyd, 21 The Beeches, Rugeley, Staffordshire

Junkers 87 Stuka Dive Bomber.

I am not very good at wording letters, but I hope that some of what I am about to tell you will be of interest. I was 8 years old when the war started and 14 when it ended. My first memory of the war was looking up at a low flying plane, and wondering why it had crosses on the wing tips!

Suddenly my dreams were interrupted by my neighbour yelling to my mother whose name was Elizabeth, "Liz, Liz, they're over", meaning the Germans. We found out later that they had been taking photos of Hornchurch Aerodrome which is close to where I lived and was of course a prime target for the Germans.

Then there was the time I was on the loo which was out the back in those days! Suddenly the peace was shattered by a large amount of planes overhead and I dived out of the loo with trousers round my ankles, looking up at the planes making a heck of a noise. As the noise died away I suddenly became aware of laughing! It was several of my school friends going round the back alley at the bottom of our back garden! It took me weeks to live it down before they stopped taking the mick.

Then on another occasion my sister, her friend and myself were playing ball in the back garden when a low flying bomber flew overhead. I was looking vertically up at it to see once again the German markings which by now we dreaded. To my horror the bomb doors opened up and several bombs were coming straight towards me.

I dived into the Anderson shelter which was close by. My sister did the same. I stuck my fingers in my ears and waited for the end which I was so sure had now come! But I did not know at that time that bombs do not come straight down but carry on in the direction which the plane is going! The higher plane the further the bombs fall. Anyhow the bombs (of which there were in fact 4) landed only 50 yards away wrecking a house and bursting a water main. Two fell on open ground. A large piece of one of the bombs landed on a roof a couple of houses away, breaking several tiles. The ones replacing them can still be seen today because they're a different colour from the rest!

We had to make our own entertainment in those days and many kids including myself collected war souvenirs such as shrapnel, hand grenades, mortar bombs, smoke bombs and bullets etc. About 300 yards away from my house is Rainham Marshes, which was partly owned and used by the Ministry of Defence as a rifle range for training with mortar bombs and sticky bombs and hand grenades etc.

Anyway my friend Roy Rush and myself used to get over the Marsh in the evenings after school and after training had ceased for the day, to see what we could find to add to our collection of souvenirs. I had a small barrel of them.

One evening Roy found something new. We found out later it was an anti tank bomb. The bottom part was missing, revealing tightly packed gun powder in the part he had. We were on our way home with it and other oddments when on crossing the Southend-Fenchurch Street railway line (which we had to do coming and going from the Marsh) we glanced each way looking out for trains and noticed smoke a short distance along the track.

So we went to investigate. It turned out to be a small grass fire probably started by one of the steam engines. At that time we put the fire out. Then Roy asked me how to get the gunpowder out of the anti tank bomb. I told him to put it in a bucket of water and ease it out with a piece of wood. That's how we got the powder out of hand grenades after getting the detonators out.

But he was the impatient type and started tapping it on the railway line. Suddenly he said "If it doesn't come out after 8 more taps I'm going to throw it on the track." I told him not to and started walking away, hoping he'd follow. I'd just got across the line and looked back to see a bright

German Bombers over West Ham, 7th September 1940.

flash, and then the blast blew me in the ditch! I crawled out clutching my forehead as a piece of the bomb had hit me there. Blood was trickling through my fingers. I looked over to where Roy had been. He was lying crumpled up on the line. I panicked and ran to get help.

I told a man working on a nearby allotment what had happened. He phoned the ambulance and police and I ran home very frightened. I later had to make a statement at the Police Station. Roy told the police I had thrown a bomb at him. But they believed the version I told them. They somehow knew that I was telling the truth. But they confiscated my barrel of souvenirs which my poor old aunt took to the Police Station on an old pushchair!

Roy's father threatened to run me down in his taxi which he then had. But he was warned off by the police. A rumour went round the school we went to that we were in fact trying to de-rail the 6 o'clock train! My friends steered clear of me for a while after that! Subsequently Roy had to have many operations to his stomach, his face and his legs, and was in hospital for several months. He died later in life when he was an adult.

Another time was when I was round my cousin's house. We were playing in her back garden as we often did, when I became aware of her gazing up speechless. A plane was coming straight at us. It crashed only 2 or 3 blocks of houses away on an Anderson shelter, between two houses. It was a smallish two-engined bomber. They got the pilot out and laid him on a nearby grass verge. He had a large gash in his forehead and he was bleeding heavily. Someone was saying "Stand back, give him air". We heard later he died on the way to hospital. But I never did find out how it crashed or anything more about it.

One day we watched a German fighter plane shot down. It landed on my next door neighbour's allotment! We saw the pilot coming down on a parachute. Looking up at it it looked like a spoon in a silver saucer for a while. Two Army trucks went belting after the pilot when he landed and took him off somewhere!

Every time a bomb fell on a house we used to go and gape at it. I bet people got fed up with us. However, I remember that one day part of our school got burned down and I remember that we not only went to look and gape at it, but we were decidedly cheered up!

John Pilgrim, 193 Wennington Road, Rainham, Essex

When I lived in Lewisham during the war I used to leave my baby son with my neighbour when I wanted a bath in case the sirens went! Well you wouldn't call it a bath really. With only about a quarter of the thing full of water – which is all we were recommended to use during the war – I had to be quick or catch a cold! On this particular day all had been quiet. The balloons were up so I felt safe and in I got. Oh! lovely hot water, and a tiny piece of soap! Still all quiet! No planes. No sirens. What was that?!!

Funny noise. Humming. Then louder. I stood up in the bath and looked out of the window. My God! A small plane coming straight at me. It was so low I could see the pilot with his black helmet on. What's more I was sure he was looking at me through his goggles!

He zoomed right over the top of the house and then the sirens started up! I have never got out of a bath so quickly in all my life. I ran downstairs and finished up in the cupboard under the stairs. The plane had disappeared and I learned later it was a lone pilot who had got through the balloons and hit a school nearby with tragic results. The only thing was that I couldn't get out of the cupboard! In my panic I had shut the door and the handle was on the outside!

So there I was, waiting in the dark, wet and cold with nothing on. Waiting for my neighbour to pop in to see if I was still in the bath. She eventually found me, but not where she expected to! And I often wonder – WAS that German pilot looking at me?!

Mrs. Joan Jolly, The Cottage, Hatch Lane, Chartham, Canterbury, Kent

Oberstleutnant Adolf Galland, the German fighter ace, with his dog.

During the late summer of 1940 and the "Battle of Britain" I was serving with an Infantry Battalion on the Isle of Wight. We moved around from place to place, but always along the southern coastline, ostensibly of course to help repel the expected German invasion. In view of the fact that most of us were raw, untried conscripts, armed only with rifles and one or two Bren guns, it may be just as well that the invasion never materialised!

Apart from watching the vapour trails from the dog fights, way up in the clear blue sky and the occasional Luftwaffe sneak raider nipping in to bomb the radar station at Ventnor, a few other incidents come to mind from those days.

At the time we were billeted in Brighstone. Myself and another Fusilier were included in a "special guard duty" which turned out to be watching over a Messerschmitt 109. It was in a field and how it got there we never found out, as it appeared to be quite undamaged! We could only assume that the Jerry pilot had run out of fuel or decided that he had had enough of "dog fights" for that day!

Anyway during the small hours I told my fellow sentry to keep a sharp lookout, and then managed to clamber up into the cockpit. With my feet on the pedals (or is it the rudder bar?) and my hands gripping the joystick, for a few brief moments I could imagine myself as an intrepid fighter pilot!

Next day I dug out my Brownie box camera and went back to try and take a discreet photograph of the ME109. Unfortunately by then it had disappeared, and I often wonder what became of it. Maybe it is still around in some museum, but more than likely it was just broken up for scrap. That's a pity!

On another occasion when we used to help out in the coastguard station and also at St. Catherine's lighthouse, two of us were off duty strolling along the cliff tops when we spotted an orange coloured object that had been washed up on the shingle and shale rocks. On climbing down we found it to be an inflated rubber dinghy. We couldn't make out much of the German wording on the various packages and cannisters stowed away in packets, but we were highly intrigued by the collapsable aluminium paddles that we were able to assemble in a matter of seconds. The whole thing was in perfect order, and had clearly come from a plane that had been shot down, and I couldn't help thinking what a smashing souvenir it would have made if only I could have kept it! But not much chance of keeping a thing like that under wraps, and it was duly reported to the coastguard and that was taken away! Again I often wonder what became of that beautifully made item of Luftwaffe equipment.

I don't think any of us ordinary soldiers had much idea of the historic events taking place during that long hot summer. Most nights were spent in a sort of well constructed dug out on the low cliffs facing out to sea, and we were not allowed to "stand down" unless the next morning we were able to see clearly "the Needles" a few miles away. Should there be a heavy sea mist, as there often was, then we just had to stay there until it cleared!

After breakfast back in the billets and a quick wash and shave, most of us would don swimming trunks and spend several hours on the beach sunbathing and getting some sleep. During the night a section (about 6 men and 1 NCO) would man the dug outs with a sentry posted outside at each end. It was the usual "2 hours on and 4 hours off".

On one occasion I remember when 2 of us were on from midnight to 2 a.m. and a few minutes before we were due to be relieved I could hear the NCO rousing the next pair of sentries. Unfortunately my pal was sound asleep and snoring loudly! We were allowed to sit at each end of the dug out and there he was with head slumped forward and chin on chest. My loud whispered warnings having no effect.

Messerschmitt ME 109 at a German airfield in France.

The Sergeant duly emerged, looked in disgust at my pal, carefully removed the rifle from his grasp and with the bayonet fixed on the end gently levered up the front of his steel helmet until he finally woke with a start.

Instead of being put on a charge my poor old mate was compelled to stagger back to the billets, almost a mile away, after we had "stood down", carrying a heavy ammunition box containing 1000 rounds of .303 bullets. This same mate I regret to say was killed in action in 1943 in North Africa.

We eventually moved to the mainland in November, but for me a humble member of the P.B.I., the period covering the Battle of Britain will always be synonymous with my time spent on the Isle of Wight. I was in the 2nd Battalion The Royal Fusiliers.

N.B. For the reader – P.B.I. means "Poor Bloody Infantry".

Albert Price, 8 Conifer Close, Whitehill, Bordon, Hampshire

I was 11 at the outbreak of war and lived in Hadleigh near Southend, which area of course saw quite a lot of the Battle of Britain. The Southend area was one of those which evacuated quite a large number of their children, but Hadleigh did not and we therefore still stayed at school and eventually, as children, drifted back to the Southend area, our schools had to take the early returners as the Southend schools had closed. After a while they re-opened as most of the children returned.

During the Battle of Britain our education suffered badly as we spent so much time in the school air raid shelters having impromptu concerts! After a while the Education Authorities decided that this should stop and the teachers had to teach in the shelters. One day during our walk home from school, my friend and I got caught under a "dogfight" between the German fighters and Spitfires. Things got a little heated and an elderly gentleman who was watching from his gate asked us if we would like to go into his Anderson Shelter with his wife. As we were a little frightened, we did this, and took shelter with him, his wife and an elderly wire-haired Fox Terrier dog. The gentleman was a little hard of hearing, but after a little while he said "listen to those machine guns, there's a hell of a fight going on up there".

My friend and I dissolved into giggles which we had to try to stifle, because it was not machine guns. The dog's stumpy tail was beating on the door of the shelter which, made of wood, was making a rat-a-tat noise! I am still in touch with my friend and we still have a laugh about this!

It's not strictly to do with the Battle of Britain, but during later raids my brother and I were coming home from our jobs in London one evening later in the war, and as we neared our home we heard a "Doodlebug" engine. We had a longish path from the front gate and as we were walking up this the engine cut out so we both threw ourselves over the garden

path until the explosion had taken place. When we went indoors, mother was just emerging on her hands and knees from under the kitchen table with her rear end covered in ceiling plaster! She hadn't quite made it under the table before the ceiling came down! The "Doodlebug" had, in fact, landed about 300 yards up the road.

Mrs. Beryl M. Kelsey, 2 Cranham Gardens, Upminster, Essex

65

Fighter pilots awaiting "scramble", with Fl. Lt. Peter Townsend second from right.

Many experts have many dates about when the Battle of Britain began. Take your pick! I believe it could be counted as a little before the middle of July 1940 when the Luftwaffe attacks on our channel convoys and ports suddenly escalated in the hope of luring our 700 plus single engine fighters into combat. Many historians tend to forget that those fighters had to be ready to defend the whole of Britain, and that in reality it was little more than the 300 planes of No. 11 Group which bore the brunt of the great air battles with the 2,600 planes of the Luftwaffe.

The whole of my working life was that of a railway man, and thus on the 17th July 1940 I remember I was removing a leaky regulator valve perched on top of a locomotive boiler, when the labourer with me quite nonchalantly remarked that there was a plane up there, and looked as if its engines were falling off! A few seconds before I heard the scream of falling bombs (some bombs had sirens fitted to the tail fins as an additional demoralising agent) it occurred to me that aircraft just didn't shed their engines like that!

I jumped the 10 feet to the ground and lay flat watching in horror as a stick of 10 bombs erupted. The sixth created a large hole in the roof of a building 200 yards away, from which shot much smoke and debris. The remaining 4 advanced in a line across the intervening field towards us. The last dropped less than 30 yards away! We duly inspected the site of that one which seemed to be singularly ineffective, and were disappointed to find only some heaped up lumps of soft clay. However, a few hours later there was quite a sizeable crater – we hadn't heard of delayed action bombs until then! However, in that raid two women and a baby were killed. The Railway Workshops which were the obvious targets were not greatly damaged apart from one badly holed roof.

The early evening of 16th September was clear and sunny, and at 6.30 p.m. the sound of a low flying plane could clearly be heard. It was instantly recognisable as a "Jerry" by its desynchronised engines, giving a quite distinctive sound from that of British planes. Determined not to miss anything the family turned out into the back garden, and there with the whole sky to itself and not so much as a peep out of the air raid sirens was a Heinkel III, leisurely cruising around Ashford at not more than 1000 feet! Even so it was rather optimistic of the over-excited Army Officer who emptied his revolver in the approximate direction of the bomber!

After a couple more circuits to select its target it turned away, and then came in at full throttle on its bombing run, plainly obvious by the gaping bomb doors which we could clearly see. Four very large bombs, which I would put at something like 500lbs each, were released which overshot the Railway Works target and killed two civilians not far from where the three had been killed earlier. Again one of the bombs was a delayed action bomb which detonated with a fair old thump a couple of hours later.

Of course there were also the spectacular mass formations typically consisting of about 80 bombers in "boxes" of 20 escorted by about 3 times that number of twin and single engined fighter planes. It was a miracle how our fighters ever managed to penetrate the escort screens to get at the bombers. But they did. Sometimes a single squadron of R.A.F. fighters would dive into these armadas of 300 or more of the enemy.

Often interception would already have taken place when the planes arrived over our town, and the battle would be raging over miles and miles of the sky with fighters milling about, sometimes only seen by the twisting vapour trails, or by the glint of sunlight on cockpit canopies as they dived and rolled and circled. The bombers would usually be sailing on with

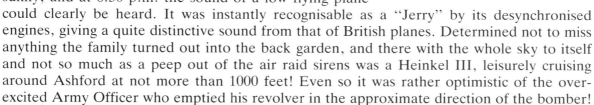

Fighter pilots after the action. The strain is clearly shown and contrasts with the picture on the previous page.

all of this going on around them, but then a reinforcing squadron of the R.A.F. might arrive and with the escort already fully engaged, managed to get in a "pass" on the bombers. We on the ground as spectators would raise a cheer because it would be unusual not to see a couple of bombers fall out of the formation heading to the ground.

On one occasion an escorting squadron of twin engined Messerschmitt 110 fighters was being heavily engaged by roughly an equal number of Hurricanes. The 110's at once formed a "defensive circle" but the Hurricanes, although slower, were far more manoeuvrable and got inside the circle quickly sending three of the 110's down streaming fire and smoke behind them. It was an unforgettable sight. As the three twisted and dived and sometimes seemed to flatten out, they remained totally out of control and their paths to destruction crossed and recrossed making a sort of giant "noughts and crosses" grid with their smoke miles high but rapidly heading closer and closer to the ground.

On what was later to become known as "Battle of Britain Day", 15th September, 1940, I was with my Home Guard Platoon sitting in a natural amphitheatre high in the North Downs near the tiny village of Hastingleigh (pronounced in the best Kent dialect as "Ars-en-lie"). We were watching a demonstration of various types of anti tank grenades. During a lull in the proceedings I became aware of that low unmistakeable but as yet distant growl of approaching aircraft in large numbers. There was a very thin veil of cloud at around 15,000 feet, and presently I could make out the bombers at that height, drifting in and out of the cloud like so many ghosts. As far as I could make out there were Dornier 17's, and Heinkel III's, about 160 in all, all in the usual "boxes" of about 20, spread out over a vast area of sky.

In the van, on each side and bringing up the rear, were squadron after squadron of single and twin engine fighter escorts. Again one could only detect the "top cover" by the occasional flash of sunlight reflected from cockpit perspex as they fought with the first squadron of our fighters which were already engaging them.

One could readily distinguish the comparatively slow "tump tump tump" of the German fighter's cannon from the throaty roar of the 8 Browning machine guns carried by our Hurricanes and Spitfires. Two fighters fell from that melee, one trailing flames and a long plume of black smoke. The other had the fuselage separated from the wings which spiralled down like two giant sycamore seeds. The significant thing I could always remember is that only one parachute opened.

As the roar of several hundred aero engines slowly faded along with the sounds of battle and the screaming whine of over-taxed Merlin and Jumo engines, there occurred a strange phenomenon which I never saw again throughout the war. The A.A. defences of the Medway towns put up a spirited barrage. The shells, well ranged, were bursting in the thin layer of cloud and each one created widening ripples of shock waves in the cloud like throwing handfuls of pebbles into a pond. The effect of perhaps 300 shells bursting in just a few minutes created a fantastic pattern which spread across fully 20 miles of the sky.

History has shown that the early engagement of fighters was to have a telling effect. Before the outskirts of London were reached the Luftwaffe fighter pilots found themselves out of ammunition and low on fuel, forcing most to turn back leaving the bombers to press on with a very depleted escort. Over London on one of the very rare occasions that Douglas Bader with his reinforcing "Big Wing" from No. 12 Group was in the right place at the right time, the unprotected bombers were met by the huge formation of 60 Hurricanes. The result for the Luftwaffe was catastrophic.

It wasn't until much later that I learned that one of our Hurricanes had crashed at Staplehurst railway station that day killing Charles Ashdown, a school chum of mine, who had not long started work there as a booking office clerk.

There was another attack of much the same strength in the afternoon after I had arrived back from my Home Guard activities, although I only saw a small part of it when 20 Dornier 17's flying low and without escort passed over Ashford flying due west. A few minutes later the rumble of jettisoned bombs was heard followed by the same Dorniers at full throttle flying east! They were no longer in formation and were in fact being shot out of the sky by a squadron of Spitfires that had spotted them. Already reduced to 18 in number we climbed

German bomber formations over Kent, 1940.

Band of 1st Battalion Kent Home Guard. Bob Barham extreme right on back row.

out onto the roof of the church hall next door to see 4 more go down before our very eyes, and a column of smoke marked the funeral pyre of each one in the Kent countryside.

That day marked the turning point. The Battle of Britain was from then all over bar the shooting. However, I progress too fast!

The previous weekend had seen the first mass bombing of London. It was in retaliation for a small raid by R.A.F. Whitley bombers on Berlin a few nights earlier, and it caught Fighter Command unprepared as a continuation of the bombing of our main airfields was expected, and our Squadrons were deployed accordingly, leaving London unprotected until it was too late to retrieve the situation.

A very strange thing about that afternoon was that I saw what I will swear to this day was a small formation of a dozen or so JU89 four engine bombers fly at a great height over Ashford towards London, and yet I have never been able to find any record that the Luftwaffe ever used that type of bomber over Britain. Be that as it may, by teatime a great pall of black smoke could be seen drifting westward from the direction of London, and we lived 50 miles away!

That night we could also see the dreadful glow in the sky as the Thameshaven oil storage tanks continued to burn to guide in another 270 Luftwaffe bombers.

I shall not forget my surprise on seeing my first shot down aircraft on the ground. Walking through some hay fields at Finn Farm, I came across a Messerschmitt 109 in splendid isolation, and completely unguarded! How incredibly small it seemed! There was no sign of a pilot. The cockpit canopy was open, and it had made a "wheels up" landing having mowed down a hundred yards swathe of hay in the process! Apart from some bullet holes it appeared undamaged, except of course for the bent propellor blades.

In the end we saw so many planes in various states of disrepair we didn't even bother to go and see them, but I never got closer to any than that ME109.

On the 26th September I saw my first bomb – close up that is! On Thursday afternoon I had "day release" for technical studies, and had just completed a test in the course when there emerged from the cloud base a Dornier 17. Again there was no air raid alert.

I counted the 4 bombs as they left the bomb bay, and from the position of the plane and its direction of flight, I calculated that the stick would not be too far away from my parents' home. I was already out of the building before the first bomb landed. It dropped in a dairy

71

Bomber and fighter trails over St. Pauls Cathedral.

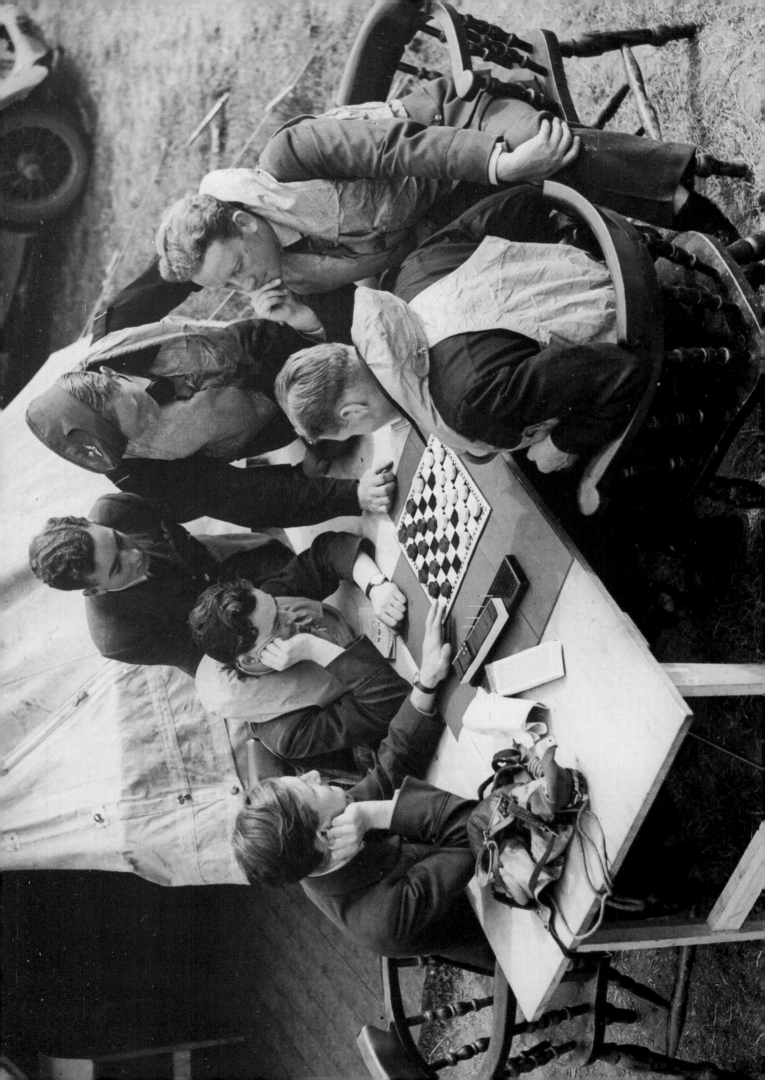

man's yard and killed 2 people. The second didn't explode. The third landed in the back garden of a row of terraced houses, and destroyed five of them killing another five people. The fourth was a 500lb bomb, which was oil filled with an incendiary device and it demolished the back of a house less than 100 yards from our house. The occupants of that house who were friends of ours had just taken cover under the stairs and were safe although they were smothered with oil from the bomb. Mercifully it all failed to ignite.

Two minutes after it had fallen I was passing the site where the second bomb had dropped and already people were being evacuated from their houses. The Military had not yet arrived, but a pal of mine who was an Air Raid Warden was on "general duties" and asked me if I had ever seen an unexploded bomb. Of course I hadn't so I accepted the invitation – just a quick peep! In the gutter was a hole about 18″ in diameter surrounded by road debris and broken kerbstones. It was full of water already from a cracked water main which was running down the road, and there down through the clear water were the ugly angular fins of a 550lb bomb. It detonated at about 9.30 that evening destroying 12 houses and leaving a deep crater the full width of the road.

One of my more hairy experiences in the Battle of Britain occurred on the 27th July 1940. The railway breakdown gang of which I was a member was called out to rerail a wagon in danger of toppling off the Prince of Wales pier into Dover harbour. We had our massive 120 ton steam crane with us, but it was decided that the wagon could be hauled upright by means of a block and tackle rig. This was duly attached, and we were merrily heave ho-ing on the ropes when the Dover sirens began to wail. Before the last note had died away a squadron of Messerschmitt BF109 fighters arrived, and proceeded to shoot down the barrage balloons which protected the harbour. Seeing 23 balloons descend in flames, each one leaving a column of black smoke, was pretty spectacular, but not as spectacular and certainly less dangerous as what happened next.

The hollow bong bong bong sound of Dover's 20 odd heavy A.A. guns hailed the arrival of about 30 Stuka dive bombers, together with fighter escort. This armada however kept out of range of the guns whilst individual squadrons came in one by one and peeled off singly to give a demonstration of what accurate dive bombing was all about! I took refuge beneath our crane while the long drawn out screaming dives followed on one after the other. It was my 'baptism of fire" with a vengeance, and within me it created a strange mixture of excitement and fear. It was a feeling I experienced only once more during the war, in 1943 but that's another story.

The attack was successful although I believe the guns claimed two Stukas. As each Stuka released its 1000lb bomb and climbed away, great water spouts a hundred feet high marked the place where each exploded in the harbour. Great columns of black smoke rose to indicate a hit on something more solid. In the next basin of the docks was the large destroyer H.M.S. Codrington which was at Dunkirk. It was hit and sunk and two other destroyers badly damaged. One of them was H.M.S. Walpole which was towed away next day in a crippled condition for repairs at Chatham.

Apart from light craft such as minesweepers and motor torpedo boats, that raid marked the end of Dover as a naval base, and the remaining destroyers were transferred to Harwich. R.A.F. Fighter Command No. 11 Group which was responsible for the defence of the whole of south east Britain including London, had 13 squadrons of Hurricanes, 7 of Spitfires and two each of Blenheims and Defiants. Just this to defend the whole of the south east of Britain! The Defiants in any case were dinosaurs, based on the World War I concept of the two seater fighter. They carried no forward firing guns, but had a four gun turret mounted behind the pilot and the weight and drag of this turret not only reduced its manoeuvrability, but also reduced its top speed to barely 300 miles an hour despite the fact that it had the same Rolls Royce Merlin engine as the 355 mile an hour Spitfire.

The turret of the Defiant made the plane look hump backed like the Hurricane. But the experienced Luftwaffe pilot always attacked a Defiant head on knowing the plane that it was, but woe betide the "rookie" pilot who mistook the "hump" for that of a Hurricane! Thus two "one to one" duels I saw had two very different outcomes.

Pilots and gunners of "Defiants" pass the waiting time with a game of draughts.

It was no surprise therefore to see a lone Defiant shot down in a frontal attack by a Messerschmitt 109. It screamed down vertically at full throttle and the force with which it struck the ground was such that its engine was recovered from a depth of 12 feet near the tiny hamlet of Hinxhill about 2 miles east of Ashford. Subsequent reading revealed that German records show a Defiant aircraft being shot down near Ashford in Kent by none other than the most famous Luftwaffe ace of them all Adolf Galland.

The second encounter was again between a lone Defiant and a Messerschmitt, which ended disastrously for the German pilot who elected to carry out a rear attack, no doubt believing he had caught an unwary Hurricane. The Messerschmitt of course ran straight into the concentrated fire of four Browning machine guns, and the result was all the more startling because at 5,000 feet the sound of firing did not reach me, until a few seconds after the visual effect. I still remember that it was like watching a silent movie. Suddenly where one moment one plane had been diving down on another, the attacker was no more! Just a big black ball of smoke. From the smoke emerged the fuselage in several pieces, and for the second time I saw a pair of wings twirling round and round like sycamore seeds. Finally and miraculously there appeared a parachute. Pilot and chute landed about a mile away, and although he was not seriously hurt, I was told that he was not too kindly treated by the waiting "reception committee"!

The most harrowing and sickening thing that I witnessed during the Battle of Britain was an R.A.F. pilot being literally shot to pieces on the end of his parachute by the pilot of a Messerschmitt 109 when he was only about 500 feet from the ground and safety.

At the end of the Battle of Britain when the bombers had been vanquished from the daylight skies, it became virtually a fighter to fighter affair, and with no bombers to worry about our Hurricanes and Spitfires acquitted themselves very well by shooting down the enemy in almost a 2 to 1 ratio with the Messerschmitt 109's sometimes going down to almost zero feet to escape their pursuers. My last memory of that great struggle is of standing on a low hill known locally as "The Warren" and actually looking down on a Spitfire chasing a Messerschmitt firing at it in short bursts. Both disappeared at a high rate of knots, and my only regret is that I never did know the outcome of that spectacular duel.

Robert A. Barham, 7 Bridle Close, Chellaston, Derby

We were married in August, 1935 in my home village in South Wales, near Swansea, and then we went to live in London at Islington. I can remember the day war was declared. We were returning home to London on the motorbike after a holiday, as that was the cheapest way to travel!

On the way we saw people queuing up for their gas masks. I thought then "fancy going back to London of all places", but for quite a time things were quiet. Sirens would go quite often, which would make one jump and listen. Quite a lot of barrage balloons were up in the sky but after I got pregnant we went to live in Finsbury Park and my husband joined the Fire Service.

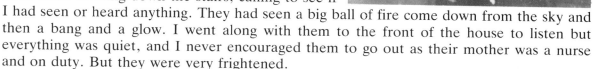

One night, quite late, I was in bed and my husband was on duty, when three sisters living on the top floor came running down the stairs, calling to see if I had seen or heard anything. They had seen a big ball of fire come down from the sky and then a bang and a glow. I went along with them to the front of the house to listen but everything was quiet, and I never encouraged them to go out as their mother was a nurse and on duty. But they were very frightened.

I was amazed the following morning when I went down to the nearby Main Street shops. There were boarded up shops and windows and house windows and burnt wood everywhere. I asked my local greengrocer man "what's happened around here?"

He said that he and his wife had not long got in from a late show when he heard a bang and what he thought was machine gunning. He went out with a dustbin lid and poker! Others apparently also took weapons out, thinking that there were Germans around, only to discover that one of our aeroplanes had been caught in a barrage balloon and caught fire, falling on a baker's storeroom behind the grocer's shop.

The pilot baled out, landed on the roof of a house, and either broke his arm or his leg, but at least his life was saved.

Royal Air Force men were soon on the scene, wanting to know what kind of a sound the plane had made when it fell. I presume that was something to do with their investigation. But the questions only made my greengrocer very annoyed as his lorry was in the garage behind the baker's store and he was anxious to get it out! So he just said "pick up a bit of paper and tear it! That's the noise!" and walked off.

One day my husband was travelling along Holborn on the fire engine when a landmine was dropped, which brought the heavy ladders and equipment on top of them. One of the men was cut rather badly with glass and the bonnet of the engine was never found!

Anyway they were taken back to the station and from there to the hospital for treatment against shock. The following day he went to our doctor because he felt that most of his ribs were broken. He was strapped up, but because he never reported back to work that day, 2/6d (12½p) was taken out of his wages!

On four occasions the fire engine team went back to their Fire Station to find that it had been bombed. They would move on to another place then. I remember one day that down in the City it was fires here and everywhere. People were grateful for the work the firemen were doing and used to bring them rolls and then apologise for not having butter on them!

75

Douglas Bader (4th from right) with his squadron.

My husband lost two of his pals in those raids. They used to work, not knowing if they were working by a live bomb, and wondering if they would be spared to see the following day.

Then things were quiet for a time. The Germans were bombing different places, but one day we were out visiting when some German planes came over and bombed the children's school at Lewisham.

After that raid my sister picked up a two leaf newspaper that had been dropped by German planes. The heading was "A Last Appeal to Reason by Adolf Hitler. Speech Before the Reichstag, 19th July, 1940".

I still have that newspaper. Like me it is getting worse for wear now because, like me, it is getting on in years and, like me, it has travelled round the world a number of times!

Mrs. Margaret Wells, 11 Mount Pleasant, Tonna, Neath, Glamorgan

Mr. Wells, back row far right.

The "phoney war" period was coming to an end by the early Spring of 1940. Until then things had been mostly quiet in and around the Dover Strait, apart from a few isolated raids on shipping. Life for a 10 year old schoolboy went on much as usual. Preparations for attack were going on all around. Barbed wire, machine gun "nests", A.R.P. posts and Field Boxes began to appear on the white cliffs and hills around the town. As in the First World War, Dover was about to be in the forefront of the battle that was already beginning to unfold on the other side of the Channel. By the middle of May, French and Belgian resistance had all but crumbled and the Germans were on the outskirts of the French ports.

Calais fell on the 27th May. The following day until the 3rd June, the Dunkirk Evacuation took place. Dover became a huge reception area for the many injured and exhausted troops. Air attacks were becoming frequent. Up to this time most activity had been restricted to "hit and run" attacks on the barrage balloons. I remember one such attack very vividly.

My father and I were walking on High Meadow, a good viewing point, as were most hills around the town. An aircraft came low over the castle from the direction of Swingate. Father asked what it was. Like all boys I thought that I was an expert on aircraft recognition, and calmly told him it was one of ours.

Almost at once there was machine gun fire and a couple of flaming balloons were on their way to the ground! I felt very shamefaced as we lay on the ground whilst the German aircraft zoomed low over our heads, the pilot clearly visible. He shot up several more balloons, including the one that flew from about half a mile away, before making his way over the Western Heights and out to sea. He had obviously caught the defences completely by surprise, so I wasn't the only one caught napping! He must have given the vital secret radar station at Swingate quite a scare.

Most other raids were much more serious. The bombing of convoys in the Strait was a regular occurrence and we could see the Spitfires and Hurricanes moving in to defend the

ships. "Dogfights" would break out and these would often continue over the coast and the skies were streaked with white. The first of many attacks on the harbour began to occur. Dover was also now within range of enemy guns on the newly occupied French coast and this threat lasted right through to 1944.

My school had been evacuated along with the others. It had been decided that I would not be going for the moment. Quite a number of children did remain all through the war and their education suffered badly.

In between raids life went on as usual, though the whole dockland harbour area was closed by now to all but essential personnel. A special pass was needed to get on to the seafront and this situation remained for most of the war. However, certain businesses and shops were very proud of the fact that they were closest to the enemy. So we had a "front line" bookshop, cafe, garage,

etc., as well as a cinema, the Granada, which I believe kept going all through the war. We also had a "frontline theatre", the famous Hippodrome, in Snargate Street close to the seafront. It kept going with nightly shows for a long time but was eventually destroyed by a direct hit one night, luckily after the show had finished.

All the four cinemas flourished in the town. All survived except one, the King's Hall, which was restored after the war. It was often necessary to leave the cinema if things became too dangerous and everyone would file into the shelter, returning when the "all clear" sounded or even sooner. I saw countless films which had two or three interruptions in this way.

By the beginning of July the Battle of Britain was well under way and much of it was being fought over the skies of Kent. Dover was a vital strategic centre for operations, the Castle in particular. Lodged in part of the East Cliff was an operations lookout post which was visited by Churchill and other war leaders. The King and Queen also came to visit the town. People made good use of the caves, medical centres were set up in some and meals and other facilities were available.

Most boys made quite a good hobby of collecting pieces of shrapnel, barrage balloon fabric, bits of shot down aircraft, cartridge cases etc., which could be found in profusion all around and we used to swap and trade for the best pieces. It wasn't usually possible to get close to wrecked aircraft though, as these were guarded until removal.

As the battle raged and things became rather too hot for comfort, I went with my mother to stay with relatives in Portland. This turned out to be not a very wise move as soon after our arrival the Germans turned their attention to the harbour there and we had several dive-bombing raids!

I remember the deafening whine of the Stukas, and it seemed as if they would land on the house as we sheltered under the stairs. We went up the hill near the well known prison to see one which had nose-dived into the ground. We had a narrow escape when a landmine came down and exploded quite close as we walked across to the mainland. The blast almost blew us into the front door of a house, and the occupant gave us shelter until the raid had passed.

We soon left Portland for London but again this proved unwise! Daylight raids were just beginning and night attacks soon followed and became a regular occurrence. Things were very uncomfortable even in the North-West suburb where we were staying, and so we decided to return to Dover. I well remember our last night being very violent with destruction all round. As we travelled out of London we passed many smoking ruins in the south-eastern suburbs, and the smoke from the Surrey Docks fires could be seen from many miles away in Kent. I remember as we passed a street in Camberwell we saw the remains of a shot down Heinkel.

Back in Dover things were moving swiftly to a climax in August and September, with "dogfights" raging overhead every day. Divebombing raids on the harbour had intensified. For much of July and August the Germans main target had been shipping. In one severe attack on 27th July several ships were hit and the destroyer "Codrington" was sunk.

The noise of the diving Stukas was deafening, even a mile or so from the harbour where we lived, and we could see the smoke from the burning vessels. It was about this time that Charles Gardner made his famous B.B.C. broadcast from the cliffs near Folkestone. He gave a cricket style commentary describing the battle over the Channel!

By this time the town's population had reduced by over half to about 15,000, and it was finally decided that I should join my school in South Wales. So I left with a number of other children and said goodbye to my home town. I was not to return for nearly two years.

Peter Elgar,
Canterbury, Kent

Flight Sergeant Harry Steere of Wallasey, Cheshire, awarded the Distinguished Flying Medal for shooting down 3 enemy aircraft, assisting in destroying 3 others and gallantry in the face of the enemy.

I arrived at R.A.F. Biggin Hill on 23rd August 1940 straight from West Kirby after a 3 weeks Basic Training course. As I was 27 years old and had held a Heavy Goods Licence for 4 years, I suppose the powers that be decided to use me as soon as possible. When I arrived late Saturday afternoon there had been quite a bit of activity, but the dust had settled so I was able to use the Mess for a meal and after making enquiries report here and report there until I found a spare bed and locker in the Motor Transport Section of the H.Q. staff and proceeded to make myself as comfortable as possible for the night.

The weekend was quiet after reporting at 8.00 a.m. on the Sunday morning, but the following days were fairly hectic with Squadrons scrambling, Ack-Ack guns going off, and Motor Transport having to disperse vehicles and then return them when the flap was over. This state continued until the Friday when I was instructed to get an early tea and report back at 5.00 p.m. as I had been assigned a Night Duty spot.

Shortly after reporting for duty, the air raid warning went. Then after a few minutes the Station Tannoy ordered all personnel not engaged in actually servicing aircraft or on ground duties to take cover. I was walking to the Motor Transport shelter as I had been shown previously, when a Corporal from the Motor Transport Office ran out shouting to me "Can you take the Fire Tender to the guard room". I was told to pick up the Fire Picquet who would instruct me where to drive to. I must admit that I felt no sense of urgency, but did as I was ordered and shortly after leaving the Guard Room the Corporal in charge shouted "Pull up and take cover". After parking I saw 8 or 9 aircraft very low approaching the Station, then the whole world seemed to erupt without warning! The noise was horrendous and as I crouched in the hedge bottom I was showered with soil, stones etc from a bomb burst which had dropped about 30 yards away. After a few minutes I returned to the Fire Tender, but as I couldn't see any of the Fire Picquet I drove it down to the Guard Room where I found it surrounded by 3 huge bomb craters.

The next few hours were spent in helping to clear casualties from a shelter which had received a direct hit. Incidentally the one I had been prevented from taking cover in by the Corporal who himself had been killed, along with 40 other airmen, mostly M.T. personnel. The next few days were spent in transferring kit to South Camp as all the water, electricity and other services were destroyed in that raid.

All this time the airfield was bombed several times although aircraft were still taking off and landing. With the Tannoy system being useless, the communication system was completely erratic, and although some state of order was obtained, it still was rather chaotic and so many Sections were being evacuated. Nevertheless the Airmen's Mess miraculously

continued to produce meals and this time no complaints were heard!

Saturday 7th September was the day that a formation of enemy aircraft tried to break through at mid-day, but were stopped although I must admit that the airfield took another bashing. About 6.00 p.m. a huge formation of enemy aircraft managed to break through and although Biggin Hill was side-tracked and little damage caused, East End of London which was visible from the airfield was turned into one great fire and as night came the enemy aircraft started night bombing for the first time. That continued for quite a few hours.

81

Spitfire pilots at Biggin Hill discussing the action.

Next day the remaining Motor Transport personnel were paraded, and I was given a Norton motorcycle, one of a lorry load especially driven down to us from Birmingham. It was my birthday and I joked "Just the job. I've always wanted a new bike". The Flight Sergeant replied "Take good care of it and when the war's over perhaps Fighter Command will let you keep it as a souvenir". I was told to contact the Watch Office to stand by ready to relay orders from Operations Room to the Squadrons at dispersal in case of loss of contact. This was necessary on many occasions over the next four or five weeks, and being familiar with my motorcycles, I had no problems in relaying orders with the minimum of time lost.

As the day raids gradually diminished I was still kept on standby at the Watch Office, and later on as winter came was responsible for inspecting the runways and take-off areas just before dawn to make sure there were no delayed action bombs or sunken bomb craters to cause a hazard to the aircraft taking off at first light.

This state continued into 1941 but gradually the Station started to come back to its former state as the services were restored. My last site had been Biggin Hill in April 1941 when I was posted overseas, and did not return until I was repatriated for medical reasons in May 1945. But that is another and much longer story.

Grenville Bottomley, Flat A, Croft House, Station Road, Otley, West Yorkshire

———————————————————

"Paddy" Finucane – a sketch. A photograph of "Paddy" ready for take off appears on page 202 together with details of his achievements.

I remember walking home along the London Road in Croydon at about 11.30 p.m. one evening, when I came across a most unusual sight. There was a pale moon in a clear sky, and a lone raider had recently dropped a cluster of fire bombs the residue of which now littered the road.

As I came near to Campbell Road church I noted that considering the late hour, the number of people in the road was considerable. However, the most striking feature was the fire engine turntable ladder!

I pressed forward into the crowd and then I saw the reason for the activity. Everyone was looking up at the tall spire of the church steeple. When I looked I could make out a man's figure about half way up the spire. I calculated he was about 80 feet up, and what is more he was stuck, being unable to go further up or climb down. In order to rescue him the extension ladder was being winched into position.

Near to me was a group of 7 or 8 young men in R.A.F. uniform, and on the breast of each of them was the "full wing" showing that they were pilots. A man standing near to me spoke.

"The man up the spire is one of their mates". Clearly their mate's predicament was not giving them concern, but great fun! Finally the lad was brought down, and he too I noticed was wearing the wings of a pilot but I failed to see the "rings" on his arm which would have identified his rank. He, with a couple of his pals, was put into a van and driven away! Knowing the area they could have been based at Croydon, Kenley, Biggin Hill or Red Hill.

This escapade became widely known throughout Croydon, and so did the lad up the spire. He was in the Battle of Britain and later became a Wing Commander! I cannot be positive but I think it was Brendan "Paddy" Finucane. I'm not certain that it would be necessary to have checked with the records at the time, but whoever he was he was quite a lad!

On the 15th August 1940 I was living near the Purley Way in Croydon. The day had been fine and sunny and at around 6 p.m. apart from the flow of traffic the evening had acquired a peaceful air. I had my evening meal and was settling down to read the evening paper when I heard the crump of an explosion which I knew came from the direction of the aerodrome about a mile away. This was followed by another crump although no warning sirens had been heard.

I rushed out into the road and looked along the Purley Way to the aerodrome which was up on higher ground than Croydon town itself. I distinctly saw several planes circling the area and could see the smoke curling up to the sky from the bomb damage.

Then the sirens blazed their warning note, but it was too late. The damage was done. There was a great loss of life because of lack of warning. Apparently the German aircraft came in under the radar screen. On this occasion they did not dive bomb, but circled the aerodrome and dropped the bombs as they chose. The heat from the blast of the bombs was so intense that when the bodies of the victims were removed the outlines of the figures could be traced on the ground. A squadron of Hurricanes was based at Croydon but, due to the

lack of warning were taken by surprise and several destroyed on the ground. Several later took off in pursuit. However, some of the raiders were shot down by units of fighter squadrons from 11 Group, probably Kenley or Tangmere, before they reached the coast. It is a fact that the leader of the raiders, a Messerschmitt 110 twin-engined fighter bomber, was the first to go down!

But at least I remember reading later that some of them had been shot down by our fighters on their way back. But I must be one of the few people who can actually report an eye witness description of that terrible raid on Croydon aerodrome.

Harry Tattersall, 50 Carluke Street, Blackburn, Lancashire

In 1940 our family, consisting of parents, two brothers and myself, lived in Chislehurst, North West Kent. We occupied a three bedroomed semi detached house – newly built and purchased in 1932 for £695! It was situated on top of a hill, some 220 feet above sea level – or in this case above River Thames level. From the front bedroom window we enjoyed an excellent view of the lower River valley, and from the rear bedroom window a clear vision of what proved to be one of the main Luftwaffe flight paths into the capital. Later, and more disastrously for us, it was also the flight path of the V1 flying bombs in 1944, one of which destroyed our home killing 4 of our neighbours.

After the fall of France the initial German air attacks against Britain were made on shipping and south coast radar, slowly moving inland to the Royal Air Force fighter bases. These largely failed to disturb the peace as far as we were concerned until, as the battle intensified, Biggin Hill, Gravesend, Croydon and Hornchurch fighter stations became the major targets for the German bombers. I recorded our first major alert on the 15th August 1940. From that date onwards raids by day and also by night were virtually continuous, so much so that when an "alert free" day did occur, I noted the fact as an "event" in my diary!

During the remainder of August, throughout September and well into October, we witnessed the full panoply of aerial warfare overhead. Interweaving patterns of vapour trails on blue skies, the whine of aircraft engines under stress, the seemingly harmless backing sounds of machine gun and cannon fire and the inevitable silvery spin downwards of a doomed aircraft. All these became common place and almost acceptable to the senses.

I think most of us watching made the easier assumption that the stricken plane was "enemy" and we were to be thrilled on a number of occasions in the early part of the fighting to see low flying Spitfires or Hurricanes, usually in pairs, rolling gloriously and victoriously towards their bases at Biggin Hill and Gravesend. Occasionally, however, we were to see others flying similarly low at hedgehopping height with faltering engines and our youthful enthusiasm for future participation in what we regarded as the "excitement of war" became temporarily at least somewhat dampened.

This innocence and naivete towards the horrors of warfare were reflected in many of my diary entries. Typically on the 31st August I recorded "Three raids this morning. Saw Jerry brought down. Fine sight. Two more raids before midnight and another after".

It is impossible to deny that at that time there was a very genuine thrill in observing the action in the skies above us. Throughout September the school remained closed and it was not until the first week in October when we were able to resume a two or three day working week i.e. attending on alternative days. But even then much of the time was spent in the newly constructed air raid shelters.

On 15th September, which is now recorded as the climax of the Battle, although fighting was to continue for some weeks after, I remember watching from our rear bedroom window as two Hurricane fighters flew at low level in pursuit of a thin bodied Dornier bomber. The two fighters were capable of greater speeds, but in view of their need to remain on the tail of their quarry, they adopted undulating flight. As each of them came into line with the bomber in front of them their wings flashed brightly as their eight machine guns were activated, and a thin trail of smoke seeped from the Dornier's starboard engine just before

it was enveloped in cloud. Although there was little chance of their target reaching its base, I remember my acute sense of frustration and disappointment at not actually seeing the plane go down!

What is surprising on looking back on those momentous days is how little they affected our daily lives in terms of normal activity. Even though our nights were disturbed constantly the slogan "Business as Usual" proved very much a reality. During some of the most hectic aerial activity in August and September I recorded ten visits to the swimming baths at nearby Eltham in South London, almost as many trips to the cinemas in Eltham

Dornier Bomber on a German airfield in France.

Do 215

and Sidcup, and various picnic and blackberry picking outings to Chislehurst Common and Petts Wood. A kind of crazy normality is reflected for example in my diary entry of 30th August. "Four warnings, the first three in day, the last from 9.30 p.m. to 4.00 a.m. In the first morning one I was in the barbers. Fights were overhead, heavy machine gun fire. 1500 aircraft in today's raids. 62 brought down". Another entry on the 27th August simply records "Air raids again last night, first lasting 2 hours 40 minutes, but we stayed in bed for the second".

The attempt to maintain a degree of normality lay also behind the frequent cinema visits. Most of these were made in daylight of course, and there was rarely any great tension within the audience when the almost inevitable message in spidery writing confirming an air raid was superimposed upon the screen. This requested anyone wishing to leave to do so with as little disturbance for other patrons as possible. Only occasionally did anyone move! Indeed there seemed little point in standing in bus queues to be exposed to the metallic "fall out" from battles overhead. It is probably also true to say that an illusory sense of security was experienced by most people in being with others within a closed environment.

There was very little evidence of fear at that time. The aerial battles overhead were seen as a prelude – an overture to the land battles to come. We already had the experiences of Warsaw and Rotterdam to ponder on, and it seemed obvious that the invasion was imminent. We lived in a world of mushrooming pill boxes, tank traps, sandbagged "strong points" and the local fields were magically occupied by overnight stakes and poles to counter glider landings. A Guards Regiment occupied large areas of Chislehurst Common and the evidence seemed overwhelming that "the worst was yet to come". At school boy level the biggest impact was a switch from the collection of cigarette cards to that of shrapnel. Cannon shell and bomb casing fragments were the most eagerly sought! Whilst it is now realised that the decision to abandon the "Sealion" operation by Hitler was taken in September, this was hardly obvious to us groundling observers. Daylight attacks continued well into October, although on 15th October I noted the German use of fighter bombers for the first time. This was a practice which was to continue into 1941 and 1942 with growing emphasis on the "hit and run" technique. The greatest raid of all, however, was to prove the opening of the Blitzkrieg on London, the now well documented raid of the 7th September 1940.

My diary entry for 7th September read "colossal raid. Huge fires over Thames, 400 killed, 1300 injured, terrible damage but wonderful sight". The attack began in the middle of a sunny Saturday afternoon. My father and brother were away from the house – shopping in Lewisham. After the sirens had sounded my mother and I stood at the entrance to the Anderson shelter waiting to dive down to join my younger brother if an emergency happened.

Aircraft noise intensified, but there was no whining of stressed engines on this occasion, simply a steady growing reverberation of power in the sky. Two separate formations of German bombers droned massively towards us and passed almost directly overhead. I estimated at least 60 bombers in each group and there were no British fighters on the scene. Anti aircraft guns opened up. Shells exploded whitely, but as the aircraft moved towards London the blue sky was left scarred with blackening smoke. The track of the planes was constant, and inexorable. The afternoon sun glinted fiercely on the perspex gun turrets at the front of the aircraft as they headed for the Docks. We didn't take cover. It was as though there was a feeling of total vulnerability and acceptance of enemy domination. Even a sense of admiration. The planes went on to the Thames creating fires which burned all night. Fires which extended from London's East End down to oil fires burning at Tilbury. The brightness of the flames enabled me to read a newspaper in the front bedroom of our house in the evening hours of normal blackout. The travelling members of the family happily returned safely, but with their own exciting and alarming accounts of the day. In October our local press reported 50 bombs to date on Chislehurst, and this was increased by early November to 200. In my diary I recorded many of these especially during October making reference to the neighbouring street where bombs had fallen. Wherever an incident occurred there was an immediate tendency of all within a radius of half a mile or so to claim the enemy missile as 'our bomb'! During that month of October alone I make reference to sticks of bombs falling on seven different occasions so the press reports were almost certainly accurate.

Derek J. South, 18 Kent Road, Fleet, Hampshire

Goering and his staff on the French coast look longingly at the English coast, clearly visible. Goering in peaked cap, 6th from right.

I was brought up in Folkestone in the 1930's, and my most nostalgic memories of those years are of school. It was a huge Victorian building on Dover Hill, and when we weren't there learning the three R's and cookery and playing netball, we were playing on the sands or diving into the harbour off the quayside to swim amongst the fishing boats. My grandfather with whom I lived was the fishing boat skipper of the trawler "Jessica", and our house was very close to the beach and the harbour and the fish market and that was our playground.

Later we moved to a new house on the outskirts of Folkestone under the hills between Folkestone and Dover, very close to the famous white cliffs. It is an area known to this day as "Little Switzerland" where we roamed the green and chalk slopes by the beach (now the site to the entrance to the Channel Tunnel!) where we camped, picked blackberries, caught butterflies, picked wild flowers, and when the tide was out harvested winkles to take home for our tea! On very clear days the coast of France could always be seen – little did we children know of the horrors which would come from across that stretch of water and soon it would not be safe for us to venture too far from home.

I was 12 years old when war was declared and we very quickly became aware of the dangers forthcoming when barbed wire appeared all along the beaches and sands and gun emplacements were set up in funny holes on the cliffs! Then we were issued with gas masks, and I remember watching a neighbour trying to put her 8 month old baby son into a special respirator, and I helped to pump it while she did it.

The first of the air raid warning practices or rehearsals quickly became the real thing when one day shortly after the beginning of the war my mother and I were digging potatoes in the back garden. It was a bright cold day and my attention was drawn suddenly to a low flying aircraft and what appeared to be a large black cross mark on it.

"Look Mum – that's a funny plane – and it's so low I can see the pilot", I said.

"Could it be a German?"

My mother laughed. "They wouldn't send one plane", she said. "In any case they wouldn't get past our chaps up there on the cliffs". But they did, as we were to learn later. That plane I saw was a reconnaisance plane taking aerial photographs.

From summer 1940 we were to experience shelling. At first the shells fired by the Germans from the French coast fell short of the towns of Dover and Folkestone, but as they became more efficient the shells began to fall all over the towns causing dreadful damage and death everywhere. Unlike an air raid at least one shell had to fall somewhere before a warning could be given, and sometimes there would be a lapse of 2 or 3 hours in between each shell. This situation made life very difficult. We seemed to be in a permanent state of alert. Our schooling was continuously being interrupted. Just when it was anticipated that the Germans fired enough shells for the day and perhaps the all clear would be given and we would come out of the shelters and either go home and continue lessons, there would be another explosion somewhere nearby and we had to stay where we were. Occasionally we were caught between shells on the way home and ran like the devil to hide in a doorway. Instinctively everyone tried to escape shells, bombs and bullets by hiding INSIDE something or somewhere! In actual fact I believe we would have been safer to have stayed out in the open!

Like many other households we had an indoor shelter called a Morrison shelter. It stood in all its glory in the middle of our living room, made of reinforced steel, with curtains around it to disguise its ugliness. But it still made a very useful table. When the air raid siren first sounded we

89

Barges assembled at Antwerp ready for the invasion.

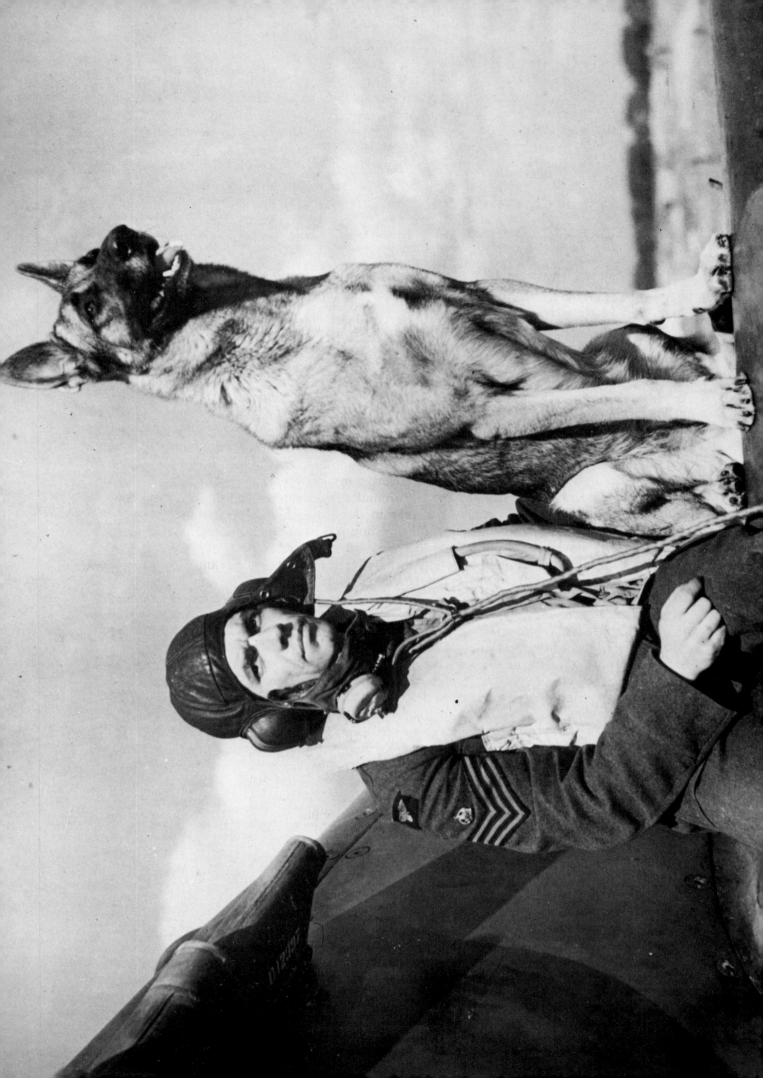

were all supposed to creep inside it. There was a mattress in it and pillows and I seemed to remember my mother often slept in there. However, my grandfather and I only made a gesture of getting inside the shelter. We just had our heads and shoulders under cover, but our bottoms and legs would be sticking out, and I think it must have been a very funny sight!

I remember in 1940 sitting on the grassy bank at the top of our garden with the hills behind me and a view of the sea in front, watching the first of many "dog fights" between "our" fighter planes and "theirs". Some planes dived into the sea – very close to the harbour area. We cheered because we thought it was a Messerschmitt!

One Sunday morning vans with loudspeakers came slowly round all the roads advising that all school aged children and mothers with babies and pregnant women should evacuate the town as there was a threat of an invasion by the Germans. The following day with one small case and gas masks in their little boxes over our shoulders and a label tied to our school blazers giving our name and school, we assembled at the Railway Station to be trundled off to far away places in Wales to live with complete strangers. But that's another story! But I do remember that there were so many children and people of all ages at the station that when our train finally moved out I didn't even get a chance to say goodbye to mum. It was nearly 7 months before we were to meet again.

When I did get back to my beloved Kent, Grandad had somehow survived all the shells and there was no invasion of England! But the towns were still suffering from German bombers releasing the last of their bombs before they flew back over the sea after raids on our cities. But life had to go on, and I remember one day when I was crossing the main shopping street in Folkestone that a German fighter suddenly appeared from nowhere and machine gunned everyone and anything that moved in Sandgate Road. I threw myself into the gutter, and using logic saved myself by covering my head with a canvas bag!

I remember another incident that comes to mind. I had been saving up for weeks for a beautiful pale blue silk blouse that I had seen in Bobbys, our posh departmental store in Folkestone, and one lunchtime I went into the shop to buy it. In fact I had just bought it when suddenly there was another hit and run raid, and a German plane swooped in low from the sea and peppered us all with bullets. Being a lunch time there were quite a few people about, including military personnel, and the whole bunch of us crouched down in the arcade entrance of a nearby shop only to be showered with glass when a display window shattered.

It took me ages to pick the glass out of my hair – but at least I had my precious blouse!

By 1944 I was working in an office in Folkestone when a land mine exploded practically demolishing the whole street of little houses near to us. The large windows in the accounts office caved in, and as I had taken shelter under a desk with my legs (as usual) sticking out, I received a small cut on my leg. Forever afterwards that was known as my "war wound"!

Once the glass and plaster and dust had settled I was sent home by my boss. The all clear had sounded and as I started to pick my way through the chaos outside caused by the disaster I saw my mother running down the road towards me still with her apron around her and wearing just her slippers! She was worried and tearful as she had heard the land mine had fallen near to my office. On that very same day she had also just heard that my only brother had been seriously wounded in North Africa. It was such a hard time for mothers.

I also have another recollection of that time. Despite the continued dangers and trauma of a coastal town in war time, there were lovely times to be had at dances held in the beautiful Leas Cliff Hall, which was set into the cliff at the "posh end" of Folkestone.

At one of these dances the Entertainments Officer for the town appealed to civilians who could sing a bit or dance or tell jokes or play a musical instrument to form a concert party to entertain service men who were based on remote gun sites or aerodromes.

At that time I had a fair singing voice, similar in tone I suppose to that of Anne Shelton. I knew the words to most of the war time songs, so I was persuaded to join the concert party. Once a week we set off in an old camouflaged lorry with the flaps down at the back as we weren't allowed to see where we were going! The bases were supposed to be top secret. Our concert party consisted of a piano accordionist, a drummer, a pianist, a comedian and 3 vocalists.

91

Flight Sergeant Cecil Unwin of Bolton-on-Deare, Yorkshire with "Flash" the squadron mascot. Awarded the Distinguished Flying Medal for intercepting a formation of bombers escorted by 30 fighters, and shooting down 2. Had previously shot down 10 other enemy aircraft.

The lorry would trundle along country lanes, across fields and up tracks until we reached the mess tent or the hut or the hangar or marquee, or whatever was to be used for this jolly little concert. I must say that all the lads always made us feel very welcome and applauded enthusiastically – but I have to admit that I cringe to this day when I think how awful we must have been. And how this captive audience probably welcomed an alert to escape with a good excuse!

I distinctly remember arriving at what was obviously an airbase – rows and rows of airmen and airwomen – and air crews who were already in their flying gear with boots and scarves etc. The Commanding Officer got as far as the introduction when red lights began to flash the alert, and there was one mad dash to evacuate the hangar. That left the concert party on the makeshift stage with borrowed tin hats! I don't blame the airmen – they were saved from a fate worse than death if only they had known!

In December 1944 I finally joined the Womens Royal Naval Service – but that's another story!

Mrs. Maureen Kenefick, 6 Trundle Mead, Horsham, Sussex

I was nine years old during the Battle of Britain and I remember an occasion when I was in the cemetery (of all places!) in Harpenden with my Mother when a "dog fight" took place overhead. We could clearly see the German and British planes chasing each other across the sky. A German plane was hit and the pilot came out below his parachute, and landed behind some trees a little way off.

We then saw a policeman riding along the lane alongside the cemetery on his bicycle on his way to apprehend the pilot!

On another day we were at home and my Mother came running in from the garden when a German fighter plane swooped across and let off some machine gun bullets. They went through our pantry window, and one embedded itself in the meat safe!

Some bombs fell on St. Albans, and property was destroyed, but I particularly remember when a string of land mines went down into Verulam Park near our house. My Father says that he can remember me calling out from my bedroom window "That was close!" From our house we could also see the sky all red with the glow from fires in London.

If the air raid warning went before we were due to go to school then we didn't go. But if it went whilst we were at school, we had to stay there until the "all clear". For this reason each child had a small tin stored at the school containing biscuits in case we could not get home for a meal. On the wall in our living room we had a map provided I believe by the Daily Express, on which we pinned small flags, either Union Jacks or Swastikas, to show how the war was going.

My Father eventually went into the Royal Army Ordnance Corps but before he was called up he was in the Home Guard and before that I believe he was in the L.D.V. (Local Defence Volunteers). Before they had rifles the only weapon he had was a truncheon! A little story about that. I asked him for a memory and he told me about one when he was out patrolling with a colleague in the Home Guard. They were supposed to stay together and had been given a particular route to follow, but his colleague decided they ought to investigate the meadows. That was down towards the river. But Dad would not do this so his colleague went off on his own.

A moment or two later he heard a voice calling out "Arthur". He made no reply and the voice called to him again and again. Eventually his colleague returned to him and said "Why didn't you reply when I called you?"

My Father's reply was, "We're supposed to be out looking for Germans, not announcing to the whole world where we are!"

G. Farmer, The Croft, 73 Sandpit Lane, St. Albans, Hertfordshire

German pilots being escorted to interrogation.

At the time of the Battle of Britain I was in 'C' Troop 373 West Somerset Yeomanry with the 55th (Wessex) Field Regiment of the Royal Artillery. After training and having been moved around to different parts of the country we were settled just after Dunkirk at New Romney in Kent, but after only a short time there we were moved two miles along the road to St. Marys Bay which was considered to be a better position.

Our gun position was actually at St. Marys in the Marsh, and our gun pits were at the back of 6 farm cottages at the bottom of the gardens! Initially our work consisted of training and then filling sandbags, and when that was done we then filled more sandbags! Certainly there was no shortage of sand because we were only a few miles from Littlestone where there were miles and miles of sand dunes, and also our own Observation Post at Popes Hotel.

When the gun pits had been completed the Regiment took possession of the guns which were American 75's with ammunition and the boxes marked "American Expeditionary Forces France 1917"! They were also from the Rhode Island Arsenal! In appearance the weapons looked pre Boer War and the sights were

Hubert Bowden at the St. Mary's site during the Battle of Britain.

completely different to the "British Dial" sights. During our period of gun training the attacks on our country intensified with more and more bombing attacks generally, but certainly we also suffered them at St. Marys in the Marsh. There we had a "front seat", and witnessed the heroic actions of the Royal Air Force against insuperable odds. I remember seeing one of our planes apparently deliberately ram a Dornier. I found out later that the pilot was a Czech who had run out of ammunition and apparently in his hate had abandoned any discipline and just taken his ultimate revenge. Because of the aerodromes that were near to our gun sites we also saw members of the Polish Air Force, and in later years we began to understand the hatred that they felt for the Nazis. The American Eagle Squadron was also stationed near to us and at times it was difficult to know who was who from all the different nationalities in the pubs and generally in the area.

One of the worst moments we witnessed, and we were powerless to act, was when a young British airman had to bale out of his stricken Hurricane fighter. I actually saw this myself. As he glided to earth a German fighter shot him to bits as he floated down. His name we later learned was Pilot Officer Brooks. He was just 21 years old.

In front of our guns we had a very deep pit for us to stand up in which housed a Lewis gun on a revolving stand. It was used for firing on low flying aircraft and I have to say that after I saw the deliberate shooting of that young British pilot in his parachute, we certainly took pleasure in firing at these aircraft as they came in.

At night we would hear the rumblings and see the fiery glow of London being bombed, and set alight, and we were helpless to assist. It seemed that day in and day out almost

Hubert Bowden on left with his friend S. J. Woodbury who served in the same regiment.

around the clock the enemy planes came. We built up such a rage and hatred towards the Germans that every time we saw a bomber crash or one of their ME 109 and ME110 fighters come spiralling down to earth we cheered and cheered and cheered. It was true that the young brave gallant and fool hardy pilots saved Britain in those days.

For us it was stand to's with long hard work. There was also guard duty day after day, and day after day after day so that we became almost walking zombies. At this time, which was about the beginning of August 1940, we were issued with the Canadian Ross rifle, and I have to say it was the most accurate rifle I have ever fired. We practised with them on the Hythe ranges with excellent results, and best of all we felt morale was suddenly rising and at the same time we could see the

95

Czechoslovak fighter pilots at an airfield in Kent.

R.A.F. VERSUS LUFTWAFFE: TO-DAYS SCORE 14 to 20

Royal Air Force was already having a profound effect in the skies and the German airman who were captured seemed to be getting younger and younger and more inexperienced. We had our moments of fun. The vast majority of our troop had worked on the land, and were quite skilled in foraging! In the St. Marys in the Marsh and New Romney region there were flocks and flocks of the famous Romney Marsh sheep around, and occasionally one found itself in our pots! That was assisted by the fact that our Sergeant was a butcher, and he usually did the honours and so we lived like lords in those cottages which still had their cooking ranges! Those meals were assisted by trips to the Battery cookhouse where we took what was needed and borrowed coal for the range, plus there were plenty of bags of potatoes and cabbages and other vegetables around the farms on Romney Marsh, and so we lived very well indeed. On occasions chickens also somehow managed to find their way into our pots!

I remember that it was about this time that we were told the name of the General commanding South East England and it was a General Montgomery. We didn't know who he was, but many of us later in our service lives knew who he was by then! Our defences improved and so did our vigilance. I remember our being told that there were Fifth Columnists in the area, and this was borne out by our signallers on occasions when they would find our communication wires cut. All these stories did not surprise us as we weren't the most favourite people on Romney Marsh being strangers to the area. Not that we were able to visit the towns a great deal, but when we did we knew from the attitudes when we went to have a pint or two what the feeling was. I remember in those days there was a drink made locally which was called "Fighting Cider". It turned out to be a concoction of cider and cherry, and it was lethal! This was usually obtained at the farmhouses where they were apparently experts on making it.

On Sunday September 11th 1940 we were hauled out of our beds at 3.00 a.m., told to get our ammunition ready and stand to. Officers came round our gun pits repeatedly as we had a visit from Colonel Ackland, which was apparently designed to keep us on our toes. Everyone was in a state of jumpiness, but no-one told us anything and we presumed it was just a "top brass" visit until we heard the steady roar of heavy bombers. But by their engines we knew that these bombers were not German, but ours, because they had a "steady" roar and not the "intermittent" noise of the enemy bombers.

This huge noise passed over us, and then across the Channel and in the distance we saw flashes and the word went round amongst ourselves "Thank God we are hitting back". As each squadron of bombers came back more were going out, but if our Officers knew what was happening they were keeping it close to themselves. Finally we stood down at mid-day and I remember that at Littlestone some bodies were picked up from the sea and placed in the mortuary at New Romney. I also remember that for months afterwards bodies in all stages of decomposition and burning were recovered from the Channel, and of course there are stories that this raid and the recovery of numerous bodies from the Channel were linked in that the raid was on the German invasion troops. This will always be a great mystery to us, but certainly that raid just across the Channel which we could see, and the recovery of so many bodies shortly afterwards remains unexplained. A couple of Sundays later we witnessed the greatest of all the air battles with our Royal Air Force triumphantly shooting out of the skies 187 enemy aircraft in one day. After that the attacks became sporadic. Apparently Hitler and Goring had learned the lesson the hard way that our Air Force was superior, and that anything they could do the R.A.F. could do better! But why Hitler never invaded England only he would know. Many books and theories have been put forward, but in our state of unpreparedness I have never been able to understand it.

Before I finish I would also like to mention that one of the things we did to pass the time when we were not particularly busy or on duty was to collect all the perspex glass from planes which had crashed in the area. In those days of course we did not know the name perspex, but we called it "Jerry glass". The perspex was about ½" or ¾" in thickness, and we would fashion various trinkets out of it. Rings, bangles and rosary crosses to name but a few. The articles we made were given away to our families and girlfriends. I still have a piece of this "glass" in my possession to this day with the splinter marks of bullet holes in it.

Soon after the Battle of Britain ended, I left the Regiment and served with the 8th Army. but I learned my lesson and kept a diary from then on! I also took part in the Normandy invasion, with my Regiment which was the 4th Regiment of the Royal Horse Artillery. But I still remember the 373 West Somerset Yeomanry, and on 3rd September 1989, on the 50th anniversary of the outbreak of the Second World War, those of us who were left held a reunion at Wiveliscombe in Somerset.

Hubert H. Bowden, 149 Darwin Road, Ealing, London

It was treated like cricket! A newspaper seller on 15th September 1940.

Although a boy of 8, coming up 9, children matured quickly in those days, and I remember the things I write about as though they were yesterday. I had declined evacuation saying "Old 'itler isn't going to make me go away".

I remember my late mother and I with some friends went for an afternoon on the Earlswood lakes near here. We were out on one of the lakes in a skiff when a German plane came over and machine gunned everything on and around the lakes! Some of the bullets made a pattern in the water very near us, just like the scenes in the films or on T.V. now only this was for real! I can see it now. The plane was a Heinkel with all the glass in the nose and some of the crew were quite clear to us. Needless to say I was pleased we weren't hit, but some of the people around the lakes were although I don't think they were seriously injured.

I remember another near miss at that time as well. My late father and I were walking near the railway bank of the London to Brighton line one afternoon when we heard a German plane approaching. By that time we were able to tell friend from foe simply by the sound of the engines. Soon we heard the whistle of a bomb falling and "hit the deck". Luckily for us the bomb fell on the other side of the railway bank. There was no damage as we were out in the countryside, but I don't think I would be writing to you now if the bomb had fallen on the side of the bank where we were!

The Royal Air Force fighter station at Kenley which was at the centre of the Battle of Britain is only about 5 miles from here, and Biggin Hill about 15 miles. Tangmere is about 25 miles, so we were well placed to see the Battle. There was also a station at Nutfield about 2 miles away, but this was used for night fighters only, although it still came in for some attention from "Jerry" attacks!

My most vivid memories of this time are the formations of German planes being attacked by our fighters. Sometimes those attacks were directly overhead, and I also remember the planes of both sides coming down, some with smoke and flames coming from them as they descended, usually from a great height. When the crews were able to get out they could be seen falling in "dead fall" before their parachutes finally opened. For much of the time there would be vapour trails leaving all sorts of patterns in the sky, and of course the sound of the guns of both sides hammering away at each other with the Ack Ack guns adding to the sound of the almost daily raids, with their puffs of smoke drifting along in clusters.

Strange as it may seem I only remember 2 German bombers crashing near here. One was at Reigate Hill and the other one was at Godstone. Both of them were about 2 miles away. Also a Spitfire came down some way away, and we actually saw the pilot bale out, but I'm not sure of exactly where the plane crashed. However, some years ago while some digging

work was going on the German plane that crashed near Godstone was discovered. Rumour has it that the skeleton of the pilot was still at the controls, but of course I can't vouch for that. All I do know is that the police would not allow anyone near to the plane.

What I do particularly recollect is how pleased we were to see the victory rolls of our fighters knowing that another "Jerry" plane had been shot down. Almost every day we, that is our family, friends and the local people, would collect the bits and pieces of planes that had fallen and the bullet cases. Some people actually made cigarette lighters from the cases. I know because I still have one!

My lasting memory of this time is the droning sound of

99

Burned out Dornier, shot down 19th August 1940 in Kent.

the German planes as they came over, and the Ack Ack guns opening up. Then the whistling of bombs falling from planes and our hiding in the cupboard under the stairs (said to be the best place to be if your house was hit) or later on the Morrison table shelter that had been installed in many houses. Some other houses had what were called Anderson shelters. These were small dug outs mainly in back gardens and before our shelter was installed we sometimes shared next door's, but it was very cramped and damp and not something to be enjoyed.

It's another story, but that Morrison shelter actually saved our lives in 1944, when a V1 "Doodlebug" actually fell near our garden about 20 yards from us. I shall never forget the screams and the sounds of breaking glass and the falling debris all around us. We were trapped for about 2 hours before the rescue services got to us. There is no doubt at all that that Morrison shelter saved us, and eventually apart from shock and some slight cuts from the glass, we were OK. But it took us a long time to pick out all the fragments of glass from our hair and bodies and in our streets there were 12 people killed and scores of injured from that one V1. The house was rebuilt, and we moved back in and I have lived here ever since!

Dennis Kent, 34 St. Johns Road, Redhill, Surrey

I had my birthday on September 11th, 1940 just four days before what is now known as "Battle of Britain" day and at that time we lived in a tenement house in Islington, London. One beautiful afternoon around this time I heard my grandparents in the back garden arguing fiercely about the identity of an aircraft overhead.

"British – one of ours", shouted Grandad. "It's a German, Tom", replied my Nan. "British". "German".

I stuck my head out of the loo window, because I'd already learnt by then how to identify different planes. "German", I yelled. They both stopped arguing to turn to me.

"Get in", they shouted together. "Before you get hurt".

Streetwise or heroic, I scoffed, "They can't see me from up there", but at the same time I looked round quickly to make sure that the loo door was bolted to avoid any possible retribution! As I did it a Spitfire appeared almost from nowhere and blew the other aircraft out of the sky in a matter of seconds. "There it was a German", said my Nan triumphantly.

To my delight and excitement 2 parachutes appeared and slowly drifted out of sight. Later that afternoon my great uncle who was a Metropolitan policeman came home and told us that two German airman had come down near the Arsenal football ground, and one of them had been captured straight away. The

other one however had managed to escape and was still being hunted. That night we slept, as usual in those days, in the basement of the house, and the adults talked about the missing German airman, wondering where he was, whilst I, feigning sleep, listened to all this with growing wonder. However, as far as I can remember, I had no fear. My Dad was a soldier and could beat the whole German Army and Airforce on his own as far as I was concerned! In the early hours of next morning the whole household was woken up by the piercing shrieks of my mother. My father had come home unexpectedly. During an escort duty to London he had found some hours spare before returning to his Unit. He had let himself in quietly, and shaken my mother by the shoulder to wake her.

She had woken to see a large uniformed figure with cropped hair and a rather square head standing over her! Her first thought was that the German airman who had escaped the day before had somehow got into the house! I remember explaining "She thinks you're a German Daddy" and was in his arms before the rest of the household knew what was going on. Incidentally the missing German had been captured much earlier. Sadly my grandparents and parents are no longer with us. The longest survivor was my father who died in 1989, still big, still square headed, and still cropped haired – and still very much loved!

David Collins, 28 Poulders Gardens, Sandwich, Kent

A German pilot at a London station en route to an internment camp, 7th October 1940.

Hawkinge being a Fighter Station of the Royal Air Force and the closest airfield to the enemy across the Channel was bombed heavily on 11th August 1940. I was biking home from work that day along the lonely lane at the rear of the landing runway. Suddenly it seemed almost without warning that the Stukas came in with a scream of noise and the air raid warning was still blaring out as the bombs detonated.

A relation of mine working on one of the hangars had no chance to reach shelter. He was later found buried under a collapsed giant metal door which had crushed him to death. He had stayed behind beyond his shift to finish a job on an aircraft. All the hangars were obliterated.

From the lane I can clearly recall having an uninterrupted view of the destruction. All the hangars were down and in a cloud of debris, smoke and flames. Buildings were smashed and the roads and runways filled with giant holes. That evening some people who lived in the village near to the aerodrome arrived at our house. Their home was roofless and gutted. The family, husband, wife, daughter and young son were to stay with us for nearly a year. They slept on the floor in made up beds, and shared our facilities as best they could. Electricity and water had been cut off in the village in the raid.

Luckily living just outside the village we had a well and we also used oil lamps plus we had a kitchener which burnt coke, and a primus stove to boil water on. Life from then on was hectic. Once I found whilst calling at a farmhouse near the aerodrome an old lady who was well into her 90's asleep on a pile of sacks under a table "air raid shelter". It was in fact a specially made table with a steel top. I was calling for some water at her back door at the time, and I remember that she thought I was the enemy, and screamed to me to leave her alone! I had to leave to pacify her! Later I learned that her family who were farmers left her under the table with tea and biscuits while they went off to tend the crops! I still remember quite clearly that she had all the mattresses piled on top of the table, and down by her side was a chamber pot! So that was how she spent the last days of her waning life. All very sad.

At the rear of our house we had a dug-out. It had been created out of a boiler room that once heated our greenhouses with its coke run boiler.

I remember that one Saturday the area was shelled from Calais, and at the same time there were overhead "dog fights" going on and the area seemed to be full of noise from the giant explosions of the shells and the roar of the shell flight, and the aircraft fighting above us. Everything seemed to be in "full swing" and the noise was appalling. We really thought the invasion was about to begin.

A Hurricane fell like a stone into the lane near our home. It ground its way through the tarmac to a depth of about 6 feet. Luckily the pilot was seen on a parachute, and landed near to Folkestone. Over at Dover we could see a great many barrage balloons. In a few moments it seemed that they were all shot out of the sky, trailing orange flames and smoke as they tumbled to earth. This occurred more than once. Each time they were replaced.

Veterans from Dunkirk were posted nearby at about this time as anti-invasion troops. I have to say that they were very trigger happy! That was especially so in darkness when guarding a blockhouse across the main road or something similar. We found it best to answer quickly when challenged! Otherwise you would hear the click of a bullet going into the breech, which showed that they meant business! Folkestone became an almost derelict town. There seemed to be hardly a civilian in the place. Troops were billeted in hotels and barbed wire was laid in the streets and along the beaches. I remember

Czech pilots at Hawkinge with the squadron mascot.

again one particular Saturday. This time it was at lunch time, and it was in September. I was on the way home from work when Dornier bombers flew low over the aerodrome dropping bombs, followed by ME109 fighters. They were flying at almost tree top level spraying machine gun fire as they came. There was only one thing to do and it was done quickly. Leap off the bike and flatten down in the kerb! The kerb was only 6" deep, but surprisingly it did feel as if I had some protection! It was all over very quickly, but a few minutes later I saw the enemy planes heading out over the Channel hotly pursued by a squadron of Hurricanes. Thus life went on!

Air raids, shellings, hit and run incidents, and on one particular day I remember the awe inspiring spectacle of a fine sunny September day when the sky in every direction appeared to harbour formations of enemy planes. All bound for London. That night the sky to the north was a dull red glow. London docks were an inferno. I recall it as a sombre and sad night. The steady throb of enemy night bombers feeding the flames of London until dawn left little to the imagination of what a holocaust it must be there.

My final recollection is that once the Italian Air Force put in an appearance! It only happened once as they were soon put to flight. Eventually October came, and with it the end of the Battle of Britain. August to October in particular was a time to look back on in later years with mixed pride and sadness. Pride that Britain had stood firm and all alone. Sadness at so many young lives destroyed and homes in rubble.

Frank G. Brisley, 31 Calland, Smeeth, Nr. Ashford, Kent

My memory of the Battle of Britain is coming home after working all night as a worker at the local colliery and after having breakfast I retired to bed. Around about 11.00 a.m. I was woken by sirens and gun fire, and I dashed downstairs to arrange to take my wife and son who was only 2 years old to the air raid shelter in the front garden of my house.

I and my family had never experienced bombs or shell fire in our lives, so you can imagine how we felt. It was absolutely hell. After being in the shelter for half an hour 2 aircraft then flew over the top on the way out to sea dropping bombs. Although you could see them leaving the planes, you could do nothing about it. There was soil, dust, paper, wood, tiles etc. flying all over the place. One bomb dropped about 20 yards in front of the shelter, and looking through a slit in the steel sheets, I could see everything. It took the breath out of my lungs and splattered shrapnel all over the shelter, killing my wife and a large piece came in one side of my leg and out of the other burning like hell. My son at this time was lying in the bottom of the shelter crying his heart out.

After about half an hour the raid was over. A.R.P. men, firemen etc. all came to help. I was taken to the clearance post and treated, and had my wounds dressed and sent on my way to hospital with a message with the ambulance men that I wouldn't last half an hour. I never saw my wife again.

My son was looked after by my family but after 3 or 4 nights in hospital I was transferred to an Army Emergency Hospital which was made up of wooden army huts. At night the planes came over when it was dark dropping bombs all over the countryside. Every night I died a million times with fright. My experience in hospital was terrible. Twice I was taken to the operating theatre to have my leg amputated, only to find when I came round that it was still there. I don't know why it was. What I do know is that eventually after months of treatment I succeeded in being discharged from hospital to try and pull myself together.

Since then all my life I have had terrible pains in my leg, and in going to swimming baths I have been embarrassed at people staring at me. After 50 years of pain and misery with my leg, and the loss of my wife, I received virtually no help at all from the Government, and what help I did get was an insult.

H. Gale, 2 Parkside Crescent, Parkside, Seaham, County Durham

Italian plane shot down, October 1940.

I was stationed in Kent during the whole of the Battle of Britain, and the invasion emergency. In my capacity as an Army despatch rider with the Royal Corps of Signals, and as part of the 167 Infantry Brigade of the First London Infantry Division, I travelled most of Kent and parts of Sussex on a motor cycle seeing much of what was going on during the air battles, and the defence for the expected invasion. Our Headquarters were stationed in Kent College just outside Canterbury on the main Dover to Canterbury road. Of course I can't give you exact dates after all these years, but I can recall incidents as I remember them.

One morning several of us were having breakfast in the Mess at Kent College when we heard gunfire and the roar of low flying aircraft. We crowded for the windows and saw 3 planes coming straight towards us. They could not have been more than 50 feet up, and we could see that the first aircraft was a German with black crosses and all, and right behind him were two of our fighters. I think they were Hurricanes. Both British fighters were blasting away with their 8 machine guns and the noise of the guns together with the roar of the screaming engines was terrific. They passed right over the roof of the Mess. They were so low that the spent cartridges were tinkling on the roof as they passed over.

I must admit that we all felt pleased and proud at seeing such a sight. We certainly enjoyed our breakfast! The enemy plane crashed a few miles away but I don't know if the crew survived or not.

Another incident I recall may be humorous although it might have been serious. One day one of the young 18 year old despatch riders came into the Barrack room grinning happily saying "Look what I've got. I found it in a crashed German plane." We looked askanced at the fins of a small bomb sticking out of the top of his battledress. Well I can't remember how many people were there at the time but never have I seen a room vacated so quickly. I never did find out what happened to the bomb, or the stupid bugger who did such a thing!

I remember approaching the coast on my motorcycle one day and I could see four huge radio masts. Of course we didn't know it at the time, but this was one of several radar stations used for tracking the German bombers. Suddenly I heard the sound of aircraft and looking up I saw 12 planes circling a few thousand feet above the tall masts. Another plane, by means of smoke, made a huge ring above the radar masts and then I realised the 12 planes circling above must be German Stuka dive bombers. There was no sign of any of our fighter planes and I was just a spectator. I saw the 12 dive bombers in line ahead formation start to dive almost vertically through the smoke ring which was obviously a marker for the radar masts. I watched helplessly at the attack on the masts. The sound of diving and screaming aircraft and exploding bombs filled the air as I drove away. There was nothing I could do and I had my own duties to carry out.

Filling up at the Headquarter's petrol point one Sunday we heard the fantastic roar of airplane engines. Looking up we saw a huge formation of bombers flying slowly in from the direction of the English Channel. They were in flights of three one behind the other. I stopped counting when I got to more than 70, and I could see scores of the smaller fighter planes wheeling above the bombers as they droned towards London. I remember somebody said "They must be ours", and someone else said "Don't be so bloody stupid – we haven't got that many!" They flew on out of sight. We heard later that they were attacked and scattered by our fighters, but we saw none of that.

Many of our fighter airfields were being attacked at this time. I saw Manston airfield the day after being blitzed, when I was on a run carrying despatches. I had to go right through the airfield, and I remember being horrified at the terrific carnage there. Permanent buildings were blasted into ruins, there were huge craters everywhere, and a great many fighter planes were scattered about and blown to bits. There were a great many killed and wounded. Yet I believe that Fighter Station was operational again in a couple of days. It was amazing.

107

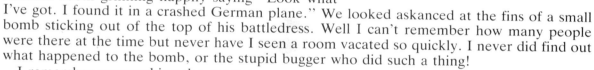
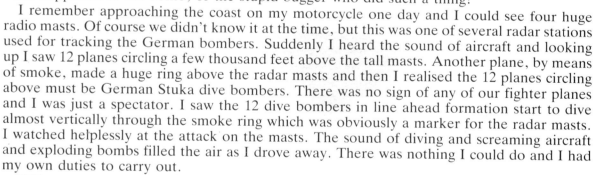

Giving a Spitfire the "once over". Note the oxygen bottle on the ground.

During the invasion emergency despatch riders were sent to the coast at night to the Headquarters of troops defending beaches and harbours. This was in case other forms of communications broke down or it was an extra means of alerting Battle Headquarters of any intrusions by the Germans.

I was very surprised indeed to find that many of our first line defenders amongst the coastal troops were mature veterans of the First World War in their 40's, of which some of these were ex-officers. Most of them were in Pioneer Battalions! I remember they were all very helpful and cheerful and keen to "have a go" at "Fritz" as they called the Germans. They waited every night in harbours and along promenades behind sandbagged emplacements and barbed wire with many heavy Vickers machine guns. I was only very young then, and was most impressed by these middle aged men, their humour and enthusiasm. They would have given a very good account of themselves and I used to leave in the mornings very encouraged and less fearful.

One night while visiting these troops, we heard a single German bomber cruising above in the pitch darkness towards Sheerness. Suddenly lots of searchlights appeared looking for him. Then we heard the heavy detonations of exploding bombs. Immediately all the searchlights went out! The Germans must have had a lucky hit on the generator or power station. However, the remarks of the watching soldiers were not particularly complimentary!

It was a wonderful summer in 1940 and hardly a day went by when there was not the sound of air battles. Yet we didn't realise how the R.A.F. was strained to the limits to contain the hordes of enemy planes crossing the Channel. Most of the air fighting took place at a very great height but you could see the various patterns of the contrails and hear the bursts of multiple machine guns and cannon fire as the aircraft wheeled and weaved and dived. Now and again a black plume of smoke would appear as planes were hit, and often several parachutes would be seen floating down like white mushrooms in the sky. One day I saw a fighter plane diving vertically at full power straight into the ground, and I'll never forget the sound of that screeching engine suddenly cutting out like an electric switch!

It was a common sight in Kent in those days to see wrecked and shot up German aircraft in garage forecourts, because they usually had plenty of lifting gear to clear the wrecks. Strangely enough I never ever saw a captured German airman or even a British pilot in those days. But I often saw them taking off from air fields sometimes nine abreast, and Squadrons got aloft very quickly even though many of the air fields had virtually no runways but just grass. Since then my admiration has grown for those few fundred pilots and their bravery and stamina and loyalty which must have been unsurpassed.

One more incident I recall just to illustrate what I said in the last paragraph, was the time when three of the most modern battleships of Germany decided to break out through the English Channel blockade from a French port to a home port in Germany. I saw a squadron of 12 ancient torpedo bombers go out to attack the battleships. They were old obsolete biplanes with a torpedo slung between the landing wheels and open cockpits held the crew. They were flying very low, no more than a few hundred feet above the fields. They looked so slow and vulnerable as they disappeared over the Channel.

I was still in the area when they returned towards their base. I counted only 2, still flying very low and slow back home. I believe that one of the warships was badly damaged. To attack three of the most modern warships in such slow and outdated aircraft makes the bravest of the brave. Yet that same type of aircraft sank a large part of the Italian fleet. I will never cease to admire such men. We were fortunate to have them at a time when our fortunes were not so good But they indeed turned the tide and it was just a handful of them that did it.

Another point of interest I remember was that in my travels around Kent I saw collecting points for hundreds of civilian buses which had been hastily brushed or sprayed with khaki paint. They were organised into Troop Transport Companies for the rapid movement of troops in case of emergency.

Also taken over at that time were hundreds of brand new civilian motorcycles. All their bright colours and shiny chrome had been sprayed over with khaki paint. We as Army motorcyclists so longed to have one of these as they were much better and more powerful than our Army machines, but of course we never got them! The reason the above was done was of course that the Army was very short of all kinds of vehicles after losing so many thousands during the evacuation from France.

109

Hurricane formation "in the clouds".

I suppose I could go on writing for hours as memories come flooding back, but perhaps I have written enough. I am 73 now and I hope this may be of some use to you. I know it is difficult to try and recreate the atmosphere of those long gone days. It was often exciting, even at times exhilarating, but it was also heartbreaking. However, I wouldn't have missed it for anything. I consider those long six years as the best of my life, even though in 1942 our Division went abroad, and I took part in the Salerno landings in Italy and took part in much heavy fighting at Cassino, before being landed on the Anzio beach head which was then under seige. That was also tough and exhausting and we had so many casualties and destruction of equipment that we were all withdrawn back to Egypt.

J. R. Gibson, 65 Rowan Avenue,
Harraton, Washington, Tyne and Wear

It was precisely 8 a.m. when I left my home village of Otford and shortly afterwards arrived at Sevenoaks Station in order to catch the Hastings/Sevenoaks/Cannon Street fast train. The front portion of the train was always very full, so I made my way to the far end of the platform. While waiting there it was not unusual to hear the drone of a "dogfight" taking place in the clear blue skies above the lovely Kent countryside. That, however, was not to be the case on this particular morning.

The train arrived and I found a seat in one of the rear compartments. Fifty years ago trains were very different! Each carriage consisted of some six independent compartments, and each compartment had two facing bench seats to accommodate five to six passengers a side, with very little floor space in between!

In a very few minutes I was aware of something happening at the windows and simultaneously a naval officer, seated by one of the windows, shouted "everyone on the floor". Of course, that was virtually impossible but I guess we automatically folded ourselves in two and ducked our heads as best we could! A funny sight had it been in the age of videos! But it wasn't funny. The pilot of a low flying Messerschmitt was machine gunning all the rear carriages! At that time the front portion of the train would already have entered the very long Polhill tunnel and, fortunately, it was only a matter of seconds (but what long seconds!) before the whole of the train was ensconced in the tunnel.

On arrival in London I made my way to my office, which was a large Insurance Company near the Bank of England. I recounted what had happened. My news spread rapidly throughout the staff. I felt embarrassed lest it was untrue and I was reproached by one and all. Maybe I had "catnapped" during the half hour's journey, resulting in a vivid dream?

However, by lunchtime the midday papers, sold at many a street corner, confirmed it all. The front page read in heavy capitals "Heroic Train Driver Guides Brave City Workers to Safety". In actual fact the driver must have been totally unaware of what was happening outside the tunnel, which he had already entered! The "brave" commuters had little time to be unduly perturbed, the rear of the train very soon becoming safely ensconced as well!

I was not aware of any passengers sustaining any injuries but sadly I found out later that the German plane continued its hedge-hopping over the pastureland of the adjoining idyllic village of Shoreham, where the pilot apparently continued his machine gunning, but this time it was the cattle that were his target!

Mrs. Phyllis K. Fellows, "Birchwood", Igtham/Ivy Hatch,
Ismays Road, Ivy Hatch, Sevenoaks, Kent

111

Flt. Lt. Percy Turner who shot down 2 enemy aircraft after his own had been damaged. He shot down 10 enemy planes in the Battle.

In August and September 1940 while the Battle of Britain was at its height, six weeks of my school holidays were spent at West Studdal Farm, Whitfield about 5 miles from Dover, helping with the harvest.

West Studdal Farm belong to Mr. Charles Roddick, whose son John was my school friend. John's elder brother Andrew had been killed during the retreat to Dunkirk, serving in the 17/21 Lancers who under the command of Lieutenant Colonel Lumbsden did their best to plug the gap when the Belgian Army surrendered. So the household consisted of Mr. and Mrs. Roddick, John and me, and a splendid bouncy black woolly dog known as Boodle. The dog was of uncertain ancestry on one side, but certainly poodle on the other! Both John and I were 17 years of age at the time. John was waiting to follow his brother into the Army. I was waiting to take examinations for Special Entry into the Royal Navy.

The younger farm hands had gone to war, but an active hardy 70 year old Mr. Poole lived in the farm cottage and there were as I recall two other old men. All three did yeoman service in bringing in the harvest. There were 2 sturdy working draft horses looked after by old man Poole. West Studdal Farm had two tractors one a Fordson and the other a Ferguson, both started by hand cranking, and with saddle driving seats!

So that I could get to Whitfield Mr. Roddick had had to get me a special pass. His farm was in a restricted area, being within 25 miles of the coast. The train taking me went slowly and often stopped. I saw many large military encampments complete with vehicles, guns and tanks. As a 17 year old I had very keen eyes in those days, and I soon realised that much, indeed most of this military might, was made of cardboard and three ply! The display was clearly laid on as a spoof for German aerial reconnaissance.

John and I worked hard and long stooking sheaves of wheat, barley and oats, and later driving tractors towing disc harrows over fields already harvested. Yet we had enough energy left to play 4 or 5 sets of tennis every evening. Once we were smuggled into Dover in the farm truck – we lacked the necessary passes to get to the coast. There we watched the film "Elizabeth and Essex" in glorious Technicolor, which was a fair novelty in those days. Every now and then a small gun near the cinema went off, so near that it sounded as though it was on the roof. Apparently it was having a go at enemy Messerschmitt fighters attacking Dover.

Daily we watched enemy air raids disrupted by our Hurricanes and Spitfires, and also by flak from the Royal Artillery guns. The anti aircraft shell exploded at the time predicted, triggered by what I later learnt was a "time mechanical" fuse. Seen from the side, a shell burst looked like a dark grey brown crescent moon, with a small cone protruding from the centre between the horns of the crescent.

Watching all this whilst driving tractors was dangerous! Do not misunderstand me. We wore steel helmets just in case, but the danger was that in our fascination with the aerial dogfights, we failed to pay attention to the tractor driving! Sometimes we failed to notice how close we were getting to the edge of the field, and often had to swing over sharply on the steering wheel to avoid a hedge or a fence!

Just once though, during the late forenoon, I stopped my tractor and dived underneath it. Shell bursts from our guns seemed too close for comfort. When the noise stopped I crawled out cautiously and took a look. I found several lumps of shrapnel, one in particular as big as a fist, embedded in the soil at a shallow angle a few feet from the tractor. I reckoned that had I still been astride the driving saddle, I might have been hit. I had been reluctant to stop. That day the tractor engine had been sluggish and the palm of my right hand was one huge blister due to the prolonged efforts on the crank handle trying to get it to go. Fortunately though when all was clear, the engine, now warm, restarted easily.

One day towards dusk Mr. and Mrs. Roddick, John and I, were on a small rise about 200 yards from the farmhouse. To our dismay we saw one of our Hurricanes gliding straight at the farmhouse. It had been hit. The pilot had baled out successfully and was slowly descending on his parachute in the distance. By great good fortune just as it seemed certain that the farmhouse would be hit, some sort of fluke in the wind took the Hurricane clear of it and it crashed in the middle of a stubble field about a quarter of a mile away.

113

There were 37 barrage balloons guarding Dover. One day at noon I remember that the Messerschmitts shot them all down! They were filled with hydrogen and burnt well! Nevertheless by dusk Balloon Command had 37 new balloons in position! These lasted less than a day! At noon next day Messerschmitts returned and shot the lot down again. Once again by dusk a third outfit of 37 balloons was guarding Dover – but that night all of them were destroyed, by lightning! There was then a delay of two or three days before they were replaced!

Mr. Roddick had had a dug-out shelter built within about 20 yards of the farmhouse. It had strong timber props and 2 or 3 layers of sandbags on the roof. One night after dark we heard unaccustomed noises, and Mr. Roddick decided we should take cover. We stayed in the dug-out for about ¾ of an hour, listening to massive explosions, followed by a weird whining noise that went on for a minute or so, followed by a deep resonant boom.

Eventually Mr. Roddick decided that, whatever it was, it was doing us no harm so we returned to bed. Next day we learned that we had heard the opening efforts of the German cross-channel guns. We were hearing the gunfire in reverse. First the shell exploding in Dover, then its noise trundling through the air, and finally the boom of the gun firing.

Every evening at 6 we listened to the B.B.C. news. Alvar Lidell was the name of the news announcer I remember best. I can clearly recall Mr. Roddick crowing with delight one evening when we heard that, if my memory serves me right, about 180 enemy aircraft had been shot down that day.

"That's the stuff to give them" he said smiling broadly. I believe later it was established that less than a third of that number had actually been destroyed. Nevertheless at the time it was a splendid morale booster.

Combine harvesters did not exist in those days. Mr. Roddick had to hire a threshing machine that was set up on a flat surface about 20 yards from the farmhouse. It was on the opposite side to the dug-out. The machine was there for about 4 days, threshing the corn and making dust! This got right in amongst me, since I suffered from hay fever, and for 4 nights could scarcely sleep due to wheezing and sneezing, coughing, spluttering and choking.

Once 3 Officers from the 17/21 Lancers visited Mr. and Mrs. Roddick to tell them about Andrew. Their caps were red, and from a distance they looked like Military Police.

It was all hard work. Once when with aching muscles we were loading the stooks onto a trailer to take to the thresher, I remember John saying plaintively "What price bread?" What price indeed.

The time came to go home. The Roddicks presented me with a freshly shot rabbit and as my memory serves me a £5 note. It was untold wealth for a young man of my age in those days. My fond Mama, despite being Australian, was none too pleased with the rabbit since she and I had to gut and skin it! However, when the job was done it was a very welcome supplement to the sparse meat ration.

Fifteen months later, just before Christmas 1941, I joined my first ship H.M.S. Rodney, with 9 16″ guns, in Iceland. As a midshipman my pay was 5 shillings a day, so as I said the £5 I received from Mr. Roddick was a small fortune. About the same time John joined up and was in due course commissioned in the 17/21 Lancers. Tragically bearing in mind his brothers death in the same Regiment at Dunkirk he was killed in 1944 during an armoured car reconnaissance in Italy.

Commander Peter Brook Cowan RN (Retired),
Tranby Cottage, 28 Broomleaf Road,
Farnham, Surrey

Barrage Balloons ready to go up.

As an Army private in the R.A.S.C. I was stationed at Shorncliffe Barracks near Folkestone with F. Company Field Bakery throughout the whole of the Battle of Britain. This area of the south east coast wasn't called "Hell-Fire corner" for nothing! In the first stage of the Battle the Luftwaffe attempted to smash the R.A.F. on the ground by machine gunning and bombing airfields and the areas around them. Dog fights were a daily occurrence and it became almost commonplace to see fighters from both sides smash into the ground, bursting into fireballs or plunging into the sea. I was always glad to see a parachute drift downwards after the plane, whether it be friend or foe, or saddened if no chute appeared.

Hawkinge airfield was only a short distance away from Shorncliffe and was attacked with monotonous regularity. But there was nothing monotonous about the sudden appearance of Stuka dive bombers. Even from places of shelter (to which we raced with all despatch at every threat of shot and shell) it was terrifying to see and hear them scream down vertically out of the sky and to watch a bomb fall away from the plane as it levelled off seemingly only feet above the ground.

But, far from being smashed on the ground, the R.A.F. hit back with stunning effect. The Luftwaffe lost so many of its aircraft (though claims on both sides were grossly exaggerated) that it was compelled to use other tactics. The Luftwaffe's answer was to launch day time bombing raids deep into the heartland of Britain.

We stared skywards in open mouthed amazement at our first sighting of a massed formation of enemy bombers and the attendant fighter escort droning in over the coast from the Channel, filling the air with awesome noisy and fearful might. It was an Armada which appeared invincible to people on the ground below.

But the R.A.F. had other ideas. As the days passed these formations were broken up by Spitfires and Hurricanes which dived in amongst the bombers, shooting many down in flames and causing others to break formation and flee for home. Spitfire, Hurricane and Messerschmitt dived, rolled and twisted with all guns chattering amongst the ponderous bombers which writhed this way and that in attempts to dodge the deadly attacks coming at them from all directions. The sight was breath-taking and awe-inspiring.

Those bombers which turned tail and headed for home jettisoned their bombs before they reached the open sea, causing death and devastation on the ground. But the daily routine of barrack life had to go on – a routine whose order was shattered one day when I was on cookhouse fatigue.

The mid-day meal was being served to the usual noisy queue of licentious soldiery when the first bombs fell nearby. The queue disintegrated as men scrambled in all directions, seeking cover. The plate in my left hand flew one way and the ladle in my right hand flew another. As a second group of bombs exploded, nearer than the first, I remember whipping round then finding myself under one of the stout tables in the kitchen without ever knowing how I got there! As the next bombs fell, nearer still, I muttered to myself over and over again "God, I wish I'd got my tin hat, God I wish I'd got my tin hat!"

I was convinced that my last moments had come. The next bombs were bound to come through the roof of the Mess Hall; there could be no escape...

And then, as swiftly as it had started, the thundering explosions stopped.

I crept from under the table feeling as sheepish as all the others looked as they emerged from whatever shelter they had found.

"Scramble" on 25th July 1940.

There was an instinctive desire to see what had happened. Without a word, everyone rushed outside, expecting to see the worst.

It was something of an anti climax when it was seen that what bombs had fallen in the Barrack area had fallen on open ground. Apart from walls pockmarked by bomb fragments and some broken windows, none of the buildings had suffered any obvious damage. Except the two storey N.A.A.F.I. block, the first floor of which was used as a snooker room.

A whole corner of the block had been neatly sliced away and one of the end legs of the snooker table was exposed nakedly to the open air, supported by nothing.

Four men had been playing snooker when the first bomb fell. Not surprisingly they promptly threw themselves under the table. Luckily, they chose the right end...!

David McKay, 9 Low Fold, Scholes, Cleckheaton, West Yorkshire

---

In 1940 I was aged 13 and lived with my parents and sister aged 17 in Cove. Our younger sister was born in early August. My brother had at that time recently joined the R.A.F. My father worked at the nearby Royal Aircraft Establishment at Farnborough.

13th August, 1940: I remember the date well because my younger sister had been born six days earlier. It was a beautiful sunny day. I think it was a Saturday. Suddenly the air raid siren sounded in the late morning. We were not sure what to expect, but when an Army lorry passed with a Lewis Gun mounted on the back and we saw a Squadron of Junkers 88 flying overhead at about 10,000 feet, my father took us to the shelter he had built in the back garden.

After a few minutes we heard the sound of the Junkers 88 roaring low across and then the rattle of the Lewis Gun. Shortly afterwards we heard the crump of several bombs. At the time I felt excitement rather than fear.

Later we learned several bombs had fallen on the Royal Aircraft Establishment and damaged the engine test beds and killed three men who were on duty with the Local Defence Volunteers. They had been very unlucky as they had been in a shelter which had suffered a direct hit.

One of them was known to us. He was Mr. Dixon, father of Peter Dixon, who had recently joined the Royal Air Force. When Mr. Dixon was buried with his two comrades in St. John's

Churchyard at Cove, I attended the funeral together with hundreds of local people. A bomb had also hit a house nearby in Albert Road, killing a lady there.

August 13th, 1940 was, of course, "Eagle Day" when the Luftwaffe began its all out attack on Royal Air Force airfields. But I suspect on that occasion that they mistook Farnborough Aerodrome for the nearby Royal Air Force airfield at Odiham or possibly Middle Wallop.

Bob Rose, 12 The Bourne,
Fleet, Hampshire

Squadron Commander Lutzow of the Luftwaffe and his Squadron Leader Captain Balthesar (on the right) at an airfield in France. Note the "victory notches" on the tail.

During the Summer of 1940, I was in the Dorset Regiment. My Army number was 5727100 and we were stationed in a tented camp at Wyke Regis near Weymouth. Our tents were in a field which sloped down towards the sea, and looked out over the Chesil Beach, and towards Portland. It was a glorious Summer with many long sunny days, and ideal for living under canvas.

I was employed as a Clerk and our "office building" consisted of a large marquee at the top of the field, fairly near the entrance. We had to dig a deep trench, partly inside and partly outside the marquee, in which we took shelter during air activity. From here we had an excellent view of many "dogfights", although we kept our heads well down to avoid being seen and wore our steel helmets as protection against falling shrapnel.

In the Summer the sea off Chesil Beach had been used as a practice area for aeroplanes. I believe they were Wellingtons. Each was fitted with a large ring, which went round the wings and under the body of the plane. They flew low over the sea, as they were intended for use in exploding magnetic mines although I don't know how successful they were!

One bright morning we had just seen one of these planes go out when suddenly it came quietly, almost stealthily, back inland. Soon afterwards we realised why. The pilot must have been tipped off that enemy aircraft were on their way and a few minutes later several German planes came in from the Portland direction, to be met by Hurricanes or Spitfires from nearby Warmwell Aerodrome. I cannot remember the outcome of this fight but there were not many days when we did not see some enemy planes. They often fought over our area although sometimes their maneouvres took them out of sight.

Many times we saw planes coming down with a trail of smoke, often not knowing if they were "ours" or "theirs". We were always relieved when we saw a parachute open as we knew then that the pilot had been saved, although once or twice they were, unfortately, too far out at sea to be rescued. I well recall the day on which the record number of enemy planes (over 150) was claimed to have been shot down, as battles were going on all day, one after the other. In the area of sky which we could watch, we counted about 36 planes come down, or at least trailing smoke, and even though we knew that some of them would have been ours, we could well believe the official figure for that day when it was given out.

The Royal Engineers Bridging Camp was nearer to the sea than we were and they also had boats, but I only know of one definite rescue. He was a German, and incidentally the first German most of us had seen! For operational reasons the Royal Engineers handed him over to one of our Officers to look after until he could be handed over to the appropriate authorities and so he spent an hour or so in the "guard tent", watched over by the Regimental Police. I gather he was asked why our camp had not been attacked, and he replied that he thought it was just a camouflage camp. Of course, there were never any soldiers to be seen when enemy planes were overhead, they were all too busy taking cover!

I remember particularly well two occasions when bombs were dropped at Portland during this period in daylight hours. The first was when the anti-aircraft ship "Foylebank" was sunk in Portland Harbour. We heard planes, explosions and gunfire, then saw a pall of smoke and knew that something had been hit, but of course we didn't know what! I now know that this was the time that Jack Mantle, who was a Gunner on the ship, had continued firing at the enemy planes even though he had been mortally wounded. For this action he was posthumously awarded the Victoria Cross.

121

Dornier shot down on 18th August 1940, under guard.

The other time we saw a lot of smoke rising from the vicinity of the Royal Navy's oil tanks, and we were afraid that one of them had been hit, and the others might also catch fire or explode. Fortunately it had not received a direct hit but a piece of shrapnel had penetrated the side of it and the oil which had escaped had caught fire on the ground outside the tank, and this accounted for the large amount of smoke. This fire was quickly dealt with and the tank was safely sealed off.

Some of the brave airmen from overseas as well as from this country who lost their lives, are buried in the little churchyard at Warmwell. The new village of Crossways now stands where the airfield was but a memorial was erected in 1989 to commemorate the part the airmen from Warmwell played in the Battle of Britain.

Graham Brunt, 4 The Rise, Weymouth, Dorset

I served in the Royal Air Force from 1940 to 1946 and trained to drive vehicles from motorcycles to Queen Marys!

One night at about 10 o'clock, whilst on ambulance duty, we were called to the sick quarters to pick up a Sergeant Medical Nursing W.A.A.F. and then to proceed to a large W.A.A.F. Centre located 10 miles away in the heart of the Fen district.

I found out that we had to collect the body of a W.A.A.F. who had died that afternoon, and the body was then to be taken to the mortuary at Stamford General Hospital in Lincolnshire.

When we arrived at the Centre a German bombing raid was in progress on our main Camp. All lights in the building were switched off, leaving just blue safety lights burning. Our W.A.A.F. Sergeant Nurse took my co-driver (Owen "Blondie" Wills) and myself, with a stretcher, to an Annexe where we

picked up the body, placed it on the stretcher and then proceeded in the semi-darkness to our ambulance, in which we placed the body of the dead W.A.A.F.

We started to proceed over the Fens using just our Hartley lights when suddenly we heard a distinct "moaning" coming through the centre door from the rear of the ambulance. Then another loud "Moan" and another followed! I pulled the ambulance up dead, looked at the other two occupants, who by the smell were having similiar troubles to myself!

The nurse switched the blue panic light on and to our amazement there was the "dead body" sitting up in the stretcher. In a real panic I turned the ambulance round and belted back to the W.A.A.F. Hospital, where it was found, after a lot of noisy accusations, that in the confusion of the Air Raid and the low lights, we had picked up a W.A.A.F. who had had an injection prior to a minor operation! Believe me all this caused quite an Inquiry! Incidentally, my R.A.F. station during my "Battle of Britain" days was R.A.F. Wittering in Lincolnshire.

Stanley Webb, 8 Huntlands Road, Halesowen, West Midlands

123

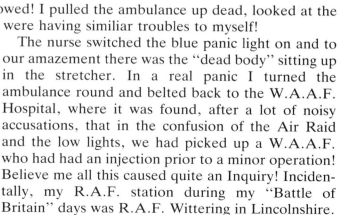

Sgt. Helen Turner decorated for remaining at her post under heavy fire. For many years pre-war she was the switchboard operator at a famous London hotel.

I was 6 when the war broke out. My family lived in a large bungalow which my grandfather gave to my mother and father as a wedding present. It was in Woodford Green which is on the edge of Epping Forest and only a few miles from East London.

My father was one of the first to enlist. He was already in the Territorial Army, and so when war was declared he went away and thereafter became a shadowy figure who took part in many of the major campaigns of the war, and from whom we had long letters from far distant places.

I was an only child. Mother and I were joined by her mother and father (My grandparents) who came to live with us. My grandfather kept a hardware shop in Forest Gate, and until the war he and my grandmother lived over the shop. With the onset of war there was a great need for coal, paraffin oil, wood etc. and the shop stocked up with big quantities of this inflammable material. As many of his staff were called up my mother went over to help in the shop, something she had never done before and so my grandmother was left in charge of the bungalow and me!

It was difficult for me to get used to all the changes. My grandmother was a formidable woman. She concealed any anxiety she must have had extremely well and certainly seemed to be frightened of nothing. My mother was a fairly easy going person and I had to get used to obeying my grandmother instantly. It was hard but I certainly felt safe and it seemed to me that she would keep any harm from befalling us!

We had many frightening experiences, some good and a lot of them very frightening.

I remember that we had an indoor Morrison shelter and an outdoor Anderson shelter. My grandmother, who suffered from claustrophobia, didn't go into either of them! If I was indoors in the Morrison shelter she would stand at the front door, with her hat and coat on, handbag on her arm, also a bag in which she kept all her important papers, giving a running commentary of what was happening! Despite all entreaties to "come into the shelter" she carried on swearing at the German planes which came over, sometimes dropping bombs on Woodford and sometimes going on to other areas.

One terrible day we were waiting for my mother and grandfather to come home from the shop. Suddenly there was a terrific explosion not far away and a terrible fear gripped my grandmother and me. Soon someone came by and told us that a No. 10A bus had been hit.

This was dreadful news as this was the bus that they caught to come home.

Hours passed by and I ran repeatedly to the gate, hoping against hope that I would see those dear figures coming down the road. For once my grandmother was silent. We really had lost all hope when I looked over the gate and right at the top of the road were my grandfather and mother running as fast as they could.

What joy. I repeated a saying which became part of my life. "I'll never be naughty again if..." That was of course until the next time!

At one stage we had a regiment of soldiers camped on the Green at the top of the road. It was quite exciting and

125

Hurricane of 615 Squadron taking off to engage the enemy.

they were very friendly and somehow you felt a little safer. One day my mother and I had been to the shops and exchanged greetings with the soldiers as usual and started off down our road. Suddenly, without warning, an aircraft zoomed very low overhead. We looked up and to our horror saw the markings and realised that it was a German plane. We started to run and I was breaking all records in an effort to get home. The plane followed us and began strafing us with bullets. What a swine the pilot must have been. We went on and suddenly a lady who lived in the road came out and beckoned us into her house where we sheltered, amazingly enough unscathed.

Another time my grandmother and myself were in the outdoor Anderson shelter. That is to say I was in the shelter and as usual she was at the door! A dog fight was taking place overhead. A British plane and a German. Suddenly the planes came very low and just above our garden it almost seemed that the German plane was hovering so that we could clearly see the pilot. It was incredibly frightening and I had to restrain my grandmother from making some effort to get this German and exact her own personal retribution! Certainly her language left a great deal to be desired! But it was all over very quickly and the pilot and the plane climbed quickly into the sky, but the imprint of it all is indelibly imprinted on my mind.

My mother and grandfather had many amazing escapes over at Forest Gate. The shop was lethal with its stock and they stayed open during every raid, knowing they stood no chance if an incendiary bomb scored a direct hit. Everyone round that area knew "Mr. Carloss" and he was a wonderful man to all his customers. He gave them endless credit when money ran out – got round the oil companies for extra oil so he would be able to keep warm. He and my mother shovelled endless hundred weights of coal and chopped firewood as well as serving all the many different items that were sold in a hardware shop in those days. They were really a lifeline to the people in that area. In fact people came from far and wide to get supplies.

One incident I have just remembered concerned a friend of ours who was a builder and built many of the houses in Woodford. He was asked to build a shelter at the school which his daughters and I attended. On this particular day I had not gone to school as I had a sore throat. The air raid warning sounded and the bombing began.

There was a terrific bang and we realised that the Congregational Church, but a hundred yards from the bungalow, had been hit. There was a great commotion and we went to the gate only to see our friends running up the road. "Where's Joan" he said to my mother.

"She's here, she's not well'.

"Thank God" he said "I hope the shelter has held".

He went on, hoping for the best. Luckily it had held and all the children were safe although they were only 30 feet away from the church. It was a good job he knew his trade.

During all this time I went to Primary School and subsequently to the local High School, and my school days seemed to have gone very normally really when you think of the dangers we faced daily and I think much of the credit must go to the adults who carried on knowing so much more about the dangers than we did. And yet they did not allow us to get away with anything and kept us under pretty strict discipline. It gave us a feeling of security and it is only when one becomes an adult oneself that you realise what a terrific task it must have been for them.

Incidentally I still live in the same bungalow which my grandfather gave to my mother and father as a wedding present, and which I referred to at the start of this story.

Mrs. Joan Challis, 18 Higham Road,
Woodford Green, Essex

The wreckage of a yellow-nosed ME109, shot down at West Witham, Kent on 21st October 1940.

I joined the Territorial Army in 1938, and joined the Searchlight Regiment when I was called up in August 1939. I was posted to a Detachment in Kent and so I literally had a front seat in the Battle of Britain. I was posted to Birchington, Maidstone, Canterbury, Ashford and Tonbridge and so we were always near to either Biggin Hill and Manston aerodromes which were constantly being bombed by the German airforce. The general area had been evacuated, and it seemed to me at the time that everyone had disappeared like snow off a roof! I remember once when our Searchlight Unit was on the cliffs of Birchington facing the

sea, and I was on guard duty. When dawn broke I remember looking through the service binoculars that I had and I saw something floating in the sea about a hundred yards out. We were always a bit jittery about things floating in the sea, as this part of the coast was generally called Hell Fire Corner because of the attacks on the shipping in the area and the shells that were constantly coming over. As it drew nearer I saw it was the body of a man, absolutely naked, but swelled up to what seemed to be twice its normal size. The thing now was to haul it up to the cliffs.

The coastguards produced a wooden coffin, but then came the question of who was going to go down the cliffs to get the body up. Being the smallest and the lightest of the lot, the job fell to me! We had no ropes, so the boys got a length of rusty fencing wire, made a loop in it for my foot, and lowered me down. I must confess that I was extremely frightened and had no great faith in the material that was holding me!

The body was by now washed to the foot of the cliffs, and my chief worry was that the tide was creeping in. I grabbed his leg to pull the body into the coffin which had also been lowered down to me, but as I grabbed it huge chunks of flesh came off. I pulled then at his arm but the same thing happened. The whole thing was utterly gruesome, but eventually I got the body into the coffin more by pushing and shoving to avoid large pieces of it coming off as I moved it.

It was then hauled up the cliffs, in the coffin, and then they pulled me up with showers of chalk and stones falling on my steel helmet. I think I perhaps now ought to add that that was on Christmas Day 1940, and it wasn't a very pleasant one! The A.R.P. warden had 2 lovely daughters, and when we had got everything cleared he invited me and 2 of our other lads to dinner, and of course we both jumped at the invitation!

I washed my hands over and over again, but somehow I couldn't forget that I had handled this dead body with pieces coming off it, and I must say that it all took the edge of my Christmas dinner that day!

When the Battle of Britain was at its height, planes of both sides seemed to be falling around everywhere, and one of the German Luftwaffe planes which was a Messerschmitt 110 actually fell near our site.

After dark it was my duty to guard this crashed plane, and whilst I was doing it suddenly bullets came flying from it in all directions. Stupidly in my fear I somehow thought that the pilot was still alive and firing at me! But all it was was the smouldering wreck had ignited the rounds of bullets from one of the belts of ammunition. You can imagine being alone in the dark with that happening, and the alarm bells were certainly ringing in my brain.

129

Messerschmitt 110 Long Range fighter.

I would also like to tell you about another incident when I was certainly not in a FORGIVING mood towards the German Luftwaffe pilots. Every tenth day one of the lads was allowed 4 hours off duty. Not that there was anywhere to go!

I was walking through a field of turnips when a plane bore down on me from behind. I thought it was "one of ours" and so I carried on walking, but it wasn't! It was a Stuka dive bomber, and he sent a hail of bullets from his machine gun streaking down behind me missing me by just a few feet. I must admit that I hurled a string of naughty language at the receding plane, making my feelings of anger known.

"Well" I said to myself "That's that. Think I'll go to the pictures for an hour".

Lo and behold the plane turned in the distance and came back again at me having another go at me, so I dived down and hid amongst a row of the turnips! He never returned.

In my declining years all these are just memories, but I do recall being sent later to Birmingham to train at the Armourers Training Centre, away from all the raids in Kent, and I remember thinking how peaceful it all would be. The day I arrived the Germans bombed Birmingham, and it was only when we were moved to Melton Mowbray to finish our training that I got peace at last!

Finally, there is one little story following on the Battle of Britain. I ended up in Keighley in Yorkshire as an Armourer Sergeant in the Durham Light Infantry. Keighley was a town noted for the woollen trade, and you could imagine that the pubs were filled every night with women from the mills whose husbands were away.

One night I was with my mate in the "Kings Arms" which was crowded with servicemen and women from the factories, and the noise was pretty deafening.

I don't wish to appear ungracious, but it was quite obvious that some of the ladies that were there were what were called "ladies of the street". One in particular across the room was obviously interested in me!

I said to my mate "I bet she's alright for half a pint of beer!"

She came over and said to me "I know what you said about me, and they call you Jack".

I said "You heard what I said in this din?"

"Yes" she replied, "All of us mill girls learn to be lip readers."

Was my face red!

Jack Goodyer, 37 Holyrood Crescent,
St. Julians Estate, St. Albans, Hertfordshire

Flt. Lt. Jessard Jeffries of Leamington Spa, Warwickshire with his dog "Hero". Awarded the Distinguished Flying Cross for shooting down 4 enemy planes and damaging another 2.

I was the youngest of four children and the only girl. In 1940, Dave, my oldest brother at 21, was serving with the Army in the Middle East; Wally, the youngest at 18, had been with the Merchant Navy since the outbreak of war; and Charles, always known as "Bub", had his 20th birthday in August. Bub was serving with the R.A.S.C. stationed in the North of England, but down south on a course at the old Tram Depot in Woolwich Road, Charlton. He and the other lads were being billeted in local houses and as we were then living in Grenada Road, Charlton, he was given permission to be billeted in his own house!

Saturday, 7th September, 1940. I was a 17 year old Cashier working at Tower House, Lewisham. During the afternoon there was the first really heavy daylight air raid. The shop was closed and the staff rushed to the shelters at the bottom of the Belmont Hill – now the present site of the Bowling Alley! At about 5 o'clock the "All Clear" sounded and we were allowed to go home. Cars were few and only for the rich – the more usual transport was the bus or pedal cycle.

I collected my bike and rode over the Heath and along Shooters Hill to find Grenada Road cordoned off with police on duty to stop anyone gaining access. I had to identify myself before I was allowed to duck under the ropes. We lived at No. 11; No. 7 had suffered a direct hit and the two houses either side were almost demolished. The rest of the street was just a mess. My father and grandfather, who was in his 80's and lived with us, were busy carting rubble out of the house and piling it up in the street. The doors and windows were gone as was the roof and all the ceilings. Everyone was trying to salvage what they could of their belongings and endeavouring to make the downstairs habitable for the night.

"Anyone hurt?" I asked Dad. "Your brother has been taken to hospital" he replied, "he's in a bad way".

We shared the air raid shelter with the Wyngrove family next door and apparently my brother had been standing outside the Anderson Shelter watching the Spitfires having "dogfights" in the sky. This was at the time of the "Battle of Britain". He was heard to shout "they've got one" and the next thing was the explosion. It was a fifty pound bomb, very small, but the damage it did was enormous. Bub was struck by all sorts of debris and lay in the garden bleeding badly for something like half-an-hour before the A.R.P. could get an ambulance through to him. My mother and the Wyngroves were trapped in the shelter until the debris was cleared for them to be freed.

Bub had been taken to St. Alpheges Hospital at the bottom of Vanbrugh Hill – now the site of the new Greenwich District Hospital – and Dad and I went down there about 8 or 9 o'clock that evening. We had to walk as the buses were out of action because of the damage. On the way the sirens sounded again and Jerry was back.

We reached the Hospital and what a sight met our eyes! There must have been about fifty or more people trying to get inside to get their relatives out. The very high metal gates were padlocked and the porters were trying to calm the crowd. We fought our way to the front and Dad said "I've come about my boy".

The harassed Porter said "yes mate, so have the others".

We managed to get through to him that my brother was an air raid casualty brought in that afternoon and we had been told to come to the Hospital. He asked our names and the big gates were opened just wide enough for us to be dragged through. The crowd tried to get through with us but the staff were able to hold them off. We were taken to the Porters Lodge where a senior member of the medical staff told us that my brother had received massive internal injuries, had lost a leg, and had been taken to the operating theatre and had died on the table.

By now there was a full scale air raid going on, with bombs dropping everywhere. Jerry

133

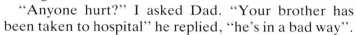
Hurricanes in formation above the clouds protecting the London area.

The German airmen being buried at Northreach. The coffins are covered with the Nazi flag.

was apparently following the Thames and trying to hit the Woolwich Arsenal. The entire riverside was on fire. The Hospital refused to open the gates to let us out so we went down into the basement where the staff were taking all the patients. Those who could walk did so. Others were pushed down in wheelchairs or in beds still with drips, etc. in place. Spare mattresses were on the floor and we were able to rest on them but it was about 4 in the morning before the raid ended and we could leave.

What chaos as we plodded along Woolwich Road, up Westcombe Hill, left at the Royal Standard and up Old Dover Road. Craters everywhere – houses and shops demolished. An off-licence had most of its stock blown through the window and for some strange reason I have a lasting memory of broken bottles of whisky, gin and beer lying about, with their contents spilling out over the pavements and dribbling into the gutters.

When we arrived home, mum broke down in tears when she saw us. She was certain we hadn't made it.

The Army wanted us to have a military funeral, but Dad wanted a family grave in Charlton cemetery so instead they sent my brother's Unit. They lined up in front, either side, and at the rear of the hearse, and lined the path to the Chapel. The coffin was draped with the Union Jack. It was a very emotional and very impressive sight.

A Major went across to commiserate with my parents, and I shall always remember my father looking at him and saying "those are the fortunes of war".

Mrs. Violet Chambers, 69 Wynford Way, London

My recollection of the Battle of Britain is one evening when my husband was on Home Guard duty and I had just put my two little children to bed. Having finished I went to the bedroom window and looked across the fields towards the Windrush landing strip near Great Barrington Farm in Burford.

It was a clear beautiful evening just about dusk and the stars were shining as I watched the young pilots practising their flying in evening and dusk conditions. They usually flew in a circle around the village and I remember that particular night thinking to myself "Oh I shan't get a wink of sleep with that row over my head all night".

Then to my horror I saw a great black object zoom down at treetop level and I knew instinctively that it was a German bomber. The engines were so familiar to us that I knew it straight away, and apart from that it was firing tracer bullets. Unbelievingly I watched as one of the trainee fighter pilots in his training aircraft turned and flew straight up at him. In an instant there was a "whoosh" as they collided, and the sky was lit up by an inferno and the explosions blotted out my mind for a time!

I know in my own mind that that young man gave his life to save the others on the Station, and later on a plaque was put up in Windrush church as a remembrance to him and to his sacrifice.

There were 5 Germans in the plane who were killed and I have photos of them being carried to Northreach church where they were first buried under the church wall until after the war when they were taken back to Germany and buried in their home towns.

Mrs. Ruby Hendy,
Flat 17 Cambray Court,
Chester Street, Cirencester

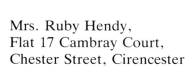

Donald Cooke with his elder brother.

Two significant dates have lived with me over the fifty years since 1940. Long afterwards when recalling the events of those two days, my family always refer to them as "That Thursday" and "That Sunday". Even when time has blurred the memory of much which followed, Thursday, 15th August and Sunday, 18th August, 1940 remain in stark contrast.

We lived at Coulsdon in Surrey, in a white house standing alone in a hillside field, overlooking the town and the valley. I was 14, and have never forgotten the build-up of tension after the fall of France. Churchill had warned us in his defiant broadcast of what to expect. The atmosphere was uniquely exciting and yet, in a curious way, unreal. The thought that enemy paratroops and tanks could come crashing through the quiet Surrey countryside during the school holidays defied imagination, but inwardly the suspense was real enough.

All through July and the first weeks of August, the air attacks were confined to the south coast and the Channel. Censorship meant that details were scant, except for the daily totals of R.A.F. and Luftwaffe losses in the air battles. From these it appeared that our fighters were successfully dealing with the enemy, and then came "That Thursday".

I spent most of the day with two schoolfriends and shortly after 6.30 p.m. we were standing in my front garden having a final chat before dispersing for supper when we noticed something unusual. The Hurricane Squadron from Croydon had taken off. There was a good view towards Croydon Aerodrome about three miles away, although the nearby tree-line obscured it. The fighters this time, instead of roaring off southwards, as had always happened before, flew in a wide circle making height above the valley.

As the minutes ticked away and the Hurricanes continued to circle upwards, the air suddenly became full of the throb of aircraft engines. Was this it? Was something going to happen? The air raid sirens hadn't sounded, so maybe the fighters had just been sent up as a precaution. It was almost 7 o'clock and supper would be ready. I was taking a final look round the sky when I saw them, directly overhead. A tightly packed formation, high up, their undersides painted a blue which was lighter than that of the sky, the standard colour of the Luftwaffe.

There were twenty to twenty-three of them. As we watched, motionless, the formation changed course with almost Air Display precision, and started to dive on Croydon Aerodrome. Within seconds the air crackled with machine gun fire as the Hurricanes rushed to intercept. What had been until then a quiet Summer evening was transformed with the thunderous reverberations of bursting bombs and the whine of tortured engines interspersed all the time with the short rapping of machine guns.

We split up then, racing for the cover of our respective shelters. As I ran down the garden, spurred on by fear, a German bomber was flying low along the valley with a fighter in pursuit. It was only a fleeting glimpse as I got to cover. Then within a matter of minutes, complete silence. Not an aircraft to be seen, not a sound, except shortly afterwards came the wailing of the warning sirens!

Later that evening my friends and I walked up to the neighbouring golf course, to the point which commanded a clear view of Croydon Aerodrome across the valley. A huge column of black smoke was pouring upwards from one of the buildings but the distance was too far to make out what other damage had been done. Obviously precision dive bombing like that must have caused havoc

137

A bomb landing on Kenley Aerodrome.

not only on the aerodrome, but also on the factories and houses clustered nearby. We stood together watching. Our mood was subdued by the sheer violence of this first experience of warfare, and we talked together about what might happen next.

The answer came three days later at lunchtime on Sunday, 18th August, at about 1.20 p.m. The family were halfway through the meal when we heard some particularly noisy aircraft approaching. I opened the window to see what was happening when explosions shook the frame in my hand. The aircraft were hidden from view by trees but the direction made it clear that Kenley Aerodrome, which was about two miles away, was the target.

I shouted to my mother, father and brother above the din to get to the shelter, but they were already on their way! Our shelter had been a garden tool store which ran under the length of the back verandah. It was protected on the garden side by a large rockery running down to the lawn and was built with brick walls and a reinforced concrete roof, all integral with the house. The only disadvantage was its internal height, which was about five feet, but otherwise it was safe from anything but a direct hit.

In contrast to the Croydon raid, this one lasted over an hour. We could hear a second wave of bombers flying very high. They were hidden from view by haze, and the whining engines and bursts of machine gun fire were muffled and distant. At one time the whistle of descending bombs was followed by a swirl of air into the shelter. We found out afterwards that several houses had been hit in Coulsdon, so that air current was actually blast from these, finding its way up the hillside.

By a coincidence, next morning I saw for myself the damage caused at Kenley. I had been in the Air Scouts for about nine months, and went regularly to meetings at the Troop Hut which was inside the aerodrome. That morning was to be the last time.

The hangars were in ruins, several of the buildings had been reduced to rubble, and everywhere was littered with broken glass. It was a sight I have never forgotten, and yet, by some miracle, our wooden hut was undamaged! However, when we had gathered there, it was to be told that the Station Commander considered it too dangerous to meet there in future. I am sure he was right!

The first two attacks set the pattern for the weeks ahead as the Luftwaffe tried to destroy the R.A.F. both on the ground and in the air. Now, since air warfare historians have researched these actions minutely, and have published their findings from British and German records in great detail, I have the satisfaction of knowing the full story of those events which I witnessed.

The Croydon attack had been by the crack German precision bombing unit, Zerprobung Gruppe 210, commanded by Hauptmann Walter Rubensdorffer, a Swiss by birth. The force consisted of fifteen twin engined Messerschmitt Bf 110's and eight Bf 109's. The Unit was unique in its use of fighters in the dive bomber role at that time, and until that evening had enjoyed considerable success. In the initial battle and subsequent pursuit over the Southern Counties, six 110's and a 109 fell to the guns of our fighters. Hauptmann Rubensdorffer and his gunner were killed when they crashed in flames at Rotherfield.

Perhaps the biggest surprise of all to emerge from Luftwaffe records was the fact that they had attacked the wrong target! It should have been Kenley! We had always assumed from the assurance and directness of the raid that the leader was an ex-Lufthansa pilot who had made commercial flights into and out of Croydon before the war. It just shows how rumour and speculation go hand in hand in wartime.

On "That Sunday" the Luftwaffe certainly made up for its earlier error. Nine Dornier Do 17's flew at rooftop height over the coast to make their low level attack on Kenley. Small wonder that they made such a racket and did so much damage but the plan went wrong again! The high level attack was to have been delivered first, but got delayed, and so the low level raiders had no alternative but to carry on. I am very glad the high level force, seeing the fires at Kenley, went for secondary targets, as we lived a mite too close to the aerodrome for my liking! Of those nine Dorniers, four were shot down by ground fire and fighters and the other five were damaged so the cost was very heavy.

The baptism of fire which I and many thousands living in suburbia had experienced, meant

Three W.A.A.F.'s awarded the Military Medal for gallantry in remaining at their posts under heavy aerial bombardment.

that the front line had moved inland and from then on we were all involved. I remember too the sudden sense of unity which the raids forged. It was first apparent after the Thursday raid when we stood on the golf course. Groups of people, complete strangers, talking together as they watched the smoke pour above the aerodrome. At that moment of crisis and for weeks afterwards social barriers disappeared. After fifty years that new spirit has long since vanished, although the T.V. series, "Dad's Army", I think, portrayed much of it successfully.

As the battle intensified, nobody then knew how stretched our fighter pilots were. When raids came in, and that was anything from three to four times per day, the Hurricanes and Spitfires were always there. Of course, to most young boys, those unknown pilots were our heroes and I can remember personally my own frustration at being only 14. But at least I had been old enough to understand what was at stake and to have witnessed events that Summer which can't be forgotten or put beyond recall.

Having never heard guns fire in anger before, I was thrilled by the sight of our fighters going into action. Fighter pilots had always been my heroes through reading about their exploits in the Great War, both in fact and fiction, and now the reality had come.

There were other realities too. The whistle of descending bombs, the awful sound of screaming engines from a stricken aircraft plunging out of control in flames, were frightening. But fear was only momentary and passed when the immediate danger had gone. Some incidents, like a crashing aeroplane, made a deep impression on me.

It came down about half a mile away, on the edge of the golf course near Old Coulsdon village. There had now been three weeks of air activity, but that sunny morning of 6th September was the first crash site that I had visited. I anticipated seeing recognisable elements of the aircraft. But there were none. The machine had hit the ground with such force that it had completely disintegrated. There was an oil filled hole with churned earth around it. The scorched grass was littered with torn and twisted fragments of aluminium scattered over a wide area.

People were standing about in groups, talking quietly. A Warden told me that it was a twin engined Messerschmitt Me 110. The gunner had baled out but the pilot had not got away. I was horrified to think that his body was in a hole a few feet away. An aspect of aerial combat which I had not seen or really thought about before and which, together with the smell of burned oil, made me feel slightly sick.

I had picked out one or two of the fragments to take as souvenirs. Boys were avid collectors of war debris! Shell splinters, spent cartridge cases, and of course pieces of aeroplane. As I was doing this an older boy calmly picked up a machine gun with a bent barrel, lying close to the hole, and started to walk off. A policeman shouted at him telling him to bring it back at once. Shortly after that incident, men wearing rubber gloves and aprons arrived, carrying a stretcher which they put down beside the hole. At that point I decided to go home.

Donald J. C. Cook, 46 Briarwood Drive, Northwood, Middlesex

I can remember the Battle of Britain well. On one occasion a train was leaving Lydd station. It was the 3.18 p.m. to Ashford and it was full of troops and A.T.S. girls going on leave. Suddenly it was attacked about a mile outside the station by a German Messerschmitt fighter plane. It machine gunned the train and flew off. Suddenly a second German fighter came down to continue the machine gunning, but it must have hit the boiler of the engine, because at that moment the engine blew up and a piece of it actually brought down the second plane because it was flying that low. It crashed in a field, and the pilot was killed. Amazingly none of the soldiers or girls were hurt. Confirmation of this story can readily be obtained from the Station Master at Ashford, Kent. I am now 87 years old but I remember it all very clearly.

R. E. Ford, 70 Station Road, Lydd, Romney Marsh, Kent

141

The remains of a Messerschmitt that crashed on 25th July 1940.

I was in the 70th (YS) Battalion having joined in 1940. At that time the Army was responsible for not only coastal defence, but also aerodrome defence as the R.A.F. Regiment had not at that time been formed. When they were then of course aerodrome defence was handed over to them.

In the summer of 1940 we (B Company) were moved to Warmwell aerodrome, not far from Dorchester. If anyone has read the "Battle of Britain" contained in "The Great Battles of World War 2" by Henry Maule, they may recall one passage which refers to "the massive raid by 45 bombers surrounded by 200 fighters". Their ob-

Albert Grice on left.

jective was in fact Warmwell airfield in Dorset. Such was the sort of place to which we partly and hurriedly trained youngsters were despatched!

During our duty there we underwent quite a few raids, but fortunately the Dorset's suffered no casualties, although a number of R.A.F. personnel did. Our Company was stationed at various points around the aerodrome.

Because of this I remember the Platoon Commanders were given the powers of Company Commanders when it came to discipline. Company Headquarters and one Platoon were in an area known as "shack" a small hut in which you could buy the usual "tea and a wad"! A second Platoon was at the "quarry" while the third was in "the woods". Platoons rotated around these places as the guards and duties varied in each area.

Although we messed with the R.A.F., normal morning ablutions were carried out at the Platoon area, and in "the wood" we had no running water! Latrines were the old bucket and hessian screen, while the R.A.F. provided us with a water tank every 2 or 3 days! Readers can well imagine what that was like as winter approached! After ablutions, in fact for every meal, we were marched to the R.A.F. Mess Hall but allowed to make our own way back afterwards. This brings me to a matter of a lucky escape.

The day in question was dull, overcast, and I feel sure that it was either misty or there was a light drizzle. It was so bad that the usual Royal Air Force fighter patrol had not gone up. Having had our midday meal, everyone, including the R.A.F. and W.A.A.F. were dispersing to our various locations, myself in a group of 3 or 4 mates, when we spotted 3 planes flying low on a direct line up the main road.

Visibility was so bad that we could not identify them, and were more or less arguing amongst ourselves as to whether they were Blenheims or not. We soon found out. They were so low that we actually saw the bombs released and fall. That was where luck played a great part. They were obviously after the hangars and buildings so the bombs dropped way behind

us. Even now I shudder to think what might have been if they had been five minutes earlier when the majority of R.A.F., W.A.A.F. and Dorsets were still among the main building area. Even so the R.A.F. personnel did have casualties including dead, but how many I don't know.

I think I perhaps ought to explain about the fighter patrol not taking off due to the weather. It was the practice, whether any raids were imminent or not, for two Spitfires to carry out a patrol both at dawn and dusk. The obvious reason being to prevent any surprise "Lone raider" attacks at these vulnerable times.

Quite often the patrol would return and perform the

143

Armourers feeding thousands of rounds of ammunition into a Hurricane ready for the next battle.

"victory roll" to show all that they had either caught a raider coming in, or perhaps a "straggler" on his way home.

This wasn't always one way traffic, as the German Air Force soon caught on to the fact that some of our planes would follow them home and shoot up their bases. They did the same thing, and it was a common occurrence for one or perhaps two dive bombers to follow our patrol in and try to catch us off guard. These were mainly nuisance raids as far as we were concerned, and apart from the sounds of bombs and gun fires, I can't recall any damage such as in the large concentrated raids. Nevertheless the particular incident I have referred to just shows what could be done when the weather was against us.

Quite often planes from other aerodromes had to make emergency landings on any airfield, due either to damage or fuel shortage. I can recall one incident where a Spitfire pilot who had landed at Warmwell before, had to do so because of fuel shortage. Unfortunately since that last time a gun pit had been constructed just inside the perimeter. The pilot didn't know this, and upon landing his wing tip caught the gun pit and he crashed. To my knowledge he wasn't killed, as I saw him carried to the ambulance, but what happened after that I don't know.

Earlier I mentioned the duties that varied in each location. They were such that at one stage we would mount guard at 9.00 a.m. for 24 hours, dismounting at 9.00 a.m. the next day, have 2 hours from 9 a.m. to 11 a.m. to prepare our kit, and carry out the remainder of the day on normal training. Then we would have a night in bed (unless there was a raid!) and back on guard at 9.00 a.m. next morning.

So in effect we were doing a 24 hour guard every other day. Good job we were young!

Finally, one matter involving our time at Warmwell aerodrome even though it was just after the Battle of Britain. One night there was a particularly severe air raid. It was so bad that the R.A.F. and W.A.A.F. personnel were evacuated, and the only ones left were the R.A.F. fire fighters and guess who? Yes the Dorsets! Imagine our horror when daylight broke and we saw the number of unexploded bombs that we had been "guarding" all night! These had then to be taken to a quarry to await the bomb disposal experts. I can assure you that they were removed very gently!

Albert Grice, 17 Birmingham Road,
Kidderminster, Worcester

I remember the Battle of Britain well because it was fought immediately over our cottage in Kent where we were living at the time.

My uncle did a very good little rough sketch of one event – while shouting at everyone else to get under cover!

One of the things that happened I remember was that a German plane came down early one morning less than half a mile from us, and my son who had just left school, but had not yet joined up except for the Local Defence Volunteers, was one of the first to the plane hoping to get instant fame by taking a prisoner! Of course he was disappointed!

Before it was all over of course a bomb landed on our place, and it was cordoned off when I got back, but I insisted on returning the next day to retrieve some of our personal belongings.

To do this we had to climb a very high "door type" gate at the back, and I always remember my husband coming out with various things strung about him and including a bottle of whisky in the pocket of his dressing gown which he was swinging about with other things! First things first! But within 6 months both my son and my husband were serving in the Royal Artillery.

Mrs. Ruby Probert, Wharf Cottage,
Bures, Suffolk

145

Pilot Officer W. McKnight, DFC; Sqd. Leader Douglas Bader, DSO; Flt. Lt. G. E. Ball, DFC.

As soon as the "All Clear" went, my mother always carefully loaded me into the sidecar on her bicycle. The care was necessary for I was getting rather large for it, having been born in December, 1935. As she mounted and pedalled off, she always had her special pole with a running noose on the end, to do her war work searching for any animals maddened by the raid which had just ended.

It was early Summer, and as we passed through the lovely Sussex countryside, which was her patrol area, we did not realise that the air raid warning had sounded again. The raiders were returning in a large formation, heading for home.

Hearing the unmistakable sound of the German aircraft about to pass overhead, my mother looked round wildly for cover but at that point there was none, not even a ditch, except for some trees at the top of the hill. She shouted at me to stay down and keep still, as to our horror fighters dropped down and fired on us.

I sat there as small as possible, hardly breathing, and quite unable to sort out the kaleidoscope of impressions beating on me. Roaring engines; afraid to look. Clattering guns. Bullets pinging on the road. Mother panting, zig-zagging up the hill, her legs going faster. Unbelievingly seeing sweat coming through the back of her coat. The heat of the sun, every muscle locked in the rictus of fear.

At the top of the hill we turned into the Warden's post. My mother, sobbing for breath, slumped over the handlebars. Silence as the planes departed. Wardens rushing out, the horror on their faces still clear to me after all these years. They helped my mother to the shelter and gave me the only injury of the incident, for in their haste to extract me from the sidecar they skinned my legs from knee to ankle!

Another clear memory is of a day out in London. I was so used to be just with my mother that I felt a little strange and rather shy about a family outing, although very proud of my father, who was on something called Atlantic Convoys on a ship that had brought bananas to England before the war but was now used for more urgent cargo. He had again been torpedoed and lost all his belongings, so one day we had to go to London to re-equip with uniform, sextants, and other things.

We set off early in the morning, arriving at Victoria Station surrounded by its barrage balloons. Before we could leave the station the warning went and as I was a small child we had no option but to go to the shelter, much to our annoyance. We lived on the Luftwaffe route to London and were inclined to ignore shelters, having developed a fatalistic turn of mind due to the dogfights overhead and the large number of bombs being jettisoned.

It seemed we spent hours in the depth of the station. Eventually my mother was reduced to taking me round the very large and very crowded shelter on a kind of showjumping course over puddles and stuck-out legs. In the end there was quite a procession of children with equally bored adults entering into the spirit of the whole thing and devising obstacles. Finally the "all clear" sounded and we poured out to the London streets about our various businesses.

The rest of the morning passed in a haze to me, being too young to appreciate the ins and outs of a Merchant Navy Officer's equipment, especially in wartime. For lunch we went to an ancient and respected place, the London Tavern, which catered for the professional and

legal population of the City. Totally unused to handling children, they had to find their old leather bound ledgers to put on the chair to make the seat high enough for me! While we had lunch there was another raid but we elected to stay put and eat.

After lunch we finished up our shopping and had a quick tea.

Hurricanes on patrol in a grey dawn.

147

As a special treat my parents had promised to take me to the cinema to see "Snow White" after tea. I was spellbound. But during the film a sign flashed up on the screen "air raid – anyone wishing to leave and go to the shelter" etc. etc. I prayed we would decide to stay on! We did, and I enjoyed to the full the story of "Snow White".

We set off on the journey home and at Victoria, which had suffered badly during an air raid since the morning but was still functioning, we caught our train for home. The hour long journey was lengthened by an enforced stop due to another air raid, but I slept through that and most of the way to our station. In the morning, on reading the paper, we learned that whilst we were lunching at the London Tavern, Victoria Station had received a direct hit on the air raid shelter, killing some 300 people. Worse, whilst we had been enjoying "Snow White" the London Tavern and a large part of the City had been demolished. Amazingly, while we had been held up on the train, the cinema had also been hit with some 200 casualties.

Our overwhelming feeling was one of wonder that throughout all this we had managed to stay one step ahead.

Mrs. Prue Elmes, 4 Coldharbour,
Chickerell, Weymouth, Dorset

It was a fine day in the late summer of 1940. I was barely 16 years old and living then in a rural area a mile or two north of Portsmouth. I had recently enrolled along with several of my contemporaries in the newly formed Local Defence Volunteers, later to be called the Home Guard. We were too young to carry arms, but nevertheless we had been enrolled (together with our bicycles!) as Messenger Boys. We were at an age when war seemed still a game, but we were eager to play our part if the invasion came.

In the skies above Hampshire on that long summer day the R.A.F. and the Luftwaffe were already engaged in deadly battle. I remember we strained our eyes to follow the tiny weaving machines high above us. A trail of smoke indicated a plane on fire plunging towards the ground, and then we saw the lone parachute, at first a tiny speck, but descending visibly towards, as we judged it, a clearing amongst some houses about 300 or 400 yards away.

A shout went up "It's a Jerry! Come on!" There was elation at the thought that a plane was down and we might capture an enemy airman!

Hearts pounding with excitement we joined a straggling line of people of all ages, some running, other walking as fast as they were able, all converging on the spot where they judged the airman would touch down. Almost everyone carried a weapon of some sort – mostly a make shift club or broomstick but in one or two cases a shotgun! I remember noticing with some amusement one man carrying a pitchfork!

He had already reached the ground while we were yet a little way off. Someone came running back towards us, shouting excitedly. I think we lads felt a momentary disappointment to learn that the enemy we had so hoped to meet face-to-face was an R.A.F. fighter pilot forced to bale out of his blazing aircraft!

Arthur M. Vincent, 51 Cherwell Drive,
Marston, Oxford

A German pilot gets a drink after being shot down, 30th August 1940.

Eileen Hanna with her mother and grandfather in 1940.

I had been evacuated in May, 1940 to Hindhead in Surrey, but in the September of that year my mother decided we would go to Wiltshire for a holiday. It was arranged that I would come home on the Friday, and on the Sunday we would travel to Wiltshire. That was one holiday that never did come off!

My home was in North Woolwich with the Royal Docks nearby and the Woolwich Arsenal across the water, so it wasn't likely to be overlooked for long by the Luftwaffe! Unfortunately for me they chose that very weekend that I was at home!

I hadn't been in the house very long before the sirens went and I experienced my first air raid. We went out to the shelter which was a brick built affair of one room, the Authorities having decided that if it was hit there wouldn't be too many bricks to fall on us and if the house was hit the shelter would protect us. Anyway, as far as I was concerned, all hell broke loose as the ships in the Docks opened fire and bombs fell. My mother's view was that it hadn't been too bad and that it was soon over! But it turned out to be an introduction to what was to follow the next day which was a Saturday.

They came around midday on Saturday following the River Thames. No sirens announced the bombers. A black cloud of bombers surrounded by silver fighters just somehow quietly and unexpectedly appear in the sky above us. At first when I saw them I thought they were ours because the sirens hadn't gone! I was only 11 years old but already had great faith in the Royal Air Force!

Through that afternoon they bombed us. The ships guns fired. A gun that I was told was

...And at the same spot in 1990!

called a "Mobile gun" seemed to rush up and down the street firing madly! A bomb was dropped two doors away that wiped out all the top half of our street and some shops.

My mother, and I remember this so clearly, decided to go to see if she could help. I clung to her, crying that she couldn't leave her only child! She removed my hands and said that I was alright with my grandparents. The people might need help and she would be back. All was as she said. My grandmother just kept putting a blanket over my head and quoting from the bible that fire would destroy the world.

It didn't exactly help.

When the "all clear" went at about 6.30 p.m. and we came out of the shelter I thought she was

151

A Spitfire of 19 Squadron being re-armed after a sortie, October 1940.

right. The whole of North Woolwich seemed to be on fire and there was no gas, electricity or water pressure to fight the fires. They had set fire to the church, our beautiful church, St. John's the Evangelist, and we stood and watched. There wasn't anything that anyone could do to put out that fire. The Reverend Garcia was out on A.R.P. duties. Later he joined the Army. He was a lovely man.

It was decided to leave North Woolwich. We knew the bombers would come back. We were going to my aunt who lived in Plumstead and it was decided that my grandfather would go on ahead and we would follow. To get across the river you went by ferry or walked through the tunnel that runs under the River Thames. Obviously at that time no ferries were running, and so we set out for the tunnel. My mother was the Police Matron at our local Police Station, and so had to report to them where we were off to. That delay kept us in the tunnel all night!

As we went down the steps the sirens went and the gates were closed. We walked through to the South Woolwich side and a young policeman who should have gone off duty at 10 p.m., found he had company for the night! He found a ladder for the women and children to sit on, rigged up a toilet (using a bucket) and made tea with about a teaspoon of tea leaves! My mother always reckoned that that policeman deserved a medal!

Right through the night the bombs fell, some seemed very close but the policeman assured us that they were miles away!

At 6 a.m. the "all clear" went and the gates were opened and in rushed the men who had come off the 10 p.m. shift at the Arsenal but, of course, couldn't get across the river to their families and homes. They wanted to know what was happening in North Woolwich, but we didn't know either. To them and to my aunt looking down from the hill, it seemed that no one could survive. The whole area seemed to be on fire.

People did survive though. I went back to Hindhead. My grandparents were evacuated to relatives in Wiltshire and my mother went back to our house in North Woolwich and her job at the Police Station. There (although this is another story) she not only carried out her duties as Police Matron, but kept the canteen open at night for the bomb disposal groups and others, when no one else could be found to do it.

Eileen A. Hanna, 12 Holcroft Road, Harpenden, Herts

My story is very short but you may find it amusing. It is certainly true. In June 1940 I was a flying instructor at No. 14 Flying Training School at Cranfield. Flying started each day at 0830, and at 0810 that day I was walking down to the hangars when I heard the unmistakeable vroom-vroom of a German aircraft. Looking up I saw an ME110 circling the airfield at around 1,000 feet, presumably taking photographs.

About 50 yards away was a machine gun post, and I ran to it. There was a gunner in the post and I remember

shouting to him "Open fire" and pointing at the 110.

The gunner looked at me and said "I can't sir".

Jumping up and down I screamed at him "Why not?" "I'm only allowed to fire with the Defence Officer's permission Sir", he replied. "Get it", I shouted. "I can't Sir", he answered, "He's gone to his breakfast"!

B. H. A. Playford, Retired Squadron Leader, Hutchins Horley, Surrey

153

Unknown pilot in a Spitfire Squadron. How young – how sad.

During 1940 I was serving in H.M.S. Brilliant in the Dover Patrol. I was involved in Dunkirk throughout the evacuation, and later watched the air battles over Kent during the Battle of Britain.

After "Brilliant" returned to Dover following the Dunkirk evacuation our job was to carry out "sweeps" in the Channel and cover convoys. On 26th July we were covering a west bound convoy when it was attacked by German bombers and German "E" boats. I believe that some of this attack was actually photographed by the newsreel cameras from the cliffs.

Anyway the dive bombers soon made a bee line for the two destroyers and we were both hit and put out of action. Tugs got us back to Dover where temporary repairs were carried out, and Brilliant got away in the darkness to Chatham. We were in Chatham dockyard for the next 10 weeks and we watched daily as the air battles took place over our heads.

I remember that the summer of 1940 seemed to be beautiful and weather wise the sky was permanently blue, but always seemed to be full of the white trails caused by the planes.

Whenever there was an air raid warning Officers and men off duty were supposed to go to the dockyard shelters, but as no bombs fell near us no-one generally bothered! However, on Saturday 6th September I was Duty Officer when the alarm was raised. Up I went on to the bridge with my lookouts, and the Damage Control Parties closed up down below.

We had no big guns aboard capable of firing at aircraft at that time. About half an hour after "closing up" at Defence Stations, my lookout, who was an old Leading Seaman from the heart of London, shouted out "Gawd blimey Sir, what's this lot coming up the river!"

And there all across the eastern sky were hundreds and hundreds of German planes. I can still hear those aircraft engines now! Believe you me all the off duty people were off the ship in double quick time and away to the shelters!

We stood on the Bridge watching those planes, trying to be brave and smoking our cigarettes in two puffs! When the last of them was directly overhead the old Leading Seaman said "They can drop their bleeding bombs now Sir, and they won't hit us!" None of us had any sleep that night I can tell you.

By morning the East End of London was ablaze. From then on until we sailed from Chatham the nightly bombing went on.

Out of a destroyer flotilla of 9 ships who started off the war in the Dover Patrol, five of us were sunk and the four remaining all damaged by the end of July 1940. I remained in H.M.S. "Brilliant" until February 1942 by which time we were serving in Freetown, West Africa. Eventually I received direct promotion to Lieutenant, and retired from the Royal Navy as a Lieutenant Commander in 1957.

Andrew K. Hall,
36 Besbury Park,
Minchinghampton,
Stroud,
Gloucestershire

Andrew Hall issuing orders on HMS BRILLIANT in 1939.

A bombed out boat in the docks.

Hellfire Corner! I was to discover the significance of that name between the ages of 6 and 13, because that is where I lived throughout the last war. More specifically in the south-east corner of Kent.

Dover was then the small Medieval-cum-Tudor-cum-Elizabethan town mentioned throughout history, even going back to Roman times. But within the first few months of the war it began to look like a ghost town by comparison as people left it for a safer place to live.

The rest of us were more reluctant to give up our homes or our way of life and so we suffered the constant shelling, bombing, straffing and such nuisances as Butterfly Bombs. These were small canisters, something like the size of a tin of condensed milk, with wings so that they caught on the rafters of the plentiful bomb damaged houses where children mostly played. Gradually the spring holding the wings would weaken and the whole thing would fall and explode like a hand grenade but we were warned to look out for them and report any sightings of them which we did.

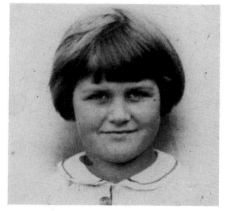

Then on the way to school one day we found the streets littered with thin strips of silver foil, apparently dropped by the bombers on their way to London. Enemy bombers of course. By doing this the Luftwaffe apparently hoped to avoid being detected by our Radar Scanners.

As if that wasn't enough, when the R.A.F. fighters intercepted enemy bombers over or on their way to London, rather than waste the bombs they had left, they usually dropped them on the coastal towns, so we had those bombs as well, thank you! At those times we had a good chance of survival, being warned by the sirens.

Shelling was different. There was no warning. Death and destruction would strike before we could take shelter, taking our loved ones and friends from us so quickly. It was the ultimate game of chance!

When I was 8 years old the Battle of Britain was being fought in the sky above Dover. I remember the clear blue sky of a Sunday morning being scribbled over by the white exhaust of diving and weaving aircraft that took part in the deadly "dogfights". Sometimes I heard a short rattling burst of gunfire and wondered why ever they were trying to kill one another. Perhaps it was a game all grown ups had to do and for a while I was frightened to grow up!

Day after day I watched both German and R.A.F. pilots lose their battle for life and plunge into the English Channel and then the motor torpedo boats (M.T.B.'s) cutting a swathe through the sea from the Admiralty Dock in Dover Harbour veering this way and that to avoid mines to reach the ditched pilots.

The destruction of our schools during this time forced the amalgamation and "upped" the number of pupils in a class to sometimes fifty-four children of mixed ability. How those teachers managed I shall never know.

Eventually to ease the burden, the powers that be decided that our schools would divide into short sessions of lessons so that for many months the children of the coastal towns attended lessons for only two or sometimes three hours each day. There would be mornings one week and afternoons the next. These lessons were taken underground in what we thought were safe shelters but, in fact, were just cellars underneath the playground! Children were not supposed to wander the streets alone at this time but many of us did whilst our mothers were out doing the work that men had to leave to go to war. In doing this we usually finished up defying Granny!

I remember when there was one raid and almost miraculously the only thing left standing of the little church at the bottom of our hill was the life-sized central crucifix hanging on the

157

Damage caused by bombs on 22nd August 1940 at Plymouth. The car is burnt from an "oil" incendiary bomb.

massive oak beams amid all the rubble. The news of it circulated the town! The rubble was fenced off for safety but the crucifix was left there as a symbol that God was indeed still in residence and people actually came to say prayers and scatter flowers beneath it.

At this time, as children do, my friends bragged about their experiences, but I was still unscathed and had nothing to say. But my turn was soon to come! Looking back it seems that a sequence of unconnected incidents came together at exactly the same time.

An ammunition train was, as usual, passing behind our houses in the early hours, but because of a lack of steam on the steep gradient the driver was forced to open the fire doors to put on more coal but at the same time a straggling enemy aircraft was making its way home with one last bomb on board. The pilot must have seen the fire glowing like a beacon in the dark night and released the bomb.

I always slept soundly as most children of that age do. Yet that night I awoke around 1.30 in the morning, disturbed for once by the drone of the plane. I went to the window and knew without looking up that it was a Dornier. Children at that time became very knowledgeable about these things.

I had no reason to think that I was in any danger, having thought that he would have dropped all his bombs on London. Nevertheless I panicked for the first time! I threw the bedclothes over the head of my grandmother who lay asleep near the window, then I did the same thing to my brother who slept in a single bed next to mine. Finally I jumped into my own bed and buried myself under the blankets and waited.

The sound and volume of noise of that descending bomb is still indescribable. It grew louder and louder until it reached ear-splitting pitch but then unexpectedly the sound stopped abruptly, and there was silence for a mere second or two and I was left confused, wondering where it had gone.

Then the terrible roar and vibrations were followed by a cacophony of so many sounds. Firstly the deafening explosion, houses falling like a pack of cards, the shattering of hundreds of windows and the sound of flying bricks and huge chunks of masonry smashing against the houses on the other side of the road, and bouncing along the street like pebbles on water in the game of "ducks and drakes". Then there was the dust, clouds of it getting in your eyes, ears, nose and mouth. Stifling! Caking hair and clothes. Finally, that peculiar moment of complete and utter silence before the crying starts!

I think that is what I remember plainest of all. That moment of silence when those who had survived waited, praying to God that was the last! That there was no more to come. In that moment the whole world seemed to stop – stunned into silence. It was at that early age I realised that although we were all bound to each other in crisis, we, all of us, would probably die alone!

Needless to say that bomb missed the train, it having gone on its way. Instead I lost five of my friends that night, maimed, blinded or killed. Our street was never the same.

In the next few years there were inevitably more deaths and I saw sad parents mourning for many more children from my school. It had an effect on our teachers as well although they tried not to show it. For instance at registration our names were called out one by one but sometimes there was no answer. The teacher would then mark that place on the register with a cross, but in pencil. There would be that certain look on her face as she did it.

We would all wait and watch at the next registration when by then, if she had received confirmation of the death of that child, she would pick up her pen and there would be that so slow movement of her hand as with a ruler she would draw a straight line through it, in ink, and slowly blot it.

I can remember her sad eyes so well. They would scan the classroom. Ominously quiet except for the weeping of a best friend before Miss closed the register until the next day. At assembly the names of the children killed would be read out and a special prayer said for them. I often wonder, as I am sure many other children from "Hellfire Corner" wondered, how long it would be before they read out my name and have to say a prayer for me!

Gwenda Harrison, 20 The Willows, Brackla, Bridgend, Mid Glamorgan

Flt. Lt. Peter Townsend with his rigger and fitter and his plane.

The year was 1940 and I lived with my parents and our Pekinese dog "Dinky" in a bungalow near to the sea at Whitstable in Kent. I was 20.

It was a lovely sunny morning around 8.00 a.m. and my mother had just brought me a cup of tea to my bed – my "Peke" was on the end of the bed. The air raid sirens had sounded. No one took much notice, as German planes often flew over the coast.

My father was standing at our back door and I can hear his voice now saying "Here come a few low flying planes, right towards the bungalow". Suddenly he could clearly see the German markings and to his horror bombs began to fall from the plane. Even now I can also still hear the deafening CRACK, CRACK as a stick of bombs narrowly missed our home.

I leapt out of my bed spilling my tea everywhere. My dog shook uncontrollably as we all made for the safest spot, a hall way in the centre of the bungalow with no windows! There were just doors leading to the kitchen, bedrooms and living room. There we were crouched on the floor, very shaken. There were several deaths that morning all at close hand. It was a pretty harrowing experience generally in those days living in what was called "Hell Fire Corner". We would watch German bombers in formation flying high above, looking like black dots. Then we would see what appeared to be silver dots as Spitfires would appear and during the ensuing dog fights many times we would see bombers shot down often landing in the sea. My parents are of course long gone, but my dear old "Peke" lived until he was almost 16 years old despite his frightful experience that morning! There is one other thing, I can remember once sheltering from bombs, in the shelter outside. There was a lull in the bombing and I volunteered to dash back into the house for tea and sandwiches. Whilst indoors I remember hearing more bombers coming and getting closer and closer, and in my haste to cut the bread and get back to the shelter I found I'd almost cut the end off the sleeve from my cardigan with the sharp bread knife!

Mrs. Joan Harvey, 4 Norfolk Terrace, Rouge, Bouillon, St. Hellier, Jersey, Channel Islands

Hurricanes on patrol.

Exactly when or where the first seeds of my military ambitions were sown is difficult to pinpoint. My earliest recollection of an awakening to the glories of soldiering came when as a small boy I was always prompting my grandfather to tell and retell the stirring tales of courage and heroism that he had experienced in the South African wars against "the blackies" and the Boers, defending the Empire and the Queen against her enemies.

I would sit spellbound in his front parlour, lit only by the dull yellow glow of a solitary gas mantle, surrounded by relics of those campaigns gathering dust on the darkened walls. The knobkerries, the assegais and native shields of animal hides were grouped around sepia coloured photographs of The Regiment, some of his comrades and one of grandfather posed outside his tent with his 'native boys'. In that atmosphere his stories came to life.

My Father who had experienced the horror of the trenches of The Somme however rarely spoke of the 1914-18 war. If I or any of my four brothers showed the slightest inkling of interest for a military career, he would come out with his stock phrase.

"I'd rather cut 'orf your bleedin' 'ands than let you fight in another war"...

But I did go to war and I've still got my 'bleedin' 'ands. I joined the Royal Air Force and I have many memories.

There was my initial trip to the Quartermaster's Stores for kitting out. Someone said that the bald headed Flight Sergeant who ran the stores had been a tailor in "Civvy Street".

TAILOR???!

I reckoned he must have acquired his skills in the mail bag shop at Wormwood Scrubs. If you weren't mis-shapen when you went in, you certainly were once you came out in uniform!

"NEXT – VESTS, 2, AIRMAN FOR THE USE OF".

"DRAWERS, 3 PAIRS, AIRMAN FOR THE USE OF".

"SOCKS, 4 PAIRS, AIRMAN FOR THE USE OF", etc, etc.

His high pitched voice sung out as he yanked the regulation issue off the shelves and slung them at us across the counter.

"NEXT! 38 chest? We've run out. Here's a 42. You'll soon grow into it son".

"NEXT! WHAT? BOOTS TOO BIG? STUFF NEWSPAPERS IN EM".

"NEXT! Even when we stood to "attention" on parade, our uniforms were still 'at ease'!

I remember having been 'neutralised' into celibate cabbages by the fear of V.D. and

Bromide laced tea, you would have thought that the R.A.F. would be more than satisfied with their handiwork. But would they leave us poor sods in our sterile wanderings around the quiet back streets of Blackpool, dodging the marauding gangs of hungry mill girls?

NO. They wanted to take away our last vestige of manhood. No, we weren't about to be castrated! Whipping the forage cap from his head, the Flight Sergeant bent forward, presenting his shorn pate to the assembled body of recruits standing to attention. He then commenced to slap the top of his head with the flat of his hand. Was he trying to improve the blood circulation to his brain? Did he have

163

...lot in "full rig". Note the tube from the oxygen mask for connection to the cylinder.

livestock in his his short hairs? Or had he simply gone 'off his rocker' under the strain of the prolonged celibacy?

"SEE THIS!...SEE THIS!" pointing to the now reddened bonce. "HAIRCUT, this is a regulation Royal Air Force HAIRCUT. Not one hair longer than an inch". He straightened, paused and slowly cast his beady eyes along the ranks of young recruits. Then softly in an almost inaudible voice he said "I want you lads to be a credit to the Royal Air Force". He paused again now getting louder. "I want you lads to get a regulation haircut". Yet another pause, "I DON'T WANT TO SEE ANY BLOODY POETS OR ARTISTS ON THIS PARADE TOMORROW MORNING". We were then dismissed!

Most of the barbers in Blackpool were many many light years away from being called hairdressers! I believe, however, that some had been on advanced courses and been introduced to a pair of scissors! The Royal Air Force regulation was achieved by the sole use of a murderous pair of clippers. With hindsight I'd have probably got a better hair cut on any sheep shearing station in the Australian outback!

Gradually chaos was replaced by habit and habit settled down to become routine as we melted into the moulding process of the Royal Air Force who hoped that we would eventually harden to become highly trained air crew. There was drilling on the promenade, P.T. on the beaches, and ten mile route marches in any direction that happened to take the Corporal's fancy! The rest of our time was spent on the first floor above Burton's Menswear shop. No we weren't learning modern ballroom dancing or developing a mis-spent youth at the snooker table. Here in the R.A.F. Signals Classrooms we were introduced to the morse code.

Morse is a method of communication using symbols made up of dots and dashes. It is an international code that overcomes language barriers and was used freely both by the Allies and the Germans. This was not a wise move by the Air Ministry. But then like their contemporary brass hats at the War Office, they had probably put all their money on Germany to win in any case!

Then I came home to London on leave. But the boy of 18 who went off to war returned to the bossom of his family still a boy who was four months older!

"You look thinner. You've lost weight, Didn't they feed you up there?" Mum was enjoying herself as she lowered the enormous king sized pease pudding into the saucepan of steaming water. Dad as usual a man of few words, hovered in the background.

"Everything alright Son?" Obviously he had forgotten my name the four months I'd been away! "Yes alright Dad". At least I'd remembered his!

The seven days leave seemed to be spent mostly tucking into navvy size meals, while Mum sat watching me, encouraging me to eat more. Dad remained hovering throughout my leave! There was an occasional "everything alright Son?" Clearly he still couldn't remember my name! But I did manage to escape from the house a couple of times between meals and my father's persistent and boring questioning!

Out there was the war, the blackout, the bombing and the "Windsor Castle", a pub that was a Mecca for troops or departing or arriving at Victoria Station. There were the 'can't wait to get into the war' on their way out, and the battle-weary disillusioned coming in on leave. Many got no further than the "Windsor Castle" with all its temptations!

So off I went, with my father's 'Don't be too late Son" ringing in my ears. Even then he still hadn't remembered my name!

Blackpool had its season in the summer months, but the immediate area around Victoria Station was always "In Séason" and so were the "ladies of the manor"! The 'Naughty Triangle' was a catchment area skirted by Wilton Road, Gillingham Street and Vauxhall Bridge Road, with the "Windsor Castle" set into it like a bright pearl.

This had always been Bonanza Territory for the "ladies". For many years they had enjoyed a good steady business from the punters commuting via Victoria Station to and from their suburban homes and suburban wives! They also had a highly lucrative source of income from the local well heeled Belgravia gentry. Continental trippers arrived regularly on the boat trains. Having 'done' Buckingham Palace and Westminster Abbey they were now able to enjoy some good old British hospitality before catching the boat train home. But since the

165

Battle of Britain Anniversary Flight – September 1945. Lord Dowding talking to Group Captain Bader.

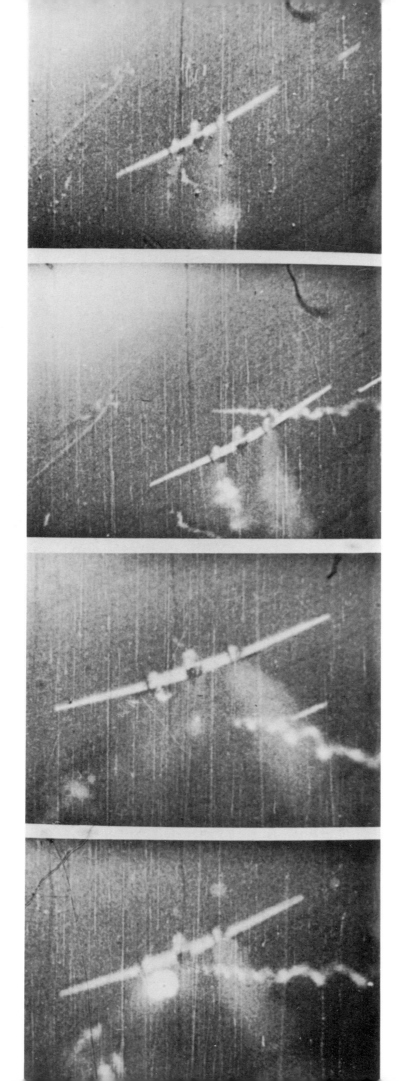

war began the only continentals anxious to make the trip were the German Army! However, they weren't likely to get the same welcome from 'the ladies'.

With the war came a bonus for the ladies. A new consumer class had been created. There was 'our boys' and 'the colonials' and now their numbers had been swollen by the Free French, the Free Dutch, the Free Belgians, the Free Czechs and the Free everything bloody else. It was "common market" created 24 years before its time together with also "commonwealth preference" trade. Yes this was Boom-Boom time for 'the ladies'. It was so good that many of the 'old brigade' came out of retirement, partly for patriotic reasons but I suspect more likely to subsidise their meagre old age pensions!

Unlike "the Bermuda Triangle" it wasn't the people that disappeared here, it was their money! The law took a pretty dim view of this, but their raids on 'The Triangle' nearly always proved to be fruitless. They would occasionally nab one or two of 'the old uns' with their varicose veins handicapping a speedy getaway. But within two minutes of the balloon going up the streets would be deserted, save for the punters left sheepish and stranded half way through their financial negotiations. Yes, Blackpool had its special way of training us for the Battle of Britain!

This article was written by Albert Kibble, known as Vic, and sent in by his wife as a "memory" of him.
Mrs. Yvonne Kibble, 1 Ayr Court, Monks Drive, Acton, London

My first recollection of the Battle of Britain was on Saturday 7th September 1940, and I remember it because it was just a few days short of my 12th birthday. It was about 5.00 p.m. on a Saturday evening when this great roaring sound of hundreds of German planes flying overhead could be heard. I remember that they were fairly low because I could easily see the crosses on their wings. I was at that time living in Carr Road, Walthamstow, East London. As we backed onto Lloyds Park we had a good view of things. There was me and my mum and dad and my sister Peg. We were stood by the shelter in the garden and watched as our fighter planes from North Weald Air Force station in Essex attacked the bombers.

Then it started to get even more noisy than it had before and so we went into the shelter, but not before we saw one plane shot down and saw the pilot bale out. It sounds horrible now, but people started cheering when this happened as they thought it was one of the bombers, but as we learnt later it was a Hurricane pilot who was a Polish airman from the Polish Airforce and stationed at North Weald. He landed safely by parachute at Loughton in Essex where I now live! Tragically his plane crashed on a shelter at Buckhurst Hill in Essex and killed a family of three who were in it. Anyway we had a few hours of quiet and then the Germans came back again and we spent that particular night in the shelter, six of us, mum and dad, Peg and me and Mr. and Mrs. Rose, the old couple who lived in the flat above us. We spent all night in the shelter just sitting on some old chairs and the shelter was cold and damp as water used to seep up from the earth and clay. Eventually we dug a sump into one corner and even then we had to keep baling this out with an old saucepan and a bucket. This became a regular job for me during the day to try and keep it dry. All the responsibilities of a 12 year old! Anyhow that's how I remember the Battle of Britain!

William R. Wheatley, 43 Barrington Road, Loughton, Essex

Camera sequence from the camera of a fighter as a Messerschmitt 110 goes down.

I was just 18 years old when war broke out in September, 1939. We heard it announced on a portable radio whilst on holiday in North Wales. Our home was at Gidea Park, Romford.

I was due to return the second year at college in London later that month but we were informed just before commencement of the Xmas term that the Army had taken over the college and our course was shut down. As a consequence I was forced to take a job! I took what I thought would be a temporary job in North Woolwich in a factory manufacturing wireless transmitting valves. This entailed travelling by road and rail from Gidea Park to Woolwich, but we only worked a five day week when everyone else worked six and seven days, because of travelling difficulties.

My outstanding recollections are of the Battle of Britain, which started in September, 1940, so far as I was concerned and the first noticeable attack began on a beautiful September Saturday afternoon. My parents, my brother and I had gone out to our caravan which was based at Frieze Hall, a farm on a hill not far from South Weald, close to Romford and Brentwood, and within easy cycling distance. The site overlooked the Thames Valley and Estuary. We could see the Electricity Crossing Towers at Barking and Woolwich Hill and on a very clear day St. Paul's Cathedral over to the right.

As the sirens went off all round us, we suddenly saw the German bombers and escorts coming up the Thames Estuary. The Spits and Hurricanes took off from Hornchurch and North Weald to meet them, the latter going over our heads. Soon there were black puffs of anti-aircraft fire around the bombers and then suddenly from the west, with the sun behind them (it was about 3 p.m.) the fighters pounced. First one bomber came screaming down in smoke, then there were numerous "dogfights" between Spitfires, Hurricanes and the German JU 88's and Messerschmitt 109's. In all we saw fifteen German bombers and fighters shot down and, unfortunately, if appeared we lost two Hurricanes in the fracas. The bombers turned as we watched, dropping their loads around Woolwich and Dagenham, and went off home. How many were ambushed on the return journey I have no idea and due to the censorship the full extent of the bomb damage was never released. But it was a fantastic sight and was talked about for days after, since from our position we had a grandstand view of the whole operation. From a safe distance!

Two other incidents stick in my mind, both occurring in the early evening. The first was when I was returning home from work. I had to travel on the train. On leaving Gidea Park Station I had to go down a road that had tall Elm trees still in leaf. It was dark, no house lights, no street lights and very spooky. There was nobody except me. The sirens had already gone, then the distant noise of a German plane was discernible above the whispering of the wind in the trees.

I happened to glance up and could just make out the outline of what appeared to be a parachute with a load at the bottom. What to do? Run on home or flatten myself on the

deck? Let's get home! Only a few more yards and into the garden shelter! Since the wind was driving the parachute away from us, I managed to scramble into the shelter with the rest of the family and had just settled down when it hit the ground. Everything shuddered and so did we!

We opened the door and bricks and glass and tiles were still falling and crashing to the ground. Fortunately the blast missed our house. We learnt later that the parachute mine, for that's what it was, had landed on the golf course about half a mile away and had caused very little actual damage apart from a huge crater; but the blast had damaged windows and tiles for miles around.

Hurricanes taking off to intercept – 16th August 1940.

The second incident concerns the time the area was fire bombed. Hundreds of incendiaries were dropped but fortunately these dropped on mostly open ground. Several persons, including my brother and I, seized buckets of sand and doused many of the incendiaries before they really went off. I think we dealt with about thirty in as many yards and all in five minutes! Meanwhile this German bomber was still cruising about overhead and flak kept falling around us from time to time. Eventually this bomber was shot down somewhere towards Grays in Essex.

Finally, the company for whom I worked evacuated part of the Works to Somerset. As I was single (and wanted more money!) I joined the Works Home Guard Unit. The Invasion Scare was still at its highest and so we also undertook A.R.P. duties and defence duties, manning an anti-aircraft defence day and night at the factory as well as working during the day. I remember one day when there was low cloud and during daylight we had a Red Alert Warning. So we manned the defences, i.e. anti-aircraft. Suddenly we could hear the plane. It was quite low but above the low cloud. Problem! To fire or not to fire! Our sole protection was a 1914 Lewis Gun. The plane sounded like a Dornier but it couldn't be identified. Was it looking for us? Then we heard "crump, crump, crump" from a stick of three bombs. Where they had landed we had no idea; later we heard that our fighters had brought the plane down some twenty miles away. We had hesitated it's true – but we couldn't see it, being shrouded in mist, and to have fired would have drawn attention to ourselves! Apart from that we had a puny and unsuitable weapon! So our conclusion was that: "Discretion was the better part of valour!" The factory was located outside the small town of Ilminster and the plane was brought down near Crewkerne.

I think we lived in dangerous but stirring times and I must add that finally I was privileged to take part in the "D" Day Landings in Normandy, the capture of Le Havre and the Crossing of the Rhine and the Victory Parade in Bremehaven in May, 1945, serving in the Royal Engineers and the 51st Highland Division.

Frank W. White, 3 Eyre Close, Gidea Park, Romford, Essex

In the beautiful Summer of 1940 I was a small child on holiday with mother and father, staying with my grandparents in Croydon. We were much in demand as raconteurs, having experienced several bad air raids in the North of England, whilst the south had remained comparatively untouched.

One afternoon my mother took me to Chiswick to visit my Godmother and on our return in the evening we passed Croydon hospital. Ambulances were rushing in and out of the gates. The attack had come at last!

From then on the air raid siren was liable to wail at any time during the daylight hours and we took refuge in the large cellar under my grandparents' substantial Victorian house. Once I stood in the back garden gazing up into the hot intensely blue Summer sky, aware of the staccato "pop-pop-pop" the little planes wheeling above my head were making as they circled one another. I was hastily hurried indoors for I had never seen "dogfights" before or heard machine gun fire and I didn't really understand it!

Fortunately our holiday was almost over and when we reached Kings Cross Station we boarded a packed train. Most of its passengers were in uniform and when we steamed out of London it seemed everybody was so exhausted that it very soon became a train of deeply sleeping people.

Daphne Stroud, 19 Clayworth Road, Brunton Park, Newcastle-Upon-Tyne

171

A Canadian fighter pilot returns from a sortie.

James Crossland's mother and sister.

My father was a Policeman during the war and had many stories to tell, some of them good and some quite sad. Here are two I remember myself.

I remember one day when a barrage balloon broke loose and drifted over our house. To get a better look at it my father went into the toilet to stand on the loo seat, and put his head out of the small window. As this had happened before and the R.A.F. had shot down a balloon we all expected to shortly hear the Spitfire's guns. Instead, all of a sudden there was a big bang on the roof, and it was the cable dragging across the slates. My father got such a fright that he slipped and his foot got stuck down the toilet. I can assure you panic took over that day. Fortunately my Dad's leg did not break, but the loo did!

During the war of course there were also very strict rules about the blackout where no light at all was allowed to come from the windows. This had an effect on children who learnt all these rules rapidly, and I can remember that the first time my sister who was then about 3, was taken out in the dark, she looked up and saw all the stars shining. Her response was "Oh, look at all the holes in the blackout".

James A. Crossland, 8 Gordon Street, East Houses, Dalkieth, Midlothian

James Crossland in 1940.　　　　　*James Crossland with his sister today.*

A Spitfire being re-armed for action whilst the pilot is already in the cockpit talking to his mechanic.

*Mr. French
far right
middle row.*

In the early days of 1940 I was stationed at Duxford as a then Flight Mechanic Engineer of No. 19 Squadron. It was whilst I was there that the then Flying Officer Douglas Bader joined the Squadron, and I was responsible for his aircraft. When at various times the Squadron was at "readiness" I naturally spent many an hour out on the airfield with him. It was during those times that I grew to realise what a great man he was, and later to become even greater.

During spells of off duty it was my great pleasure to be able to fly with him in our Squadron. Not once in any of the flights did he ever take any liberties. I still take this as a great honour, because there must be a few people who can actually say that they have actually flown with him in an R.A.F. aircraft.

I am sure that before he died he must have remembered often those days at Duxford, and in particular a time in the hangars one evening when he asked me to fit a piece of webbing across the windscreen so that he could rest his chin when looking through the gun sight for firing the gun. This was to prevent him falling forward when the hammer was released.

We also had a particular technique for getting Douglas Bader into an aeroplane almost as quickly as an able bodied pilot. For those readers of this story who at this stage don't realise what this is all about, Douglas Bader had lost both his legs in an aircraft accident prior to the war, and had yet fought through all the bureaucracy of the R.A.F. to take part as a fighter pilot in the Battle of Britain.

He was a lovely chap to talk to – an Officer and a gentleman in every respect. No. 19 Squadron was in fact his first posting in the R.A.F. after recovering from the amputation of both his legs. The flights I had with him were in a Miles Magister 2 seater plane, and he would fly from the back and let me sit in the front.

Sir Douglas Bader when visiting Newton Aycliffe.

Before he died I always used to say that a book should be written about Douglas Bader and now it is being done. It just remains for me to say what a great joy it was for me to serve with him. His death in September 1982 came as a very great shock to me because I worked so closely with him for 18 months.

E. W. French, 47 Westward Road,
Cains Cross, Stroud, Gloucestershire

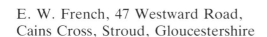

Squadron Leader, later Group Captain Douglas Bader, DSO, with his Hurricane. He led his squadron despite having lost both legs in a pre-war flying accident.

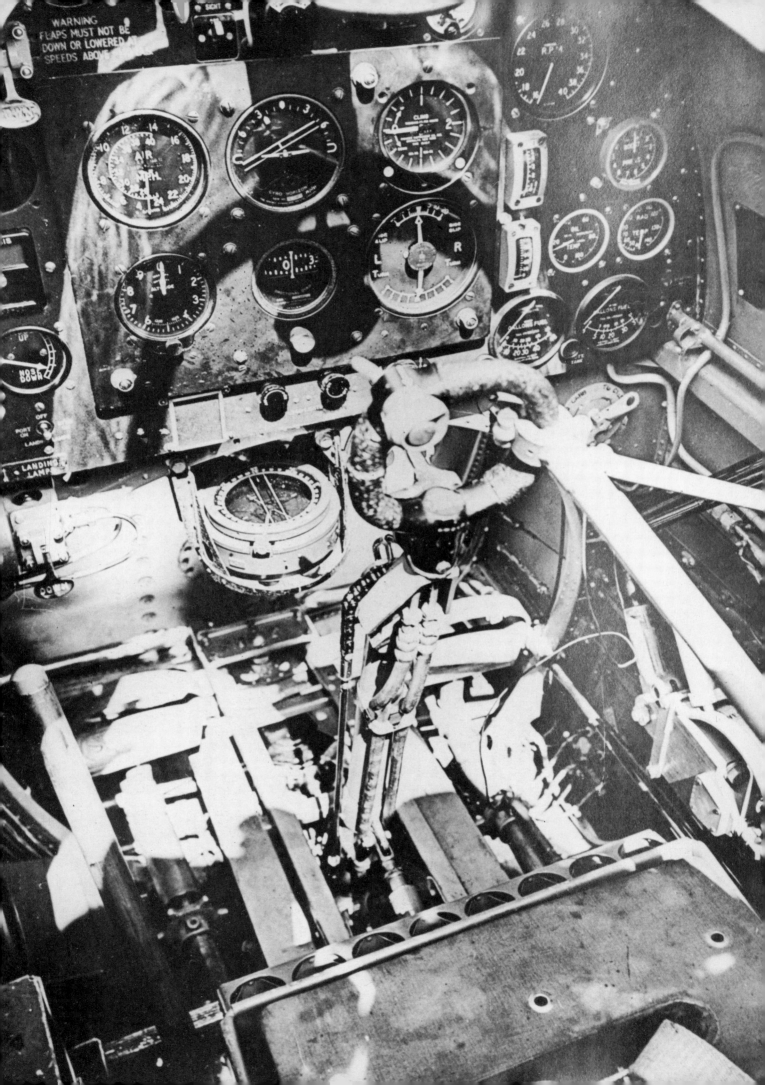

Jim the Home Guard with his wife Marie at their daughter's wedding.

I can well remember a Saturday afternoon in late September or maybe it was early October when Canterbury was being heavily bombed. We lived 4 miles from Deal on a hill, and we had a lovely view towards Pegwell Bay and Manston airfield etc.

The usual air raid warnings were sounding, and suddenly there was a mighty rushing sound coming from our back gardens, and I turned round and looked out and suddenly saw German aircraft passing low over the top of the gardens.

My husband was in the bath and he jumped out and stood on the back door step still dripping wet with only a towel round him and I can remember him swearing at every plane that was passing overhead.

Our neighbour was in the Home Guard and he ran up the garden firing his rifle and also having a good swear up! His French wife stood on the door step and I can still hear her voice calling out to him "Jim you silly bugger, why don't you hit them" and then turning to me and shouting "Look Vera he can't bloody shoot straight".

None of us saw any danger but when the last plane had gone over we looked out of the front garden and we could still see the planes in the distance but there were also parachutes coming down where planes had been hit. My six month old son slept through it all!

We still live near to Manston and every time I pass it I think of that day and how much we owed then and in later years to the Royal Air Force and our fighting forces.

I can always have a laugh now about it, but on that day even though we saw no danger it was frightening. I can remember celebrating afterwards with a well deserved cup of tea all round which included our neighbours and Jim from the Home Guard.

Mrs. Vera Giles, 58 Chapel Road,
St. Lawrence, Ramsgate, Kent

The instrument panel of a Spitfire.

I was 17 years old when the war began and lived on the outskirts of Ashford in Kent where the Battle of Britain was fought. I remember well those days and at 17 it was a very exciting time for me, not realising the seriousness of it.

It seemed that at 10 o'clock every morning the siren would sound and a few minutes later the sky would be filled with German bombers on their way overhead. The fighters would wait around to escort the bombers back after their raid and it was then that the action really began for the R.A.F. The Spitfires and Hurricanes used to tear into the German fighters, sometimes only two or three against a dozen or more Germans. My sister and I would stand on the roof of our garden shed, jumping up and down with excitement when one of ours shot down one of theirs! Finally, however, my father would drag us indoors if the fighting got too close, but mostly it took place nearer the coast and over the fields of Kent.

One particular time I remember vividly. It was when my best friend got married. I was a bridesmaid and it was a beautiful Summer's day. All went well until after the ceremony and we were ready to leave the church and then the sirens sounded and almost immediately there was a sound of gunfire overhead. As we got to the church door we could hear the spent shells of machine guns rattling down in the churchyard like rain. So we had to shelter in the church for the next hour! Finally we made it to the reception.

As the bride and groom and myself and the other bridesmaids started off to the bride's house for her to change into her going away outfit, the siren went again but we drove off thinking we would have time to reach the house before the action began again and we got there just in time. However, the fighting above was so severe that we dashed across the road to the garden shelter. In the shelter there was a large bed, a small bedside table on which was a candle and matches and torches, but very little else as the bed took up most of the room.

There we lay, the bride and groom and two bridesmaids huddled together, listening to the noise outside. The bride and groom wondering if they were ever going to get a honeymoon! That marriage seemed doomed from the start. Sadly after three years, most of which time the groom spent abroad, it did end in divorce.

It was at this time that I remember the evacuees started arriving in our area. How odd some of them seemed to us. Some of them had never seen outside of the London street that they lived in. They seemed amazed to see vegetables growing, like potatoes coming out of the ground, and they thought that onions grew strung up in bunches the way that they had seen them at home! Everyone felt so sorry for them and tried to help them but finally they were re-evacuated because it was too dangerous for them in Kent, and then children were evacuated from Ashford eventually, but we never went. We all decided that we would stay put!

Our everyday lives carried on, of course, as best it could, but hardly a day seemed to pass without someone getting a telegram from the War Office to say someone was missing or killed. The nice thing was that people clung together and gave help and comfort whenever they could.

Mrs. Vivianne J. Hambley, Pendene,
Middle Lane, Nether Broughton,
Melton Mowbray, Leicestershire

179

Hurricanes returning from combat.

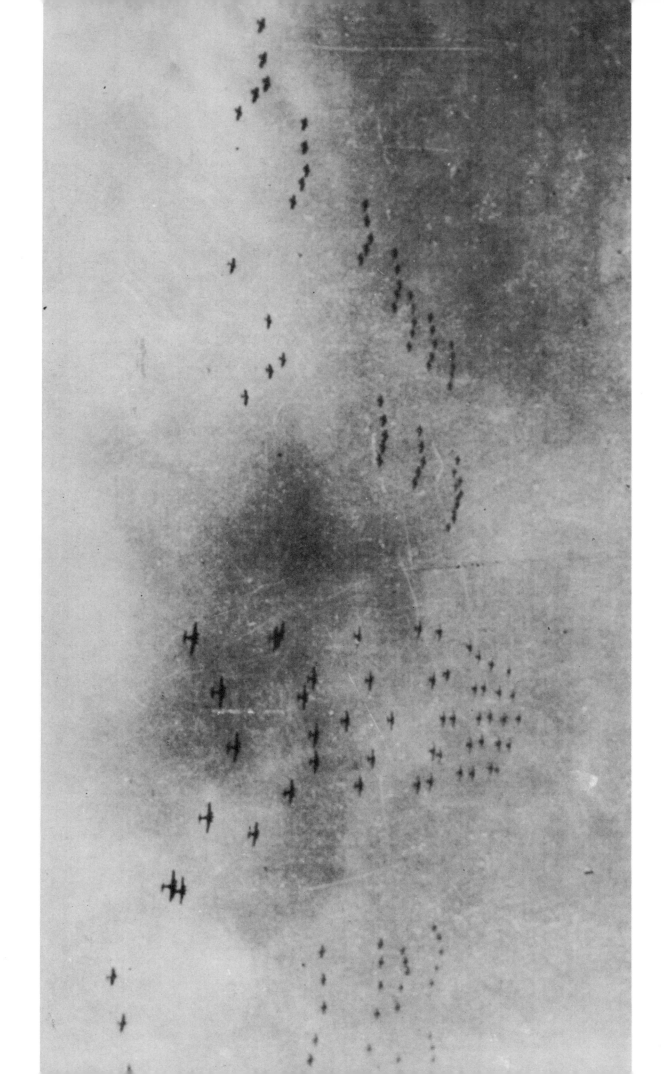

I have memories both of Dunkirk and the Battle of Britain in early 1940. I was stationed on a gun site not many miles from where the Germans broke through at Sedan in May 1940. We were cut off from the main thrust of troops heading for Dunkirk. We made our own way under frequent machine gun fire by enemy aircraft across country, and eventually arrived at St. Marie some miles inland from St. Nazaire.

One half of my Battery went forward to board the ill fated ship S.S. Lancastria, and the result was that many of my companions were drowned. On 17th June 1940 which was a Monday, at about 4 o'clock in the afternoon, the Lancastria crammed with thousands and thousands of British troops was just leaving St. Nazaire when she was struck by German bombs and sank within a matter of 20 minutes. This was logged in the Guinness Book of Records as the greatest disaster ever at sea. Fortunately I was in another group that made its way to Marseilles where we boarded a "coaster" the "Alma Dawson" and were evacuated to Gibraltar, exhausted, half starving and covered in coal dust!

By July 1940 I was stationed at a gun site at Westerham Hill in Kent manning 3″ anti aircraft guns. There were eight guns in total. Our Headquarters were at the "Kings Arms", Westerham!

From our gun position on the hill looking south we could clearly see the German bombers as they came in in waves like a huge aerial convoy on their way to bomb R.A.F. Biggin Hill and London.

Our Spitfires and Hurricanes were few in number but could always be seen bravely challenging the might of this aerial onslaught, and weaving and diving in their efforts to destroy the enemy. And of course we gunners were doing our very best to get a "Hit" with the antiquated 3″ guns that we had and that had been used in the 1914 war. The 3.7 inch gun was by then just about off the secret list!

Whilst on this station we had a new intake and you'll never guess, but they were all epileptics. I mean no disrespect to them, but poor chaps they were quite incapable of dealing with the work that we had to be doing, and naturally we couldn't keep them so they were despatched to more suitable locations. I mean no disrespect, but it just shows the dire straits that we were in at that time. It was a very traumatic period.

Douglas A. Harvey,
3 The Old Walk,
Otford,
Sevenoaks,
Kent

German bombers over Biggin Hill.

In 1940, at the age of 15, I was a part-time Auxiliary Fire Service Messenger at Wallington Fire Station in Surrey. The Brigade had two Leyland fire engines which had been purchased two years previously, and of which the Borough was very proud. So much so that at the time they had failed to comply with an instruction that all fire appliances had to be painted battleship grey. They remained brilliant red with gleaming brassware!

When on duty I was allowed to hang on to the side of one of these machines and travel to fire calls. On arrival at an incident my job was to attach myself to the Chief Officer or Senior Officer present so as to send messages back to the Station. There was no radios in those days. The messages would be sent via the nearest telephone or fire alarm post.

The 15th August, 1940 had been a lovely Summer's day. I had reported for duty shortly before 7 p.m. when the bells went and we were speeding towards Croydon Airport. On the way I could see three aircraft in the sky and saw objects dropping from them. I hadn't realised they were bombs and the aircraft were German Messerschmitts.

No air raid warning had sounded and this was our first taste of war. The German aircraft had scored direct hits on factories on the airfield, making aircraft components and aircraft. On arrival the Chief gave me the message to send back – "Make pumps 20".

Over 100 people were killed in that raid and it is something that I will never forget. Within three weeks bombing raids were to become a daily occurrence but we became quite blase about the whole thing. My strongest recollection is still of that first day when I saw bombs falling and people dying.

Roland E. Lambert, 21 Yaverland Drive, Bagshot, Surrey

183

Aircraft being overhauled on the edge of an airfield.

I was in the Army (the Queens) stationed at Denge Marsh just west of Dungeness during the Battle of Britain. Here are one or two things I remember from that time.

We were on guard in one of the little tarred wooden houses at Dungeness soon after we arrived, when the beach was bombed by a Dornier bomber which went out to sea. Apparently it was in trouble and had got rid of his load. Some time afterwards the sentry on duty called out the guards saying the local fisherman had got a "Jerry"! We went out rifles and fixed bayonets expecting trouble.

There was a pilot who had been washed up on the beach, and he was dead. We were told that he was buried at Lydd. He was the first of the enemy we had actually seen, and it seemed strange.

Another time 2 of our men were on Ack Ack duty which meant being in a pit dug in the local beach, with a Bren gun mounted on a tripod. I was there when another Dornier flew slow and rather low over us, and the gunner fired a burst from the Bren gun, and hit the bomber which went into a steep dive into the sea. As no other services then claimed to have damaged the plane it was credited to the Bren gunner as his own personal "hit", and he was given two weeks leave as a reward!

Leave was rare in those days, and after this no plane was safe! In fact we had a message from the R.A.F. that any of their planes that were fired on in future would retaliate!

There was a small boat filled with pit props that had been sunk near the shore, and stuck out of the sea at low tide. This was often bombed and straffed by the enemy planes, and it also happened to the local fishermen a lot in their boats, and we certainly admired their pluck.

During this time the numerous planes flying high caused us no trouble. It was the odd one or two planes that did the "hit and run" raids, flying very low and fast often so low that you could see the pilots. Lydd was the nearest town and it was often raided. We used to sit in the canteens, and even the local cinema there, with our rifles with five rounds in the magazine as invasion was of course still expected at that time.

Lydd is a very quiet part of the world. But it certainly wasn't in 1940!

F. G. Ramsden, 2 Viaduct Terrace,
Hamstreet, Ashford, Kent

Spitfire being "turned" for take off.

"THE FEW"

Across a clear blue sky
Grey ghosts of Spitfires fly
The Hurricanes they still zoom low
As back in time I go

The bombers they came droning
At least a thousand strong
To pulverize and shatter
But these fighters proved them wrong

The R.A.F. were dauntless
And to the battle flew
Like hornets roared and gathered
Remember just "The Few"

Do not forget these heroes
Don't let their memory die
For they shall never sleep
Where only the valiant lie.

This poem was sent in by Eric Seddon and it is a poem he wrote in 1940. He was a Gunner in the Royal Artillery, 11th Armoured Division from 1939 to 1946.

Eric Seddon, 47 Holts Lane,
Tutbury, Burton-on-Trent, Staffs.

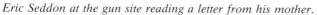

Eric Seddon at the gun site reading a letter from his mother.

Fighter ace Bob Stanford-Tuck with his "notches" alongside his cockpit.

Ruby Worboys with her husband and three children.

We lived in a very small cottage, opposite the recreation ground in Ashwell. My late husband was in the Home Guard. This particular night (can't remember the date) we were awakened by a terrific bang. My husband jumped out of bed, said "look after the children" and went to join his mates in the Home Guard.

I was terrified. All was pitch dark. We weren't allowed any lights. I gathered the four small ones together and ran next door to an elderly couple (who were up because of the crash). We sat huddled up and drinking tea until early light, then we found a German aircraft had crashed on the field at the top of our garden. Bullets and shrapnel were everywhere, whole rows of bullets and great lumps of shrapnel on the children's bedroom window-sill.

We were so lucky that it didn't break the glass. The recreation ground was littered with clothing which hung from the trees, and smashed limbs everywhere. I don't know how it happened. I kept thinking how lucky we were and felt sorry for the parents of the dead.

Mrs. Ruby Worboys, No. 11 Bungalow, Back Street, Ashwell, Baldock, Hertfordshire

The cottage where Ruby Worboys was living in 1940.

Ruby Worboys' garden – the plane crashed behind the hedge at the top.

Where the plane crashed.

189

A group of fighter pilots, one wearing an Italian helmet as a trophy.

In the early days of the Battle of Britain, two or three times the German aircraft were bombing Manston Airfield and all around even before the air raid siren had finished sounding. We had an Anderson Shelter in our garden, and we ran to it pretty quick I can tell you. We spent quite a lot of time in it, and once when my mum and I were down the town shopping, the siren went and we took shelter in an old wine cellar which was used for the public. We spent the whole day down there, not even a cup of tea to be had!

As the days went by the battle seemed to be getting bigger and bigger. We had "dogfights" in the sky nearly every day. It was very exciting at times, but also very frightening.

11th August, 1940: I was taking a cover off the washing line, which we used to take down the shelter with us. I was looking in the Manston direction when the siren was still sounding and I could see all those bloody, great big aircraft, very low over Manston, bombing, and the anti-aircraft guns were firing at them, and one of the bombers seemed to break in half and crash down, and another one fairly close to it wasn't looking too good at the time, and that came down as well. In our local paper that week there was a report about two aircraft being shot down by one shell, which I presumed to be what I had witnessed. The report reads as follows:

Dick Hambidge, in white shirt, seated on his Anderson Shelter.

One Shell Brought Down Two Bombers
A dive-bombing on a Kentish aerodrome on Wednesday gave anti-aircraft gunners the chance they had been waiting for. Here is the Ministry's account of the action. "There was only one mass raid, when large formations of enemy bombers and fighters appeared between midday and 1 p.m. on the south-east coast of Kent. In this and other attacks, 20 raiders were shot down, 3 of them by anti-aircraft guns.

"Only a few of the German aircraft taking part in the noon raid were able to cross the coast and attack aerodromes in Kent.

"A Light Anti-Aircraft battery at one Kentish aerodrome brought two bombers crashing down near them. Then a Heavy Battery attacked two others. They saw their shells damage one. the other to get out of range, dived low, only to be destroyed by Lewis Gunners.

"A single anti-aircraft shell exploded between two of the bombers, shooting off the tail of one and blowing the other to pieces.

"The Mayor of a south-east coast town, wearing a steel helmet, was amongst those who watched British fighters engage the raiders in furious 'dogfights'."

That is the end of the press article. Living fairly close to Manston we often caught the tail end of the German aircraft, mainly Messerschmitts strafing the 'drome. They would come over so low, machine gunning, and the bullets sounded like heavy rain. It was very frightening and it certainly made you shake a lot!

24th August, 1940: It was mid-afternoon. My mother and I were sitting in our Anderson Shelter. We could hear the guns firing and the aircraft zooming around, and all of a sudden there was a terrific loud "zoom" right over the top of us. It frightened the life out of us but it was all over in a split second. A little while after our Air Raid Warden called into the garden and told us that it was a Messerschmitt that had just gone over, and it crash landed in a cornfield which was about a quarter of a mile away from where we lived.

I scrambled straight out of the shelter and told my mum "I'm going out to the crash to have a look for myself". I hadn't ever seen a Messerschmitt on the ground before. When I got there you could see where the Messerschmit had struck a concrete post alongside the

191

The Intelligence Officer receives pilots accounts of the combat.

cornfield and had ripped off part of the left wingtip. The concrete post was bent right over and the aircraft must have spun quite a bit on impact. The cornfield was off Minster Road at Westgate-on-Sea in Kent. All the open fields around this part had either concrete or iron posts stiking out of the ground and I understand that they were part of the plan to stop Germany aircraft landing if ever there was an invasion. that was why they were put there.

One of my old schoolmates worked on the farm. His family cottage was about fifty yards from where the Messerschmitt finished up and he was one of the first out to the crash. He told me that when the Pilot got out of the Messerschmitt, he was shaking like a leaf, but he was O.K. and not injured at all. He was very lucky after hitting that concrete post! Now the interesting part is that after all

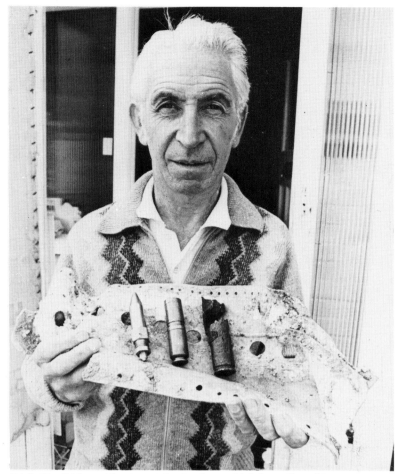

Dick Hambidge with pieces of a Junkers which he collected.

these years, I am now writing to that Pilot out in Germany, and he has told us that he would like to come over and meet us one day so that I can take him out to the site where he crashed!

September, 1940: Sometimes during the Battle of Britain, my mother and I slept in the Anderson Shelter in the garden. I remember once we were both fast asleep and it was about 6.30 a.m. Suddenly we were both awakened by a very loud crackling noise and a sound of aircraft, and then quite a big explosion not very far away it seemed.

The very next thing was a bloody great boot coming through the entrance to our shelter and my first thoughts were that we were being invaded by the Germans! I really believed it was a German soldier coming after us! It was also my mum's thoughts as well as she confessed later. But it was only our milkman coming for cover from the bombs! He was delivering our milk when this crackling noise started and we found out later that day that it was a bomb that fell about half a mile away. I think there must have been some kind of device attached to that bomb. I will never forget that morning as long as I live. The fact that I was only half awake at the time made me even more frightened, and also my mum, but we had a good laugh about it afterwards.

14th November, 1940: Later on during the battle this afternoon, we could hear a lot of aircraft activity and we were wondering what the hell was going on when suddenly we could see all these aircraft in the distance and when they got closer we could see that the one in front was a Messerschmitt and all around and behind it was a mixture of thirteen Hurricanes and Spitfires. The Messerschmitt had a little black smoke coming from the tail but our aircraft were not firing at it at that moment. They seemd to be giving the German Pilot the chance to give himself up and land at Manston but that didn't happen, so two of ours had a go at it, and the Messerschmitt was shot down in flames and crashed at Sacketts Hill Farm, Poorhole Lane, Margate. The Pilot was burnt to death.

This smiling pilot has obviously had a good sortie.

I remember this incident particularly because it was something quite different from what we were used to seeing. It was usually our aircraft that were so outnumbered!

10th April, 1941: We had a day of "dogfights", like many other days we had already experienced but this one ended quite different. It was just before 5 o'clock teatime and we could see a "dogfight" going on up so high in the London direction, much too high to recognise which machine was which, but we could hear the machine gunning of the aircraft in battle.

Suddenly one of them caught it, and down it came with black smoke behind, dropping straight down just like a brick. Then one of the other aircraft in the battle started to dive straight down towards Westgate-on-Sea. When it got down low enough, we could see it was a Spitfire and it swooped right low over the Pilots Billets at Manston and straightened out and then shot straight across towards Manston, almost at rooftop height, and did the Victory Roll, but sadly the Pilot was much too low and the Spitfire crashed on the parade square and the Pilot was killed.

The Messerschmitt that the Pilot had shot down crashed with its Pilot at St. Nicholas-at-Wade about four miles from here. The next day I cycled out there to have a look and see if I could see some bits of the Messerschmitt for souvenirs. I used to make rings and badges and lighters etc. out of some of the pieces. I did get quite a lot of pieces, including some tubing, which was always handy for making rings.

When I got home with all my bits, I started to clean some of the dirt off them, including a short piece of tubing about 6" long which I had thought was full of earth. I pushed a bit of wood up the tube to push the earth out, and to my shock I pushed out a piece of the dead German Pilot's flesh. The smell was hard to explain but it rather put me off making rings for a while!

All the Pilots from Manston were billeted at Westgate-on-Sea. The Officer Aircrew was at the old Doone House School in Canterbury Road, and the non-commissioned officers and the Sergeant Aircrew at St. Gabrails Home, Elm Grove. The two billets were only about 300 yards apart.

We also had W.A.A.F.'s billeted in Westgate-on-Sea and I used to look after the Pilots. I was having a chat with one of them the day after the Pilot killed himself doing the Victory Roll, and she told me that the dead Pilot's dog was sniffing round the wreckage of the Pilot's Spitfire. I thought that was very sad.

The W.A.A.F.'s often used to tell me about the times when they would lay the tables ready for evening meals etc. and there would be empty seats where some Pilots hadn't returned from the day's battle.

I lost my brother in the R.A.F. It makes you think.

Dick Hambidge, 6 Wellesley Road,
Westgate-on-Sea, Kent.

NOTE: See following two pages for recent events.

Operations Room, Fighter Command HQ, Stanmore.

On pages 191-195 Mr. Dick Hambidge tells the story of the German plane shot down near him and of his recent contact with the pilot.

Opposite is a letter he has received from the pilot Herbert Bischoff now living in Nuremburg, and is reproduced exactly as written.

The photographs show his crashed plane on 24th August 1940 and with his colleagues in France on 10th May 1940.

The two on the outside were killed that summer. The other on the inner right was taken prisoner, as was Herbert Bischoff who is seated inner left.

The running boar insignia and white '9' proclaim this Messerschmitt Bf 109E-1 as an aircraft from the 1st Staffel of JG52. Based at Coquelles, France, this particular specimen crash-landed in a field of stubble at Minster Road, Westgate on Sea after suffering engine failure on August 24th.

Dr. Herbert Bischoff   85 Nurnberg
                                         Siedlerstrabe 9
                                         Tel 40 38 55
                                         22-4-90

Dear Richard

You can hardly imagine how happy I was to receive your letter, reminding me of my "second birthday" in 1940, 24 August. I still remember every detail of the Spitfire which shot my Messerschmitt wrong over London in 15000 ft. high, and of the crash, but it is even more interesting to read about it, described by an "eye-witness" who still lives close to the place where I went down.

I am answering very, very late and I beg your pardon. We had any problems during the last 8 months (sickness). Thanks for the newspaper-clipping, I feel sorry for the constable who got into trouble for talking an unauthorized picture of the wreck of my Messerschmitt – but at least he came out of it without being found guilty, the photo of the wreck I already found in the book "The Battle of Britain, Then and Now". A friend has bought it for me in London. Thanks anyway, my "second birthday" is so important for me I cannot hear, read or talk enough about it!

As to myself, I retired from my job as head Psychologist in 1979 and find my present state very comfortable. Of course, as most retired men, being master of my time and in good health, I am engaged in on many personal projects that I am busier than during my working days.

In the last ten years, my wife and I have been travelling many month per year by caravan through whole west-europe, especially through France (My France is much better than my bad english, I am sorry and excuse me).

Unfortunately, my wife still suffers from the consequences of a stroke, and it will take time and patience until she will be able to travel again. We hope it will be possible to travel again, but it is not sure. During these weeks she is in hospital again.

My wife and I would like much to come to England, to see you on all the places I still remember so well but now we shall have to wait, how long time – I don't know.

Yours very gratefully and sincerely

Herbert

I am afraid I am too young to remember the war as I was only born in 1943 but my father was in the Home Guard and kept a diary of events throughout the war years. His whole story was published in a local volume of historical reminiscences called "Faversham Miscellany" but as it was all so vivid and interesting, I feel a wider audience would find it entertaining and valuable. Unfortunately he died a few years ago, but he would have been very happy to know that some of his notes could be published in book form.

The following are the extracts from the story of Cuthbert Terence Spurling: He was born in 1904 and so at the time of the Battle of Britain would have been aged 36. He had served as a Curate at Faversham Parish Church from 1935 and continued to do so until 1944, when he was appointed Rector of St. Nicholas Otham with St. John's at Maidstone. Subsequently he was placed in charge of three parishes, and retired on the 18th October, 1971. He was a regular Diocesan Correspondent for the Church Times, and wrote an historical guide to Otham Church which went into two editions, and published also a number of other booklets. He was Honorary Chaplain to the City Company of the Plaisterers of which he was a Past Master.

The following are the notes from his records of the Battle of Britain period.

September 7th, 1940: Mother and I went by car, in the afternoon, to tea at Mr. and Mrs. Miles at Goodnestone Court near Faversham. It was a beautiful warm day and I played tennis with others who had been invited. An air raid warning had been sounded and very suddenly the battle developed overhead. We were trying to pick out the planes and saw one crash with the pilot coming down in a parachute. Overhead there was a sudden burst of fire. I ran with others into the house, only just in time, for a rushing, crackling noise rent the air. We all thought that the farmhouse had been hit. Down in the cellar we waited for some more explosions but the only sound was the roar of planes overhead and machine gun fire. The tap-tapping was like hail on the roof. When we had sufficient courage to get up and investigate, we found that an aeroplane had come down in flames on the barn. From one the wings of the plane the machine gun was still firing bullets into the roof. The old barn was well alight as a crowd of people rushed up from the village. I telephoned Newton House, the Headquarters of our Civil Defence, and put through my report and called the Fire Brigade. Soldiers from a nearby Searchlight Unit came running up to help put out the flaming mass of steel. Meanwhile we were all feeling thankful to find ourselves unharmed, and also to see the Pilot descending in his parachute some way off. It was an English plane shot down in air combat. Unfortunately we were told afterwards that the Pilot had been machine gunned by the enemy as he was coming down and though still alive when he reached earth, he subsequently died.

The extraordinary effect of the exploding aeroplane, for that is apparently what had happened over the farmhouse, was that particles of canvas and engine pipes and metal were showered all over the grounds of Goodnestone Court. My car and another were untouched and not even scratched, although fragments of the plane were lying all around the drive. The same afternoon another plane, also English, had crashed at a neighbouring farm with the Pilot dead at the joystick.

Two baby chicks were rescued alive from the courtyard where the engine of the plane had buried itself about eight feet into the ground. The old mother hen had been killed. Luckily

Spitfires with flaps down returning from combat.

for the Miles family, their dog and horses were safe. We ourselves had escaped from death or injury by about forty yards. The air-raid on this occasion had lasted from 3.45 p.m. until 7 p.m.

September 12th: Mother and I went to Brenley, close to Faversham, to pick hops under the Land Army Scheme. After arriving at the farm, enemy planes came over and a battle with our planes ensued. It was a bit too lively to sit out picking hops just then! We took cover meanwhile in the Oast House until the fighters had passed over. We found the hop picking very interesting and it was quite peaceful in the "gardens" as it was after 5 p.m. and most of the workers had finished. The Reverend F. D. Foster, my fellow Curate, was with us and the three of us picked two "skips". One of the farmhands came along to demonstrate how the hops should be picked, and with his advice we got on well, considering we were all novices at this kind of field work.

Daylight raids affected the Day of National Prayer, but we managed to conduct services at 8 a.m. and 6.30 p.m. The siren warned us again at 2.05 a.m. and the raid continued until 5.15 a.m. There were no newspapers published on Monday morning but they appeared again on Tuesday.

September 11th: During a severe barrage put up by the guns on the Isle of Sheppey, a shell exploded on the roof of a house in Wallers Road, Faversham. One child was hit by a fragment of brick, but recovered later in hospital. There were eleven people in the room downstairs at the time – some of them had come out of London, but all were unhurt.

Sunday, September 15th: We had services at 8 a.m. and 6.30 p.m. but the rest of the time was given to watching air battles. 185 German planes were destroyed on this day alone. There was a nine hour raid in the evening lasting until 5.20 a.m. on Monday. It has since been announced by the Air Ministry that Hitler made an attempt to invade this country on the 16th, but the R.A.F. foiled it by a huge bombing attack on the Channel Ports.

September 17th: We had five air raid alarms. The last being a 9½ hour raid. During it, four bombs were dropped on Faversham without anyone being hurt. One was an oil bomb which did not light up. Another a time bomb exploding after four hours at 8 a.m. I was on night duty at my post.

September 27th: We had the usual series of raids and air battles overhead. We saw several planes come down. 133 enemy planes were destroyed today.

October 4th: At 9.12 p.m., bombs were dropped on Faversham and severe damage was inflicted on houses in East Street. Three bombs fell on the town and the same number on playing fields beside London Road. Mother and I were at home at the time and we both went down flat at the rushing sound caused as the bombs fell. The enemy plane was low at the time and it was a windy night. Four people were killed and others were injured. A Pilot was rescued alive from the debris of one house. One of the bombs was an incendiary and burnt out a house entirely while another, falling on the playing fields, never exploded. Much glass was broken over a wide area and a beautiful timbered house dated 1589 was completely ruined. The local doctor and his wife living here had miraculous escapes as I saw for myself when they pointed at the place where they had been standing. Soldiers and rescue parties had a strenuous time removing the rubble from the next door house, where the occupants had

201

A Sergeant fighter-pilot waiting take off.

been killed while playing cards. I was on the site at 2 a.m. to see if there were any rendered homeless who needed shelter. We found that most of them had already been taken care of by friends. One couple, an aged mother and her son, spent the night at the Queen's Hall air raid shelter, the Relieving Officer providing them with blankets.

October 8th: During an "all clear" period, a lone raider suddenly dived out of the clouds and dropped three bombs near the canning factory at Faversham. None of them exploded. One of them was an oil bomb which did not catch alight. The military, afterwards, rendered them harmless.

October 10th: Mothers and children who were being evacuated, had only just left Faversham Station when it was the target for enemy bombers. Only one railway official was slightly hurt and there were no casualties amongst the passengers.

October 11th: My mother and I were out walking a mile out of Faversham and we saw thirty or more enemy fighters on their way up to London. They were met by a heavy barrage.

When we returned to Faversham we learnt that one or more German fighters had made a power dive on the town and released four bombs; one of them falling in open country did no harm but the others caused a good deal of damage to a row of houses. One man died of shock and there were minor casualties. The Vicar, Canon P. A. L. Clarke, had a narrow escape when a bomb dropped outside the Queen's Hall, close to where he was standing. It made a gigantic crater and destroyed a potting shed in a neighbouring garden. The gardener was blown into the crater by the blast and sustained a broken leg. Pieces of the bomb, stone from the garden rockery and portions of the iron railings around the Queen's Hall were picked up streets away from the explosions. Amazing escapes from flying glass were noted and one of the bomb fragments weighed 16 ounces.

October 20th: Today I saw a German fighter at close quarters, with all the markings – the cross on the wings and the middle of the body clearly visible as he flew low over the marshland near Seasalter.

October 25th: A great battle with the Nazis in the air, in which everyone is engaged. The Londoners are at present suffering most from the bombardment, although the coast towns have their share. Canterbury Cathedral has so far escaped damage, although nearly 100 bombs have dropped on the city. There have been some very near explosions which have broken glass in the cathedral but the ancient glass windows are being carefully preserved. They were removed from the frames soon after the declaration of war.

Airfights in the Hop Fields: During September when the hop picking was in full swing, there were constant battles overhead. Some of the women, who had come from London to help gather in the hops, were very afraid and took shelter during those fights. Others went on with their work, apparently unconcerned with what was taking place overhead. The chief danger was from falling bullets and crashing planes. One of these – an enemy fighter – came down close to a hop field, and luckily for the Nazi airman, our soldiers were soon on the spot to take him prisoner. Otherwise he would surely have been mauled by these women from the East End of London!

On one occasion a man who had been picking hops got up from his stool to take cover. When he returned after the fight was over, he found a bullet wedged in the seat of his stool!

Another time a woman dived under the bins when she heard a plane roaring overhead, much to the amusement of her friends as they said her legs were stretching far out behind and would have been a conspicuous target for its machine gun!

It was reported that several times Nazi airmen dived out of the clouds to machine gun the hop pickers, but I did not hear myself of any casualties in this neighbourhood. One thing at any rate is certain – the rates of pay were increased owing to the added danger of working in the hop fields.

At Owens Court not far from Sheldwich, a village about three miles from Faversham, was the scene of three plane crashes, two enemy and one Spitfire.

When a German bomber landed on the marshland near Faversham, the crew of five were about to set fire to this new type of machine when our troops surprised them. There was a sharp duel but after being shot in the legs the German airmen gave themselves up. They

Flt. Lt. "Paddy" Finucane ready to take off. He was credited with 24 victories, Note the shamrock decoration. This is the RAF pilot referred to by Mr. H. Tattersall in his story on page 83.

were quite surprised to see our men as they had been told in Germany that *their* Army held Canterbury.

After an air battle over our house, we picked up a German bullet in one of our flowerbeds. The boys round here have been very active in saving souvenirs from the crashed planes, but the Police and Military are usually first on the spot and forbid such collecting.

In the early days of the war the Germans sent over large masses of bombers at a time (50 or more escorted by fighters) and we watched them flying along in perfect formation until they got within range of our guns. Then they would scatter and our fighters (Hurricanes and Spitfires) waited for them, chasing them off like terriers after a rabbit. Later (in October) their tactics changed and bombers of a heavy type were chiefly used for night operations, Messerschmitt 109 and 110 being used as bombers during daylight raids. This was a disadvantage to the enemy as these fighters could not carry a heavy bomb load.

November 11th, 1940: A very different anniversary – the second Remembrance Sunday of the war – from what it was before September 3rd, 1939. The Vicar of Faversham had arranged to conduct a short service at the Parish Church in order to observe the customary two minutes silence. At 9.22 an air raid alarm was sounded when Italian and German planes attempted to raid London. One hundred and fifty of them came across the Kent coast. The consequence to us was a heavy barrage of guns, which were still firing as we went in to church to observe the two minutes silence. Earlier in the morning we had been to the air raid shelters attached to the district schools, and visited the children of the different classes, each with their teacher. They were all very happy and seemed not to mind their new place for learning lessons. The only complaint from them was "cold feet" – literally, not metaphorically!

November 21st: A German Heinkel bomber with a crew of four was brought down by a Spitfire at Buckland – two miles outside Faversham. They were all killed, and the Spitfire Pilot lost his life in ramming the wing of the bomber after two of his fellow Pilots had fired long bursts of machine gun fire. One of the bombs exploded after the plane caught fire and another bomb exploded about an hour afterwards. Unfortunately the first explosion killed one of the Faversham Firemen as he was attempting to put out the flames. The noise of these explosions was terrific and shook our house considerably. Another Faversham Fireman, who was seriously injured, died later in hospital.

Cuthbert Spurling's stories then continue with the reamining years of the war.

Nicholas Spurling,
Pharendon, 18 West Road,
Berkhamsted, Hertfordshire

The Pioneers come in; cheering evidence that the mess will soon be cleared.

Spitfire of No. 19 Squadron taking off.

My story is about the Battle of Britain but really more a remembrance of the Royal Air Force in France. I am one of that generation who served in the Royal Air Force from August, 1939 right through till 1951 and in that time I served in France from January, 1940 to June, 1940, with subsequent service in Palestine, the Desert Air Force attached to the 8th Army from El Alamein to Tunis, Sicily and Italy, eventually coming back to this country in November, 1944 after four years abroad. As I have mentioned, my memories in this particular article are of my service with the R.A.F. in France in 1940, immediately prior and leading up to the Battle of Britain.

At this time, funnily enough, one of my memories is of a dear old lady who lived not far away from us where we were billeted and who seemed particularly friendly towards us. She spoke English with a French accent rather than the other way about, and eventually she informed us that she was English and that she had spent some 20 or 30 years in France, having been a Nanny to a local family. This was in the "phoney war" period and she seemed very concerned about the possibility that the Germans could over-run the country again and occupy Colemiers as they had done in the 1914-18 war. I asked her one day why she had never returned to England. She said that she had no one to return to so she might as well stay, as indeed she had done throughout the 1914-18 war! Anyhow she concluded "I am too old now". But she made us a lovely cup of tea whenever we were near her house.

After the "phoney war" my first recollection is of looking at a headline on a paper and seeing the words "Evacuation Du Dunquerque". I thought what the heck do they want to evacuate to Dunkirk in Scotland for! It was now mid-May and there were rumours that we were going to move. Where to I didn't know. I didn't know whether we were advancing or retreating and quite frankly I don't think anyone else did either. It turned out to be a retreat! Headquarters were packed up into lorries, together with personnel. My memories are vague about the journey, but I can't think of any special thing happening, except that the roads were packed with civilians who were escaping from the German advance into North-Eastern France.

Our first stopping place turned out to be Orleans. My limited knowledge of Orleans cannot help me to identify where in the city we were halted, but all I can remember was spending the night in a hayloft full of cobwebs above a grandiose archway entrance to a big palatial house with a large courtyard. I shall always remember that hayloft with its smell of chicken manure and cobwebs and no lighting and musty old hay, with the roof having seen better days!

Next day even more confusion seemed to reign than had before. Only this time, I and five other Airmen were detailed to GO BACK to Colemiers from whence we had just come, under the command of a Liverpudlian Corporal. As we were all unarmed the Corporal was issued with a revolver! I never found out whether or not he had ammunition for it, but by coincidence that very day we were issued for the first time with Ross rifles but, of course, without any ammunition! I don't know what we were supposed to do with it and I certainly don't remember what happend to my rifle eventually, but our mission was apparently to burn all documents and generally sabotage anything of value that may have helped the Germans.

We got back to Colemiers and spent about a week there doing everything and nothing in relation to our mission. One afternoon I remember seeing about 200 German aircraft flying over us in the direction of Paris. They must have been flying at only 2,000 or 3,000 feet and yet not one gun could be heard firing at them. On or about the Friday of that week we were hurriedly advised by a French Captain to get out of town quickly. Apparently the Germans were on their way to our site and were only a few miles away.

We didn't need any second telling! But our journey back to Orleans was marred by an accident in a French town, caused by a chap coming out of a side street on our left. There seemed to be quite a lot of blood about and the people in the vicinity of the incident got very stroppy. The Corporal advised us to get back in the lorry and we made off in great haste. Eventually we arrived back in Orleans and made our way to the area where the Unit had last been when we left them.

After crusing around we concluded that they must have left the area to go elsewhere. We couldn't find any trace of them. We spoke to one or two people in the area who could comprehend English, and with our little understanding French, it transpired that the Unit had left the day after we had left them. It was at this juncture that I began to realise that not only were we retreating – we were retreating in total confusion and intent on getting out of France! Apparently our Unit eventually got to Brest. A number of them were loaded on to a ship called "The Lancastria" but which was sunk off the coast with over 7,000 dead, many of whom had been in my Unit at Colemiers. Of course, at that time, back in Orleans, we didn't know about and we rapidly got to the stage where, with all the confusion and all the fifth column work that was going on, we didn't know who to believe, what to do or where to go!

Eventually we set off in the direction of Brest, stopping on the way for food. I remember in one village we stopped at a bread shop and they refused us saying that we were cowards, leaving the French Army in the lurch. On another occasion we were chased off a field by the locals, bearing pitchforks, after just asking them for a drink of water. I don't think we had much to eat or drink for two or three days. Maybe we had two or three tins of bully washed down with whatever water we could find suitable to drink. That was the total confusion and chaos that the British Army and the British Royal Air Force was in at the time.

It was on this journey to Brest that we came nearest to the actual combat area between the British troops and the Germans. We had come up to a major crossroads – straight on to Brest, to the left to Nantes. On this crossroads stood a solitary Military Policeman mounted on a motorcycle. He stopped us, asked where we were going, and we said "To Brest to join our Unit".

He said "Hard luck, if you go down that road about 200 yards round the corner you will end up in Jerry hands. Take this road to Nantes. There are still some R.A.F. on the airfield there".

The road to Nantes was chock-a-block with vehicles of all sorts and sizes, both military and civil, and here and there on either side of the road were vehicles that had been ditched and many were burned out. Pedestrians were walking down the roadsides and in ditches, dodging the moving vehicles.

We arrived in Nantes and eventually found our airfield. It looked, instead of an operational airfield, like a totally deserted place with fires burning everywhere and things being burned instead of things being salvaged. Of course, there was the odd exception. We drove up to where there were a few R.A.F.

chaps and identified ourselves and asked if we could tag on to their rear party. The result was that the officer in charge who was a Flight Lieutenant, simply ordered us to unload our lorry and set fire to it! We loaded our personal belongings on to an aircraft transporter, which is known in the R.A.F. as a Queen Mary, which is a 60 foot long low loaded articulated vehicle. We then planted ourselves on it! We were the last vehicle to pull out of Nantes Airfield in a convoy of about 15 vehicles and set out in the direction of St. Nazaire. By this time all planes had left and there was just one mad rush to evacuate France. Looking back it was as well because a month later we would need everyone of those R.A.F. men and our R.A.F. pilots and certainly our R.A.F. planes, for what would become known as the "Battle of Britain".

The run down to St. Nazaire was not interrupted by enemy aircraft, but the nearer we got to our destination the more obvious became the scenes of desolation and ruin. As Army and Air Force vehicles ran out of petrol or seized up, they were pushed off the road. They were piled up on each side of the road. One town we were passing through produced a sight for sore eyes and dry throats. As I said we were last in our convoy and we were passing through this town which had a right hand bend in the road with a steepish right hand camber. I happened to look back just in time to see a civilian lorry loaded with crated bottles of beer or wine, turn completely over, with crates and bottles spread all over the road. To say it fetched a lump to my throat is an understatement!

We got to within three miles of St. Nazaire and pulled off the road into an area that appeared to be an emergency landing ground with two hangars. It looked quite deserted and we were to spend two or three days at this site awaiting entry to the dock area to re-embark for England. Whilst at this landing ground I cannot recollect any organised feeding arrangements and there was certainly no accommodation. We slept near to the doors of the hangars covered with one or two blankets, with our gas masks as pillows!

Jerry paid us a visit on the first night when he started strafing us on the way to bomb St. Nazaire. Needless to say you don't stop in an aircraft hangar when an air raid is on. It was a case of run, and run anywhere! That certainly happened to one unfortunate lad when he suddenly found himself up to his neck in a slit trench that had been used as a latrine! You see it was night time and only half moon and there was no hot or cold running water either, so if you were dirty, you stayed dirty! You can well imagine he wasn't the most popular member of our group and certainly not someone you stayed close to!

The officer in charge was spending most of his time running back and forth into St. Nazaire, trying to get us on to any boat available to get us out. Apparently we were the last of the R.A.F. to leave and I remember he came back one day to tell us there was a ship coming into harbour with a Division of Canadian troops ready to form a rearguard around the town and he had been assured that he would be able to get us aboard after the Canadians had got off.

At this stage we were ordered to abandon all our transport and to stack our kitbags in the hangar as we prepared to march down to the docks about three miles away. Most chaps believed what was told them – that our kitbags with our personal belongings would follow us on transport. This would then leave us free to march in comfort! I am still awaiting my kitbag after 50 years!!

Arriving in the dock area we were ordered not to leave the area as we could lose our place on this boat that was due in. We spent the night waiting, just lying down where we had haltekd, within a few hundred yards or so from the moorings. In the distance we could hear the heavy guns firing. Later on in the night we had an air raid on the docks. I can also remember, funnily enough, a spectatular fireworks display! Next morning we were told that was for the Canadians who came in and disembarked! But they were instantly re-embarked to be sent back to England because by that time it was apparent that the cause was lost and France had fallen.

Consequently we had another day and night in the docks area and our Flight Lieutenant must have worked like hell on our behalf to get us away from there. We were given permission to break ranks and go up into town to stretch our legs, which a couple of us did. Whilst walking in the streets nearby we had an air raid which was quite concentrated. I dived across the road to an air raid shelter but would you believe it I was actually refused entry by a French official, apparently because it was for civilians only! So I dived back across the road to a shop entrance – anywhere to escape the machine gunning that was going on. There was a young French woman in the doorway who pleaded with me to try and get her aboard a ship to get out of France. It was a fruitless request. We couldn't even get out ourselves! After the air raid it was rumoured that parachutists had landed in the area, just out of the town. We returned to the embarkation area just in time to be told to prepare to move out.

Apparently a British destroyer had slipped in during the night and would take out as many as possible. Whoever that Flight Lieutenant was, he must have worked miracles because he got about 100 of us aboard and no sooner was the ship packed full that we pulled away and out to sea. During the trip out we transferred to another larger boat by climbing up rope ladders which, for Royal Air Force men, was rather awe-inspiring! We felt it was like climbing up the face of a rock whilst an earthquake was doing its utmost to make you fall off! The only difference was that these two ships were as close as possible one minute and yards apart the next, which would mean hard luck if you let go and fell between the two. For some time after boarding this ship we seemed to be taking on more and more survivors from all kinds of smaller craft, both civilian women and other British service personnel. Eventually all seemed to be calm and so we sailed for what turned out to be the Irish Sea and Liverpool.

That is my recollection of events some 50 years ago. It was immediately prior to the Battle of Britain, but it is an indication of the mess we were in by the time the Battle of Britain started and the fact that the Royal Air Force very wisely pulled everything out of France at the earliest opportunity and tried to get itself reorganised. I think it did reorganise itself and that's why the Battle of Britain was won.

But there were some other aspects. For instance we didn't know that the Germans advance down the coastal area had been so rapid. We didn't know that Paris was occupied when we were at Orleans and was, in fact, surrounded when we were at Colemiers. We didn't know that our Headquarters Unit had boarded the troopship "Lancastria" and that over 200 of them were either killed or drowned when the ship was hit and exploded. In fact, only about 20 of our total Headquarters Unit survived, so on reflection I consider I was lucky – if I had been there I certainly wouldn't have made it. You see I can't swim!

Bill Parry, 109 Caradoc View,
Hanwood, Shrewsbury, Shropshire

When war was declared I was only 13 years old. Our home was one of a group of little cottages on the Cornish side of the River Tamar. Being only 100 feet from the water's edge, it had a good panoramic view of about 90% of the city of Plymouth, with the distant Dartmoor in the background. Also, just about one mile away on the opposite side of the river was the Royal Naval Dockyard at Devonport, with its slipways, docks, cranes and wharves; also some of His Majesty's ships! Some were tied up against the wharves whilst others were secured to their moorings in the river. Luckily we lived in this house through the four years of the worst air raids on Plymouth and so we were lucky in avoiding the worst of the bombing.

After the collapse of France, the raids that we had already suffered to some extent became steadily worse. After all, by now, the German Air Force was now only 85 miles away.

The first heavy attack was made on the large oil terminal and its surrounding area in the south end of the city. Many fires were started and several of the large storage tanks could be seen for miles. Consequently the Germans made it a prime target.

My first narrow escape from death came about 7.30 a.m. It was a nice bright sunny morning with a little low cloud about. I was up and dressed and finishing my breakfast before heading off to school. My brother-in-law, who was staying with us, went to open the front door and leave for work. At that time Plymouth Sound was used by the Royal Air Force as a base for the Sunderland Flying Boats, which used to take off from there for their patrols. It was usually about that time of the morning and we had got used to it. Occasionally, depending on wind and circumstances, one would swing round after take-off and come over Devonport, where we could see it doing its turn on to course to head west into the Atlantic Patrol.

This morning, however, this familiarity didn't turn out quite like we expected. We heard the drone of the approaching low flying aeroplane and, of course, took little notice of it. But as my brother-in-law opened the door, I remember he shouted with great surprise to my mother, "Come and look at this silly ....., flying low in his Sunderland. He is almost on the water!"

Although he wasn't talking to me I was aeroplane mad and so I rushed to the front door to see it. The plane was between us and the dockyard, flying straight towards us about half a mile away and starting to climb from about fifty feet above the water. It was having to climb in order to avoid the tall chimneys and the hill which was behind us. The aircraft now loomed large and very black and instantly I recognised it as being a Heinkel 111. As soon as I realised what it was I shouted "It's not a Sunderland it's a Heinkel!" and I had hardly got the words out when we heard the chatter of its machine gun. No warning had been given as it had slipped in unnoticed.

Thinking he was shooting at us we scrambled back into the safety of the thick walls of the house just as it passed on its way overhead. Its guns were still blazing away. Then the firing intensified as the Nose Gunner joined in. Apparently the Tail Gunner had taken it upon himself to spray the village as he passed over!

It flew on over Whitesand, where it turned around and came back, spraying the village once more and bringing its attention back to the ships. As it cleared the village the crew must have noticed the chimneys and works. At this stage we had gone outside the house and stood talking to the neighbours, not realising it was almost on top of us on its way back. Then we heard the firing again but what was worse was the whistle of the bombs as they left the aircraft.

Everyone dived for cover, except the Air Raid Warden who lived next door, and the Works Manager and his son, who were standing talking just around the corner some forty feet away. They literally didn't have time to move. About a minute had passed and we could hear the plane going further off into the distance as the useless raid warning was now being sounded!

It occurred to us at this stage that we had not heard any explosions and wondered why. My brother-in-law who had remained in the doorway said that they had fallen into the river just up the bottom of the garden and pointed to the splash marks that were still circling in the water. "I could see them coming down" he said, "They looked like shiny milk bottles".

The Warden came round the corner looking very worried and asked if anyone had a long crowbar or a metal rod. My father said that he had one, but asked what he wanted it for. He replied "I'm not sure, but I think we're in trouble".

Apparently whilst they were talking and the bombs fell, the Manager's son said he felt something brush his coat, so he examined it for bullet holes, but there were none. He then went to turn round and his heels sank into what should have been very hard ground. The Warden said he thought a bomb had gone into the ground at his feet and he wanted the bar to use it as a probe to see how far it would go down into the ground.

We went with him. He gently removed some loose soil and it seemed to reveal a hole about six inches in diameter. Then he probed gently into the hole and about a foot down he made contact with something metallic. He cleared around it and gently lifted the soil out with his hands and confirmed all our fears by then revealing the fin of a bomb.

Immediately he made us all evacuate to a safe distance out of harms way, which I would consider was a bit late in the day for that instruction! The Army was then telephoned and they sent an Officer to examine the find, and weigh up the situation. He confirmed everything but allowed us to go into the house and collect some clothes and our food as we would have to move out while it was being dealt with. My brother in law was talking to the Officer and told him what he had seen, namely 8 or 10 bombs go into the water, and that we thought that this was the only one. The Officer told us that they would have to make a search as that type of plane carried up to 21 bombs of this size that the Warden had found.

The search in fact revealed 5 more all within 150ft. of my home! The nearest one was found only 25ft. away from our front door and had gone into the neighbour's garden. One had landed just outside the perimeter wall of the big house about 150ft. away. A second was found behind the wall in the garden of the house and only 50ft. away. The third was the one in the garden. The fourth was found on a little beach just at the bottom of our garden some 60ft. away. The fifth amazingly was in full view and was wedged beween the large slates forming the wall of a small dock just about another 20ft further on. Each bomb turned out to be 110lb. high explosive. The Bomb Squad told us that if they had all exploded none of us would have survived as they were too close to the houses and where we were standing exposed us all to the blast.

That is not the whole of the story though! We had to spend 3 weeks up in the village while these bombs were dealt with. We found out while we were there that only one person was grazed by one of the bullets fired into the village, and he was a boy that went to our school.

We returned home but we had only been home for one day and I had been out with my friends and was just returning for tea when my father who was a keen gardener asked me if I had been digging the garden. When I told him that I hadn't he said that certainly someone had and had thrown soil all over his cucumber frame. He appeared very reluctant to believe me, and made me go with him to show me.

Between each garden there was a little hump of soil with a few short poles and odd strands of wire for a fence. It was to make sure that I didn't walk on his hallowed ground! I walked along this hump to where he had built his frame. I stopped 4 or 5ft. from it while he walked between the rows of potatoes. He told me to take a look at the soil on the glass. As I moved forward to see better my foot went down a hole in what had been a fairly hard hump. I was told in no uncertain terms by my dad to be more careful! He then came over and had a look at where my foot had sunk into the ground.

Then he examined it a little more carefully, and then sent me for the Warden. Again the bar was put to work and about 3ft. down sure enough it struck metal. He had found No. 6 bomb! The Bomb Squad was called again, but this time they said they would allow us to stay at home while they dealt with it. They explained to us that we were very lucky because the bomb had been released so low that the arming mechanism had not been fully operated. During that period many times my friends and I had run up and down to the beach passing within 15ft. of this bomb, and even used the garden shed just 6ft. away to change in before going swimming. To my knowledge the ones that fell in the water are still there as it is impossible to dig them out, so its simply a case of waiting until the mud pushes them to the surface!

During one of the raids on the city centre I remember one of the planes being hit and catching fire and coming down. Suddenly we saw two parachutes blossom and float slowly downward. Later we heard that the three crew had got out. One was captured when he unknowingly ran into one of the city police stations! The second wasn't so fortunate as he got hung up on his shute high up on a hospital roof and had to be rescued. The third was the most unlucky of all. He was found quite some distance away from the other two, he was dead beneath a tree which he had crashed through when his shute failed to open. The aircraft itself crashed just a few yards away from him and in the front garden of a house that belonged to Lady Astor. I understand that she wasn't too pleased!

It was about this time that I left school and started work as a mechanic apprentice in a garage of the owner of the local village bus and boat service. The garage office had been made into a central A.R.P. point. It had the siren operating switch installed. It was manned by us during the day and by a Warden at night. This meant that when the telephone rang it had to be answered as quickly as possible just in case it was a raid warning, and the siren had to be sounded. One day the phone rang and I scrambled to answer it, and was given instructions to "hit" the siren button. As I did so we could hear low flying aircraft overhead, but we couldn't see them for the low cloud. But the roar of the engines was suddenly accompanied by the chatter of machine gun fire. Being nosy I turned around to look out and see what was happening just in time to see a twin engine plane coming out of the clouds with its starboard engine burning, and rapidly losing height. Very close behind it came two Spitfires and they were still firing as the three of them disappeared below the cliff top about a mile away. About a minute later the phone rang again to give us the all clear. So again I hit the button and we all returned to work quite elated.

The full story came out a couple of days later. Apparently an experienced pilot was flying in the area with two trainees when he was given the warning of enemy aircraft in the vicinity and so he told his two trainees to return to base but only one did! Also we learned that only one member of the German crew got out of that stricken plane. He was captured on the cliff face after a short chase by the Home Guard volunteers who were guarding the cliffs against invasion. Another eventful day!

Finally another one of those comical situations. I remember another time when we were "fire bombed" and some of the bombs had fallen into a field just at the back of the houses. So some of the men volunteered to go and try to put them out. This field had been ploughed recently so it was a big help. A rather portly gentleman neighbour had gone up with them, but he had been left somewhat behind. On his arrival, sweating, excited and out of breath, he removed his jacket and started to try and beat one out with it. One of the men shouted over him to try and smother it by covering it over, meaning of course to do it with earth. But he was misunderstood and the chap promptly dropped his coat over it. The inevitable of course happened! His coat went up in smoke in about 2 seconds. I remember distinctly that having lost it he returned home immediately, grumbling loudly as to his loss, but worse still that his wallet had been in his pocket and had gone up in flames with the coat!

R. E. Hammond, 75 Deramore Drive, Portadown,
Craigavon, Co. Armagh, Northern Ireland

In July, 1940, I was posted as a Despatch Rider to join an "A" Battery of the Royal Marines at Folkestone. The Battery of seven 3″ guns occupied three sites around Hawkinge Airfield, the nearest airfield to those of the German Air Force.

Over the next three months, practically all enemy aircraft crossed the coast between Dungeness and Dover. The gunsite, which I now regarded as my home, was perched on the cliffs overlooking the town of Folkestone and therefore provided a grand-stand view of the Battle of Britain. As a Despatch Rider I was one of the few men who was allowed to leave the site during the next ten weeks. Unless the weather was unfit for flying, the guns were manned throughout. When not in the saddle of the B.S.A. 350, I served ammunition for the guns. Normally this meant that I spent two or three hours as part of a gun crew on most afternoons.

The two guns were manually operated and controlled from the Command Post where a "Sperry" Predictor and a Range Finder were operated. My task in action was simple. A man behind me took a shell from the ammunition rack, I took it from him, swung it up and dropped it in the loading chute. The Loader punched it into the breech with his leather gloved fist. The breech was closed, the round fired and the empty shell case ejected.

At times there were so many targets we were literally ankle deep in shell cases. At every pause in the firing we all worked quickly to throw these cases over the sandbag walls, trying to clear the ground underfoot but not always succeeding.

Sometimes this task had to be neglected as fresh supplies of ammunition had to be carried from the dump fifty yards away. Five or six men would form a line with an ammunition box between each man to carry the boxes back to the guns. If during the operation another target approached, the boxes would be dumped as we raced back to man the guns!

These short bursts of frantic activity contrasted with long periods of time when no enemy planes were within range. We were then able to watch, or more often listen, to the sound of the aerial battles above. The rattle of machine gun fire and deeper boom of cannons was frequently heard. The blue skies of that Summer always seemed to be marked with the white vapour trails left by the opposing planes.

Planes would fall from the sky like dud fireworks and a column of smoke would mark the place where they hit the ground. We were always relieved when we saw a parachute slowly descending after the plane. At the height of the battle it was common to see several parachutes in the air at once. If a parachute landed near the site, two men would be despatched to bring in the survivor and, whether friend or foe, he would be given a cup of tea whilst awaiting transport.

Occasionally a bomb would land on the site, and once a low flying bomber hobbling home dropped five that stitched a near line of craters across the field close to us! No damage was done but it allowed the Marine manning our "low flying defence" gun to fire several long bursts at the intruder. That gun was, in fact, a Lewis gun and a relic from the First World War! One afternoon a Hurricane trailing smoke flew low over the site. It cleared the barrel of No. 2 gun by only a few feet and brushed through a hedge and landed in the next field. I was one of the two sent to help and as we ran through the gap in the hedge, the Pilot was scrambling to the ground.

Before we reached the scene there was suddenly a loud whoosh and the plane literally became a sheet of flame. When we reached the Pilot I remembered that there were tears in his eyes, which I thought was the effect of the smoke but his first words when I reached him were "I'm an idiot, I've left my mascot Ted in the cockpit." Apparently the tears were for Ted!

We slept in bell tents and when there was a "red alert", the other members of the tent would slip on trousers and boots and then run to the guns clutching the rest of their clothing in their hands. Only when the guns were made ready to fire would we be allowed to continue dressing. As Despatch Rider I was left to sleep on! The first time the guns fired at night I almost leapt out of bed. The crack of the 3″ shells woke me and the brilliant flash of their explosion lit the tent brighter than sunshine. I sat bolt upright wondering where I was. After a few weeks, however, the sound of the guns was so familiar that I slept on whether they were firing or not!

A few days after I arrived at the site a westbound convoy, escorted by Destroyers, was badly mauled by enemy planes. Soon after passing Dover, Dornier bombers, escorted by ME109's, made a high level attack. This was followed by Stuka dive bombers and several ships were sunk or damaged. From our position high on the cliffs, the action was clearly visible, but the guns couldn't help as at the angle at which we would have had to fire, there would have been no accuracy at all.

During the next few weeks we watched helplessly as two or more convoys, some of the ships carrying barrage balloons to deter dive bombers, were again attacked and suffered losses. Hurricanes from No. 111 Squadron were involved in the aerial battles over the convoys. I read later that more than 100 fighters were in combat over one of these convoys. Area Headquarters were stationed in Dover and I rode there several times a week. The town suffered badly from bombing raids during July. The worst raid was at the end of the month when 125 dive bombers attacked the harbour. One morning as I rode towards the town, a dozen ME109's swooped out of the clouds and attacked the barrage balloons protecting the harbour. About two minutes later they had gone, leaving all the balloons except two sinking slowly down, most of them in flames. These balloons were often attacked during the next two months, often the prelude to a bombing raid.

At the end of July, all warships were withdrawn from the harbour. By this time the heavy guns installed at the French coast were regularly shelling the area. Although Dover bore the brunt of the attacks, shells fell all over a wide area. In fact, one of the first fell on Hawkinge Airfield but this random shot was the only one to fall there.

The only official warning of this new danger was a blackboard erected near the main road into the town. It carried in chalk letters the cryptic message "Shelling in Progress"!

Life in Dover went on normally during the shelling. People would pause as a whistling shell passed overhead. After the crump of the explosion, estimates where it had landed would be made from the rising cloud of smoke and dust.

Two 14″ naval guns were installed under the cliffs at Dover, manned by Royal Marines. They were christened "Winnie" and "Pooh" and when the Germans opened fire, it inevitably followed that a duel across the Channel would take place. I visited a number of coastal towns and most of them seemed almost deserted by the inhabitants and taken over by the Services. The invasion was expected at any time. Beaches were mined and festooned with barbed wire, concrete pill boxes and sandbagged defence points were built on seafronts. In contrast, Dover seemed to typify the "business as usual" attitude. There was a large civilian population and most shops and cafes were still open, although strict rationing was now in force.

One tactic of enemy fighters was to fly very low. It was called "hedge-hopping". They would then machine gun any target on the ground as they made their way to the coast and home. All servicemen carried arms at all times and we were ordered to fire at low flying aircraft at any opportunity! I carried a rifle and a bandolier of 50 rounds when riding the motorcycle. It wasn't very comfortable but on three occasions I at least had the satisfaction of firing. One of these was when ME109's shot up the gun site. Our only casualty was a man who had the heel of one boot shot away and suffered a twisted ankle!

214

I had a shock one morning when I rode into Folkestone to visit a small cafe. This was one of the few cafes still open in the town and I often called there for a cup of tea. On this occasion I found that a landmine had been dropped during the night and the whole area was a heap of rubble. I stood behind the tapes watching the emergency services at work, trying to estimate where the cafe had once stood. I then realised that things were so bad that I couldn't even work out where the street had been let alone the cafe.

Hawkinge was attacked several times and on the 15th August at about 11 a.m., the biggest raid of all took place. I arrived at our site and joined No. 2 gun just before the first bomber came within range. Then suddenly it seemed that there were waves of Stukas, those ugly black bent-winged planes. They attacked from different directions. They came down almost vertically, sirens screaming a high pitched wail and the noise of the 1,000 pound bombs they dropped was like a continuous thunder. In the gunpit, our ears rang with the crack of the guns as we fed them with shells. Empty empty cases piled up beneath our feet and we kicked them aside as we worked, everyone concentrating on his own particular task.

This was the first of many raids that day when the sky seemed to be full of planes and the constant sound of air battles overhead. Food was eaten at the guns as we worked and snatched as we could. During one spell of firing, three bombs dropped on our site but their explosions were hardly noticed as we worked the guns. It may sound amazing but it's true.

In the late afternoon the ammunition stock was getting low and, with two other men, I was sent in the lorry to the Shornecliffe Depot to collect more. We drove off in a hurry, loaded the lorry, and drove back through Folkestone. There was still a "red alert" and plenty of aerial activity, but amazingly the town was quiet and so were we. Sitting on a load of explosives in a raid is not conducive to idle chatter!

The situation was critical when we arrived at the site. The area around the guns was by now totally covered by empty shell cases. Our load was used to fill the almost empty racks in the gunpits. But this was the most successful day for the Battery which was officially credited with nine planes destroyed. That must be a record anywhere for one day's shooting. The success could have been due to every Battery Commander breaking standing orders. These stated that shrapnel should not be fired over the airfield. Although the dive bombers were very fast when diving, they were slow to climb. The guns laid a ceiling of shrapnel over the field which the bombers had to pass through and many suffered as a result. As well as the nine shot down, many more were damaged. The lucky ones limped home across the Channel. The unlucky ones met the Hurricanes whose base they had attacked!

The following morning I delivered a package to Hawkinge. I was able to see the damage inflicted on the airfield. Several large buildings, including a hangar, had been flattened. Others were badly damaged and the whole area pitted with craters. A report later gave the number as 248. Men were working everywhere. There were Army, Air Force and civilians, all using shovels or driving machines and the place resembled a giant anthill. Many of the men had toiled through the night and their efforts were rewarded when the field was operational again in 24 hours. From this time the base was used only for refuelling and re-arming in daylight hours. Planes were held at a base further inland during the night. Almost every night we heard the sound of our bombers flying to bomb the ports where invasion craft were by now being assembled. Many times we saw the flashes and heard the rumble of exploding bombs in the distance on the French coast. Some time after the big raid on Hawkinge, the Germans mustered the largest formation of planes ever seen to attack London. There were almost 1,000 bombers escorted by fighters. When the news was received in our Command Post from R.D.F., as Radar was then known, it was greeted with disbelief and then ultimately dismay!

"Three groups of approximately three hundred bombers, heavily escorted, now forming over France" was the message. If this was true we believed it could only be the beginning of the invasion. Soon this aerial Armada was crossing the coast, flying in layers one above the other, they seemed to fill the sky. The grinding noise of their engines was loud but soon guns were booming and machine guns rattling as the ground and air defences went into action. We had a busy twenty minutes and then the action moved inland. A few planes had been seen to crash but none near us. More had turned back for home, too badly damaged to continue, and the bombs they jettisoned fell a long way from us. One of the planes that went home early bore Italian markings. I recall it because it was the first time I had seen one and I only saw one other after that.

The heavy daylight bombing raids continued throughout September and although the main target was London, Kent and the coastal towns were always a target as well. By the end of the month the Germans had decided that the loss of planes was too heavy and switched to night attacks. From the site, on two occasions, we saw the sky in the north turn red, coloured by the huge fires of burning London. That was seventy miles away. I have to admit, however, that for 24 hours our gun site was put out of action. However, it was not by enemy action but by a friendly Kent cow!

One morning about two hours after breakfast, 90% of the personnel, myself included, were suffering severe stomach pains and vomiting. The Medical Officer from Hawkinge visited the camp and instantly diagnosed food poisoning. As the fit men were those who had not drunk milk, it was obvious that the milk was the cause. Our milk was delivered by a friendly farmer each day, and the poison probably came from something one of the cows had eaten. We were certainly suffering but I do remember that we wondered how the cow felt! By the next morning everyone was fit for duty and it was back to business as usual.

One day the materials for two Nissen huts were delivered and several men began to erect them. In a few days the first hut was in position but no doors or window. That night a strong wind arose and was soon blowing a gale. In spite of extra pegs, first one and then another tent was blown down. By this time the whole Battery was out holding guy ropes and hammering pegs, but the wind grew wilder. Several more tents capsized, and then two were plucked from the ground and sailed away like kites. So the order was then given to strike all tents and move them and all gear into the hut. In pouring rain we moved kit, blankets, rifles and equipment under cover and then stood around hoping the wind would not blow the hut away! The wind eased before dawn. The cooks had lots of help and breakfast was swiftly prepared. By the time the workmen arrived, tents had been re-pitched, the hut emptied and clothing and bedding was hanging on a makeshift clothes line. The Germans certainly helped us – they stayed away all that morning! A week later both huts were ready and we moved in. Living in a hut was much more comfortable and when mattresses were issued, life was absolutely luxurious. There was a round cast iron stove in the centre of the room, and lying on the bed, with a good fire burning, was very cosy indeed! There was no lighting, but in a short time everyone had a bedside lamp, consisting of a tin of paraffin with a piece of string protruding through the lid as a wick. In the October the danger of invasion receded and leave to visit Folkestone from 4 p.m. in the afternoon until 12 at night was granted to ten men each day. For most men this was the first time they had left the site for three months and although everyone still had to carry a rifle, it was wonderful to be off duty.

Although most bombing was now carried out after dark, there was still daylight raids on Kent. Hawkinge was raided several times during the month, and one Sunday three attacks were made on Folkestone. Our guns were often fired during the night too, so the Battery was certainly kept busy. A duty "Spotter" would sound the alarm by striking a dangling, empty shell case with a hammer. The gun crews then stopped whatever they were doing and ran to the guns. Two minutes was considered the maximum time from the alarm being sounded to the guns actually being ready for action. As a "spare number" I did not have to answer the alarm. But nevertheless I often carried an armful of clothing to the gunpit which my tent mate had left behind. One cool afternoon my friend the Loader was very pleased to see me. He had been washing down at the tap when the gong sounded and arrived at the gun site wearing underpants, pumps and a towel!

In December the Battery moved from Folkestone and less than two months later was in the Atlantic en route for the Middle East. When we left Kent the Battery had been credited officially with 98 enemy planes shot down, and many more than that damaged.

Mr. A. Clarke, 2 Grange Park, Albrighton, Wolverhampton

"Theirs was the Glory"

Theirs was the glory of an age long gone by
When young men spread their wings and fought in the sky
They fought in machines so noble by name
That they called them the Spitfire and the Hurricane.

"Yes" theirs was the glory of an age long gone by
Like knights on chargers they fought in the sky
They jousted their enemy o'er sea and land
Skyward they flew to protect old England.

"O yes" theirs was the glory of days long gone by
Some lived – some died as they fought in the sky
They fought death in the sky with scarcely a care
Machines and minds weary and in want of repair.

Well the years have passed since those war torn days
And these men are older in a great many ways
But they never forgot all those that died
And their love of freedom is still their great pride
But when history is written of all these men
What finer words can it tell them
"That theirs was the glory of an age gone by".

Written by a Yank,

Patrick O'Donoghue,
186 Grand Street,
NEW MILFORD 076 46,
NEW JERSEY,
U.S.A.

*Sir Douglas Bader reading
Patrick O'Donoghue's poem*

217

BATTLE OF BRITAIN DAY
15th SEPTEMBER 1940

R.A.F. FIGHTER COMMAND LOSSES

No.	Squadron	Details	Time	Pilot	Aircraft
1.	1 (Canadian) Sqdn., Northolt	Shot down by Bf 109; pilot baled out with head wound.	12.04 hrs.	Fg. Off. A. D. Nesbitt	Hurricane
2.	1 (Canadian) Sqdn., Northolt	Shot down over South London; pilot killed.	A12.00 hrs.	Fg. Off. R. Smither	Hurricane
3.	1 (Canadian) Sqdn., Northolt	Damaged by HE 111 south of London; pilot landed at base	14.13 hrs.	Fg. Off. A. Yuile	Hurricane
4.	19 Sqdn., Fowlmere	Hit in glycol tank by Bf 109 and force landed; pilot unhurt.	14.50 hrs.	Sgt. H. A. C. Roden	Spitfire
5.	19 Sqdn., Fowlmere	Damaged by Bf 109 and force landed; pilot unhurt.		Sub. Lt. A. G. Blake	Spitfire
6.	19 Sqdn., Fowlmere	Missing after combat with Bf 109s; pilot presumed killed.	A14.55 hrs.	Sgt. J. A. Potter	Spitfire
7.	25 Sqdn., North Weald	Accident at night; no casualties.	At night	Plt. Off. B. G. Hooper	Blenheim
8.	41 Sqdn., Hornchurch	Shot down by Bf 109 near Gravesend; pilot crashed with aircraft and was killed.	12.20 hrs.	Plt. Off. G. A. Langley	Spitfire
9.	73 Sqdn., Castle Camps	Shot down at Mounds Farm, Lynstead; pilot killed.	11.50 hrs.	Plt. Off. R. A. Marchand	Hurricane
10.	229 Sqdn., Northolt	Pilot hit in leg; baled out at Sevenoaks.	12.04 hrs.	Plt. Off. R. R. Smith	Hurricane
11.	229 Sqdn., Northolt	Shot down by Do 17; pilot killed and aircraft crashed into Staplehurst Railway Station.	12.07 hrs.	Plt. Off. G. L. J. Doutrepont	Hurricane
12.	238 Sqdn., Middle Wallop	Shot down by Bf 110 near Tunbridge; pilot baled out but killed when parachute failed to open.	A15.00 hrs.	Sgt. L. Pidd	Hurricane
13.	238 Sqdn., Middle Wallop	Damaged by Bf 110s over Kent; pilot unhurt.	A15.00 hrs.	Plt. Off. V. C. Simmonds	Hurricane
14.	238 Sqdn., Middle Wallop	Damaged in action over South London; pilot unhurt.	A14.50 hrs.	Not known	Hurricane
15.	238 Sqdn., Middle Wallop	Damaged in action over South London; pilot unhurt.	A14.50 hrs.	Not known	Hurricane
16.	242 Sqdn., Coltishall	Shot down by Do 17 over South Coast; pilot baled out with dislocated shoulder and admitted to Rye Hospital.	A14.15 hrs.	Flt. Lt. G. S. ff. Powell-Sheddon	Hurricane
17.	253 Sqdn., Kenley	Shot down by Bf 109; pilot baled out unhurt at Hawkinge.	15.10 hrs.	Plt. Off. A. R. H. Barton	Hurricane
18.	303 Sqdn., Northolt	Damaged by Bf 109; pilot wounded in leg.	12.01 hrs.	Plt. Off. W. Lokuciewski	Hurricane
19.	303 Sqdn., Northolt	Shot down by Bf 110; pilot baled out at Dartford unhurt.	14.55 hrs.	Sgt. M. Brzozowski	Hurricane
20.	303 Sqdn., Northolt	Believed shot down by Bf 109 over East London; pilot killed.	14.51 hrs.	Sgt. T. Andruszkow	Hurricane
21.	310 Sqdn., Duxford	Shot down by Bf 109 over Billericay; pilot baled out unhurt.	14.52 hrs.	Sqdn. Ldr. A. Hess	Hurricane
22.	310 Sqdn., Duxford	Shot down by Bf 109 near Chatham; pilot baled out slightly wounded in leg.	14.54 hrs.	Sgt. J. Hubacek	Hurricane
23.	501 Sqdn., Kenley	Shot down by Bf 109 near Maidstone; pilot baled out unhurt.	12.04 hrs.	Sqdn. Ldr. H. A. V. Hogan	Hurricane
24.	501 Sqdn., Kenley	Shot down by Bf 109 over Kent; pilot killed.	12.00 hrs.	Plt. Off. Van den Hove	Hurricane
25.	504 Sqdn., Hendon	Shot down by Do 17 over London; pilot baled out and landed at Victoria.	A11.50 hrs.	Sgt. R. T. Holmes	Hurricane
26.	504 Sqdn., Henton	Missing after combat with Do 17s over Longfield, Kent; pilot presumed killed.	A12.00 hrs.	Plt. Off. J. V. Gurteen	Hurricane
27.	504 Sqdn., Henton	Shot down by Do 17s at Dartford; pilot baled out grievously wounded and burned.	A14.00 hrs.	Fg. Off. M. Jebb	Hurricane
28.	602 Sqdn., Westhampnett	Shot down by Do 17 over Beachy Head; pilot baled out unhurt.	15.04 hrs.	Not known	Spitfire
29.	603 Sqdn., Hornchurch	Shot down by Bf 109s over Kent; pilot killed.	15.07 hrs.	Plt. Off. A. P. Pease	Spitfire
30.	603 Sqdn., Hornchurch	Shot down by Bf 109s; pilot baled out unhurt.	A15.10 hrs.	Sqdn. Ldr. G. L. Denholm	Spitfire
31.	605 Sqdn., Croydon	Shot down by Bf 109s over West Malling; pilot baled out slightly wounded.	11.56 hrs.	Plt. Off. R. E. Jones	Hurricane
32.	604 Sqdn., Croydon	Collided with Do 17 over Marden; pilot baled out unhurt.	14.40 hrs.	Plt. Off. T. P. M. Cooper-Slipper	Hurricane
33.	607 Sqdn., Tangmere	Shot down by Do 17 near Appledore; pilot baled out slightly wounded.	14.51 hrs.	Plt. Off. P. J. T. Stephenson	Hurricane
34.	609 Sqdn., Middle Wallop	Shot down by Do 17 over South London; pilot killed	12.12 hrs.	Plt. Off. G. N. Daunt	Spitfire
35.	611 Sqdn., Digby/Duxford	Damaged by Bf 110 over West London; pilot unhurt.	14.50 hrs.	Not known	Spitfire

BATTLE OF BRITAIN DAY
15th SEPTEMBER 1940
LUFTWAFFE LOSSES

#	Unit	Remarks	Type
1.	1/KG 1	Crashed at Le Houdrel after combat with fighters.	Heinkel He 111 H-3
2.	5/KG 2	Crashed into English Channel after combat with R.A.F. fighters. Time not known.	Dornier Do 17 Z-3
3.	5/KG 2	Shot down by Spitfires of 19 Sqdn. (Duxford Wing), over London at approx. 15.00 hrs.	Dornier Do 17 Z-3
4.	5/KG 2	Slightly damaged by Spitfires of 19 Sqdn. (Duxford Wing), over London at approx. 15.00 hrs.	Dornier Do 17 Z-2
5.	7/KG 2	Slightly damaged by Hurricanes of 17 Sqdn., over London at 14.58 hrs.	Dornier Do 17Z
6.	7/KG 2	Slightly damaged by Hurricanes of 17 Sqdn., over London at 14.58 hrs.	Dornier Do 17Z
7.	8/KG 2	Shot down by Hurricanes of 242 Sqdn. (Duxford Wing), near London at approx. 15.00 hrs.	Dornier Do 17Z
8.	8/KG 2	Shot down by Hurricanes of 242 Sqdn. (Duxford Wing), near London at approx. 15.00 hrs.	Dornier Do 17Z
9.	8/KG 2	Slightly damaged by British fighters near London at approx. 15.00 hrs.	Dornier Do 17Z
10.	8/KG 2	Shot down by British fighters south of London at approx. 15.10 hrs.	Dornier Do 17Z
11.	8/KG 2	Shot down by British fighters over Sussex coast at approx. 15.20 hrs., and crashed into Channel; pilot rescued by *Seenotflugkommando*.	Dornier Do 17Z
12.	9/KG 2	Shot down by British fighters over Surrey andfl'†dbFgerald.....0000 21297 's.	Dornier Do 17Z
13.	9/KG 2	Shot down by British fighters over Sussex and crashed into Channel at 15.27 hrs.	Dornier Do 17Z
14.	4/KG 3	Shot down by Hurricanes of 501 Sqdn., south-east of London at 11.50 hrs.	Dornier Do 17 Z-2
15.	4/KG 3	Shot down by Hurricanes of 501 Sqdn., south-east of London at 11.50 hrs.	Dornier Do 17 Z-3
16.	4/KG 3	Damaged by Hurricanes of 501 Sqdn., south-east of London at approx. 11.50 hrs., and landed at Calais.	Dornier Do 17 Z-3
17.	4/KG 3	Shot down by Hurricanes of 501 Sqdn., south-east of London at approx. 12.00 hrs.	Dornier Do 17 Z-2
18.	5/KG 3	Damaged by Spitfires of 19 Sqdn. (Duxford Wing), over East London at 12.05 hrs.	Dornier Do 17 Z-3
19.	5/KG 3	Shot down by Hurricanes of 504 Sqdn., over Central London at 12.10 hrs.	Dornier Do 17 Z-2
20.	5/KG 3	Shot down by Hurricanes of 504 Sqdn., over Central London at 12.10 hrs.	Dornier Do 17 Z-3
21.	5/KG 3	Shot down by Hurricane flown by Holmes of 504 Sqdn., over Central London at 12.10 hrs. Crashed on Victoria Station.	Dornier Do 17 Z-2
22.	6/KG 2	Damaged by British fighters in Greater London area shortly after mid-day.	Dornier Do 17 Z-2
23.	6/KG 3	Damaged by British fighters near London at mid-day.	Dornier Do 17 Z-3
24.	II/KG 4	Damaged by British fighters and force landed at Eindhoven.	Heinkel He 111 P-4
25.	I/KG 26	Damaged by *flak* and fighters near London.	Heinkel He 111 H-3
26.	I/KG 26	Damaged by *flak* and fighters over London.	Heinkel He 111 H-3
27.	I/KG 26	Shot down by Spitfire of 72 Sqdn., near Dartford.	Heinkel He 111 H-4
28.	6/KG 26	Damaged by British fighters over Sussex after raid on London and crashed in France.	Heinkel He H-3
29.	6/KG 30	Damaged by fighters; force landed at St. Omer.	Junkers Ju 88 A-1
30.	6/KG 30	Suffered engine failure and crashed in France.	Junkers Ju 88 A-1
31.	I/KG 51	Landing accident at Villaroche after combat sortie.	Junkers Ju 88 A-1
32.	I/KG 51	Shot down by British fighters over South London. Probably during afternoon raid.	Junkers Ju 88 A-1
33.	II/KG 51	Shot down by British fighters over South London. Probably during afternoon raid.	Junkers Ju 88 A-1
34.	Stab/KG 53	Shot down by British fighters south of London during afternoon riad.	Heinkel He 111 H-2
35.	I/KG 53	Shot down by British fighters south of London during afternoon raid.	Heinkel He 111 H-2
36.	3/KG 53	Shot down by Spitfires of 92 Sqdn., near Hornchurch at 14.32 hrs.	Heinkel He 111 H-2
37.	3/KG 53	Force landed at Boulogne with damage from fighter combat over London during afternoon raid.	Heinkel He 111 H-2
38.	II/KG 53	Shot down by Spitfire of 92 Sqdn., near Hornchurch at 14.35 hrs.	Heinkel He 111 H-2
39.	II/KG 53	Shot down by British fighters in Greater London area during afternoon raid.	Heinkel He 111 H-1
40.	II/KG 53	Shot down by British fighters in Greater London area during afternoon raid.	Heinkel He 111 H-3
41.	III/KG 53	Force landed at Armentiers following fighter combat.	Heinkel He 111 H-3
42.	III/KG 55	Shot down by British fighters into English Channel.	Heinkel He 111 P-2
43.	III/KG 55	Damaged by British fighters over Southern England.	Heinkel He 111 P-2
44.	1/KG 76	Crashed at Cap Gris Nez following fighter combat.	Dornier Do 17Z
45.	1/KG 76	Shot down by Hurricanes (believed of 303 Sqdn.) south of London during afternoon raid.	Dornier Do 17Z
46.	2/KG 76	Crashed near Pox following fighter combat.	Dornier Do 17Z
47.	3/KG 76	Shot down by Hurricanes (believed of 303 Sqdn.) in London area during afternoon raid.	Dornier Do 17Z
48.	8/KG 76	Shot down by British fighters in London area during afternoon raid.	Dornier Do 17Z
49.	8/KG 76	Shot down by British fighters in London area during afternoon raid.	Dornier Do 17Z
50.	9/KG 76	Shot down by British fighters in London area during afternoon raid.	Dornier Do 17Z
51.	9/KG 76	Shot down by British fighters south of London during afternoon raid and believed to have crashed off Sussex coast.	Dornier Do 17Z
52.	13/LG 1	Shot down by Hurricane flown by Ferič of 303 Sqdn., over North Kent at 15.50 hrs.	Messerschmitt Bf 110
53.	13/LG 1	Shot down by Hurricane flown by Kellett of 303 Sqdn., over North Kent at approx. 15.50 hrs.	Messerschmitt Bf 110
54.	14/LG 1	Shot down by British fighters south-east of London during afternoon.	Messerschmitt Bf 110
55.	I/LG 2	Shot down by British fighters near London in evening.	Messerschmitt Bf 109
56.	I/LG 2	Shot down by British fighters near London in evening.	Messerschmitt Bf 109
57.	Stab/JG 3	Believed shot down by Dover A.A. defences.	Messerschmitt Bf 109
58.	I/JG 3	Crashed into Channel after combat with British fighters; pilot picked up by *Seenotflugkommando*.	Messerschmitt Bf 109
59.	1/KG 3	Shot down over Sussex by British fighters.	Messerschmitt Bf 109
60.	2/JG 3	Shot down over Sussex coast by British fighters.	Messerschmitt Bf 109
61.	1/JG 27	Shot down over South London by British fighters.	Messerschmitt Bf 109
62.	1/JG 27	Force landed near Lille short of fuel after combat.	Messerschmitt Bf 109
63.	2/JG 27	Possibly ran out of fuel and crashed into Channel.	Messerschmitt Bf 109
64.	2/JG 27	Crashed at Guines-West short of fuel after combat.	Messerschmitt Bf 109
65.	7/JG 51	Shot down by Hurricane flown by Currant of 605 Sqdn., near Maidstone at approx. 14.40 hrs.	Messerschmitt Bf 109
66.	9/JG 51	Shot down by British fighters south-east of London.	Messerschmitt Bf 109
67.	Stab I/JG 52	Shot down by British fighters over Margate.	Messerschmitt Bf 109
68.	I/JG 53	Shot down in flames over South Kent by British fighters.	Messerschmitt Bf 109
69.	1/JG 53	Force landed at Etaples with combat damage.	Messerschmitt Bf 109

70.	I/JG 53	Shot down by Spitfire flown by Denholm of 603 Sqdn., near the Isle of Sheppey at approx. 12.05 hrs.	Messerschmitt Bf 109
71.	1/JG 53	Shot down by Spitfire flown by McPhail of 603 Sqdn., near the Isle of Sheppey at approx. 12.05 hrs.	Messerschmitt Bf 109
72.	3/JG 53	Missing from sortie over South-East England at about mid-day; believed shot down over Kent.	Messerschmitt Bf 109
73.	3/JG 53	Missing from sortie over South-East England.	Messerschmitt Bf 109
74.	III/JG 53	Force landed at Etaples after combat; aircraft burnt.	Messerschmitt Bf 109
75.	III/JG 53	Force landed in Channel after fuel ran out; pilot rescued by *Seenotflugkommando*.	Messerschmitt Bf 109
76.	1/JG 77	Force landed following engine failure caused by combat with British fighters over Dungeness.	Messerschmitt Bf 109
77.	3/JG 77	Missing from sortie involving combat over Dungeness.	Messerschmitt Bf 109
78.	*Wetterkun dungsstaffel 51*	Shot down by Hurricanes flown by David and Jay of 87 Sqdn., off Bolt Head at approx. 09.00 hrs.	Heinkel He 111 H-3
79.	3/406	Crashed on taking-off from the sea off the south coast of Ireland; crew rescued.	Dornier Do 18
80.	*Seenotflug-kommando 3*	Landing accident in sea at position Square 117.	Heinkel He 59

THE AIRCRAFT COMPARED

	Maximum Speed	Climb	Ceiling	Range	Armament
ROYAL AIR FORCE					
Hurricane	320 mph	9.8 minutes to 20,000 ft.	34,200 ft.	600 miles	eight 0.303 machine guns
Spitfire Mk. I	355 mph	9.4 minutes to 20,000 ft.	34,000 ft.	575 miles	eight 0.303 machine guns
Spitfire Mk. II	370 mph	7 minutes to 20,000 ft.	37,200 ft.	500 miles	eight 0.303 machine guns
Defiant	304 mph	10.2 minutes to 18,000 ft.	30,200 ft.	600 miles	four 0.303 machine guns in power operated turret
Blenheim	260 mph	15 minutes to 15,000 ft.	24,000 ft.	1125 miles	six 0.303 machine guns

	Maximum Speed	Climb	Ceiling	Range	Armament
LUFTWAFFE					
Fighters:					
Messerschmitt 109	354 mph	6.2 minutes to 16,500 ft.	36,000 ft.	412 miles	two 20 mm cannon two 7.9 machine guns
Fighter-Bombers:					
Messerschmitt 110	340 mph		32,500 ft.	565 miles	1102 lbs.
Bombers:					*Bomb Load*
Dornier	265 mph		26,740 ft.	745 miles	2,200 lb.
Heinkel	255 mph		25,000 ft.	1,540 miles	4,400 lb.
Junkers Ju 87	232 mph		24,500 ft.	370 miles	1,100 lb.
Junkers Ju 88	286 mph		26,500 ft.	1,553 miles	3,968 lb.

FLIGHT LIEUTENANT D. J. NICHOLSON
ROYAL AIR FORCE

It is fitting that this book concludes with a photograph and story that perhaps typifies the courage or heroism of "The Few"

In his very first combat on 16th August 1940 Flight Lieutenant Nicholson won the first V.C. to be awarded to a fighter pilot. On patrol in the Southampton area, he was detailed to attack three Junkers 88 bombers.

Before he could take action they were engaged by a Spitfire squadron. But his aircraft was set alight by cannon shells from a Messerschmitt. Nevertheless he attacked the enemy plane. As he pressed the gun button he recalled seeing the skin being burnt off his hands.

He continued to fight in his burning Hurricane and eye-witnesses saw the Messerschmitt crash into the sea.

Because of his injuries Flight Lieutenant Nicholson had difficulty in baling out, and it then took him twenty minutes to reach the ground. Doctors fought to save his life for forty-eight hours, but he recovered from his wounds. He was born at Hampstead, London and was 23 years old at the time.

When we remember "The Few" and those who kept freedoms flame alight, remember that they were usually young men like Flt. Lt. Nicholson and that we can never repay the debt we owe.

Long after the dust of the Battle of Britain has settled the events of those far off days are still with us in the shape of unexplained sights and sounds around some of the airfields used during the Battle.

Places like Hawkinge in Kent. Around 1947 the Station was put on a care and maintenance basis and some buildings were used as a W.A.A.F. Depot. A W.A.A.F. reported seeing a Fighter Pilot on the airfield late at night – a few weeks later another W.A.A.F. again saw the ghostly figure of a fighter pilot walking on the airfield as if wounded. Some people think that it was a pilot who was killed when his plane crashed near the airfield during the Battle of Britain. Even in the last few years the sound of an aircrft engine has been heard revving up near the gates of the Museum. No explanation could be given.

North Weald in Essex was one of the famous Battle of Britain Fighter Stations. One day in September 1940 after an operation over the Channel a Spitfire landed in a very poor condition and on landing turned over and caught fire. The pilot was pulled out of his plane still conscious and he was taken to the Operations Room before being taken to Hospital. He was attended by the Squadron Doctor who decided he could be left for a few minutes, and went next door to fetch the Senior Controller. The Doctor had only left the room for a moment when there came the noise of heavy footsteps, followed by a crash and a bump.

The Doctor hurried back into the room only to find the pilot slumped on the floor near to the desk – the telephone was off the hook and dangling to the floor. He had died trying to make a telephone call to someone – but who?

The sounds of heavy footsteps followed by a crash and then a heavy fall have since been heard by Telephone Operators coming from the Operations Room at the end of the corridor, and on examination the phone has been found dangling from its cord. Around 1949 a test was made by locking all the doors and windows and thread was put across the door. The Staff on duty that night sat and waited. At about 12.30 a.m. the same noises were again heard – they ran down the corridor and opened the still sealed door. All was quiet but the phone was off the hook and dangling to the floor – the last call had still not been made.

Another story connected with North Weald is about the Museum and the picture that will not stay on the wall. The Museum is securely locked every night but when it is opened next morning the picture is found on the floor, and it doesn't matter which wall it is hung on the same thing happens. Also the covers over the display cases are often found on the floor. No explanation has been given for these events.

Many other stories are told of strange happenings around these old airfields and whether you believe them or not it certainly makes you wonder, especially when the events have been experienced by a number of people at different times.

Roy Smart, 39 Mount Close, Mount Lane,
Kirkby-la-Thorpe, Lincolnshire

BLACK-OUT
ZERO
HOUR
TO-NIGHT
UNTIL **6.3** A.M.
MOON RISES **5.19** P.M.
MOON SETS **3.10** A.M.

Daily

No. 12,576

Thursday, Sep

Mr. Churchill (in a broadcast last night reported on Page Five) gave war

Every man—and woman—will therefore prepare himse
pride and care . . . With devout but sure

TERRIFIC LON
MEETS GRE
While Navy and RAF pound

SUPER-BLITZ GETS A SHOCK

HITLER'S PLANS FOR IN-VADING BRITAIN ARE NEARING COMPLETION.

Mr. Churchill last night said the invasion may be launched at any time.

Next week must be regarded as "very important."

Germany, he said, is massing barges and ships in ports from Hamburg down to the Bay of Biscay. Preparations have also been made to carry a force from Norway.

While the Army stands confident and ready for the assault, the Navy and R.A.F. are shelling and bombing every one of Hitler's invasion ports. Barges and harbours are being continuously and heavily bombarded. This has been going on since Tuesday night.

LONDON BLITZ NIGHT No. 5 WAS A SENSATION.

It began at 8.34 after three daylight raids. Goering intended it to be a Super-Blitz night.

He sent over bigger-than-ever formations of bombers, and sent fighters to protect them.

AND WHAT A SURPRISE THEY HAD!

All round them broke the biggest anti-aircaft barrage London has ever seen.

From every part of London A.A. guns flashed and roared. Only a few raiders got through to drop bombs on inner London. Most had to drop their bombs haphazard on the outskirts. And all the time the intense gunfire drowned the noise of the bombs.

The indiscriminate bombing of London now stands revealed by the Premier as part of the invasion plan.

9
DO
400 peop
Monda

NAZI squ
twice y
noon and ev
home attack
and on the I

They paid
at least nine
of the most s
of the war.

As many
brought dow
Goering lost
men.

The two r
gether about
that the "de
an hour.

This news
midnight. Ear
that our losse
fighters, with
Here is the c
by the Air Mi
try of Home S

Fuller repor
able of b
enemy activit
area. Althoug

CHANNEL BASES SHELLED

Gunfire louder than the bombs

FEWER searchlights but MANY more guns